# UNIVERSITY

# *of*

# MOTHERHOOD

## *Undergraduate Degree*

*Cathy Kotow-Dockman*

*EA, BHSc*

 FriesenPress

Suite 300 - 990 Fort St
Victoria, BC, V8V 3K2
Canada

www.friesenpress.com

ISBN
978-1-5255-7143-5 (Hardcover)
978-1-5255-7144-2 (Paperback)
978-1-5255-7145-9 (eBook)

*1. FAMILY & RELATIONSHIPS, PARENTING, MOTHERHOOD*

Distributed to the trade by The Ingram Book Company

# TABLE OF CONTENTS

I wish to dedicate this book to my family members of today and days gone by. To my ancestors who immigrated to Canada and worked tirelessly to build better, safer lives for their loved ones. To my parents and my siblings for their endless support, wild humour and inescapable creativity. To my children who shine bright light into my heart.

# INTRODUCTION

Why write a book about motherhood? Is motherhood really that important? Of course it is! Motherhood is an institution and a formidable position that's been passed on from generation to generation throughout human history. Matriarchs have dominated, encouraged, and supported families since time began. Motherhood is the procreation and the evolution of our species.

A mother has an instinct for the survival and protection of her offspring, which leads her to develop certain values, morals, and skills. Being a mother is the epitome of the survival of our species, and it's an education in life. Motherhood has evolved through changing times, and change is necessary for human growth and survival.

Why call this book *The University of Motherhood*? No mother has earned an official degree in motherhood. It's not a four-, seven-, or even nine-year period of education that results in some form of certification. Other college and university degrees have immense value in their own right to the individual recipients and their contribution to society as a whole. A degree in motherhood is different. It's the very fabric of life. It's an intense degree taking twenty-five years and more—with ongoing upgrading!

The significance of our profession can add pressure, fear, and power to motherhood. A mother's actions, words, and thoughts mould her children's characters, which become the fundamental building blocks of the world they will create. Our children become this world's next phase of thinkers, leaders, followers, inventors, and spiritualists who will build or break our future. The philosophies our children learn and the paradigm shifts they initiate will kill or save our planet.

I have invested twenty-five years toward this degree from the University of Motherhood. I've learned plenty, with loads more to come. I've gained knowledge about myself, my world, and my children. I anticipate the next fifty years of motherhood to be more of the same. *No!* Of course not! Nothing stays the same; change is inevitable. My years of motherhood will be a continuous process, with new learning and a multitude of experiences yet unknown. There will be more graduations, possibly marriages, hopefully grandchildren and great-grandchildren, and growth challenges of all kinds. So here's to you! My hat goes off in praise of you parents, grandparents, and great-grandparents who have graduated with this degree. Congratulations! You made it through with blood, sweat, and tears, and with pride, accomplishment, and joy!

There are so many questions—questions I've asked myself and have been on a quest to answer throughout my life. Are parenting methods passed on through the ages from generation to generation? Is parenting done blindly, based on our learned habits and environmental influences? Can we choose how we parent? Can we change? Can we change how we think about ourselves, our parents, our children, and the planet? Can we teach our offspring new concepts? Where do we go to learn to be parents? How do we deal with the feelings, responsibilities, stress, and physiological changes? What about emotional, financial, spiritual, and physical stability? Do we automatically repeat what our parents did and how they raised us? What about learning, evolution, and growth? Am I doing what is best for my children? There's no school to teach us to be parents.

Sooo many questions! Too many questions. It's very mind-boggling. As I parented, I found myself asking these questions more frequently. They are important, life-changing questions about the development of these human beings. I felt a responsibility to do the very best I could to support my children to be whole, well-adjusted people. How do we find acceptable, useful answers that *work*? This is my story of how I searched for and found answers to these questions and many more. It's the story of the decisions and discoveries I made and the conclusions I came to as a result of those experiences.

At the age of nine, I decided that I would have four children. First, I would travel the world, do some schooling, and learn as much as I could about life and the world's workings. Then at twenty-five years old (after I figured out how the world worked, LOL) I'd have my first child. Forty-one years after making that choice, I can say that I've lived that plan successfully in many ways, but not without mistakes and discouragement. I dealt with those challenges, the forks in the road, and the blockages in a variety of ways. I drove at high speeds at times, and at other times was at a standstill, along the very jagged, twisted, winding road of my life. I became a better person because of the unexpected turns and surprises life presented me with. I wouldn't change anything. Every piece of my life has contributed to who I am today.

Who I thought I'd be and who I am aren't necessarily synonymous, but I mustn't be too hard on myself. This is a lifelong journey. Living and enjoying the journey are as important as the destination. As I reflect on my learning, growth, and the choices I've made so far, I revel in the incredible pride and feeling of accomplishment I derive from my journey through motherhood.

Searching for meaning in my life, I am led to write. I write in order to record personal history for interest, understanding, growth, and the possibility of helping other parents. I've kept journals for years. Journaling helps me formulate ideas, gather my thoughts, de-stress, and solve problems. In hindsight, my journals helped me establish a deeper awareness of myself, my thoughts, my actions, and the areas I needed to change. Later, I realized my journals had also become historical recordings of my life.

I wrote the journals not to document my life but to live my life to the fullest on that day, in that moment. I wrote to help me cope with life when I was overwhelmed and to be aware of and express joy when I felt it. At that time, I didn't intend to use the notes to write a book. That idea came much later, and the journals became invaluable resources for dates, events, and emotional details. As a young person with an incredible memory, documenting events for the future wasn't important to me, because I knew nothing of aging and the effects of time on memory. Many of the minute details of my life experiences would have been lost had I not recorded them.

Some of my story is universal, while other parts may be unusual, for this is my story, my perception of my life events. This is the story of how I chose and acted on becoming a conscientious parent. When I made a mistake, I worked on admitting it and doing my best to correct my error. I regularly ask myself this question: What is the best decision, step, or process that would work for me and my family right now?

Life speeds by, so it's important to live this moment, right now, with all of its pain and glory! This moment is all we have. As a society, we do have many things to which we can escape, but they can lead us to a variety of social and emotional problems. When I remember to remain in this moment with gratitude, I live!

Being a mother has been the most challenging and the most rewarding "job" I've ever had. I often questioned my actions: Is this useful? Is this damaging? What are the consequences? I wanted my children to learn to make decisions, to make mistakes, and to learn from those mistakes. I wanted them to grow into interesting, confident, and independent adults who felt worthwhile, needed, and loved. I wanted them each to feel that they were unique and added value to our family and world.

My children became more precious to me and more of a challenge because I made these choices. Free will gave them choices, like freedom of thought and speech, which afforded them the opportunity to question the prevailing philosophies of society and the family unit. My children often wanted to know why life worked the way it did, so I strove to provide or help them find the answers. They looked at the world with such wonder and curiosity that it continually amazed me. It was lovely to watch and participate in my children's wonder.

I felt a need to grow and develop with my children in order to understand them as I tried to assist them in understanding their world. I wanted to be able to accept each child's different perspective, and I'm grateful for that process and the outcomes. This task took every ounce of my energy, love, and creative intelligence. My goal was to develop a loving environment surrounded by interesting things and people that encouraged awareness, understanding, enlightenment, and joy. I wished to provide educational opportunities that aligned with my children's strengths and passions.

We had potent fun times when we laughed until we cried and our sides ached. There were crazy, nutty times when we were all very silly and giggled at our own dotty antics or were giddy for no particular reason. At other times our sadness brought bouts of weeping and emotional distress. We grew together through these experiences into a loving, caring family unit. I cherish all those times, and I wouldn't have missed them for the world.

I offer this book as a history of events, a mapping of sorts of the progression of my thought process throughout my years of motherhood. I feel immense gratitude and appreciation for my wonderful children: Annalisa, Johnathan, David, and Rachel. I love you to the moon and back, to the sun and back, and to infinity and back!

With all my pride and love to you, my four lovely children, Mom.

Cathy Andrea Kotow-Dockman XOXOXO

Kotow Homestead aerial, 1950s

Dad, Andy and Mom, Elizabeth (Betty) playfully courting, 1950

Andy and Betty's wedding. St. Mary's Church, Maidstone, Ontario, 1950

Andy and Betty's honeymoon in Niagara Falls

Betty on honeymoon

Andy on honeymoon

Kotow Homestead, 1980s

Andy, Betty, Babka, and newborn Crystal (Cris), 1951

Andy with his mother, Babka, at his wedding

Betty's parents, Mimi and Pipi Malenfant

Babka enjoying farming, caring for a calf

Cathy as a newborn at her christening on Babka's dining
room table, 1957. This antique table I still have and use

# CHAPTER 1

## *My Early History*

I was a quiet, thoughtful, mischievous, intelligent, and creative child. I grew up on a farm in rural southern Ontario. My grandparents purchased the quarter section in Sandwich South township after emigrating from Europe. I attended a Catholic school from Grades 1 to 8 and then a public high school from Grades 9 to 13. Yes, we had no kindergarten and we had Grade 13, which was like a preparatory year for university. I was the middle of five living children, sandwiched between two brothers. My brother Francis (Frank) was a year and two months older than me, and Joseph (Joe) was a year and nine months younger. My two sisters were Crystal, four years and nine months older, and Mary Beth, six years and six months younger.

Beth, Cris, Cathy, Joe, and Frank on our side porch. What a crew!

JULY 1958

Looks like Frank is in trouble again.

Kotow family: Mom, Dad, and five kids with neighbor child

Cathy, Frank, Beth, and Joe in front of the old brick farmhouse during its demolition

I was a tomboy and spent most of my childhood doing what my father and two brothers did. As a toddler I spent much of my time riding on the seat of the tractor with my dad. As I grew older, I spent time in the barn, tending to the cows and other farm chores.

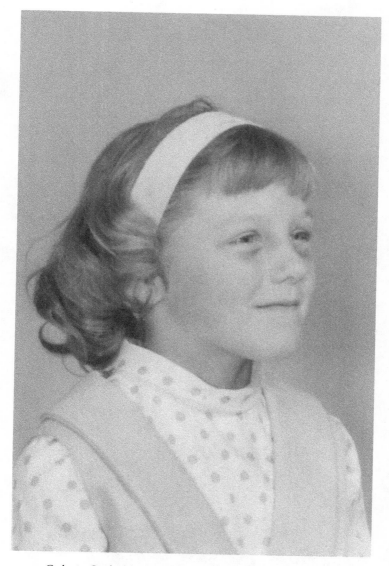

Cathy in Grade 4 with two black eyes from a baseball accident,
dressed in an outfit our mom sewed for Cris and me to be matching

Really, I just followed my dad around. I was much happier doing outside farm work than inside housework or cooking, with the exception of learning how to sew, which I loved to do. I learned to sew with a passion and a purpose—I wanted fashionable clothes. We couldn't afford to buy them, so I improvised. I took the used clothing that we received from our cousins, or our old, outdated clothes, and remade them into modern outfits. Being able to visualize an outfit and then create it turned out to be a useful skill later in life.

As a child, I was very motivated to do schoolwork. My Grade 4 teacher took me under his wing and encouraged me to utilize my potential, which he saw and I didn't. He saw more in me than I saw in myself. Over the next few years, I thrived under his guidance and graduated from Grade 8 with an A plus average, tied for top marks with my best friend, Joanne.

Cathy's Grade 8 school picture, St. Mary's school, Maidstone

In Grade 9, I discovered boys, and they became more than just hockey or baseball teammates—much more. This created worry and fear for my parents, as I was very naive. That year, I dated a guy who had already graduated from high school. He had a white Chevy muscle car with white leather seats and a powerful engine. It was exciting! I was having a blast! My parents had reason to be nervous about this relationship.

That's when they decided to appoint Frank, my older brother, as my "protector," my bodyguard. He was to watch out for me and keep me out of trouble. They trusted me to make decisions on the condition that my older brother and I went out on double dates, which was a wise choice on my parents' part. The fellow I was dating was five years older than me and experienced in sexual matters. I was green and lacked knowledge about matters of love, sex, and relationships. Fortunately, the relationship didn't last long, and I didn't get into trouble with him.

High school was an intensely fun time. We were footloose and fancy free with no cares in the world. I was active socially with friends and boyfriends. We roller skated, danced, went to the beach, threw bush parties, and went to movie theatres and drive-ins. We drank alcohol and smoked cigarettes because it was "cool," and we skipped school to go to bars and dances in the afternoons. We made fake ID cards so we could buy alcohol at the liquor stores and bars. We had no fear and saw few consequences of our activities. We never got caught, so we got bolder and took more risks, like keeping bottles of alcohol in our school lockers and drinking while we drove our parents' vehicles. It was a crazy time, and we were lucky that we weren't in accidents or suspended from school for our shenanigans.

My priorities changed from schoolwork to my social life in Grade 9; therefore, my marks fell drastically from the high nineties to the mid-seventies. I spent some time on the honour roll, which required an average of 75%. I didn't do any drugs, due to a warning from my brother, whom I trusted to protect me. Turns out I dated one of my brother's best friends from Grade 10 to Grade 13. He was one year younger than me. We were extremely compatible and enjoyed each other in all ways. He was my first love.

After I graduated from Grade 13, my boyfriend of four years wanted to get married, build a house beside his parents', and settle down. I believed I loved him and that we could build a life together, but I wasn't ready to be married and have children. I wanted to go to university and travel the world. I had grandiose ideas. I declined and broke off the long-term high school relationship. It was very difficult, because I cared deeply for him and felt we were soulmates.

So I trotted off to the University of Waterloo to take kinesiology, and I lived with a girlfriend, Maureen, in her off-campus apartment. After six months, I discovered that kinesiology and university weren't what I expected or wanted to do. Getting a job in human kinetics was nearly impossible in those days, so I didn't see the practicality of my studies.

At that time, I was introduced to a company called Bestline, a direct sales business, and I chose to try it. At nineteen years old, I went to my parents for money to start this business. My parents investigated the business and loaned me the $4,000 I needed to pursue the endeavour. Thank God for free enterprise! I worked hard and was rewarded with great income, many promotions, and lots of travel. I loved it! I took management seminars as well as sales and personal development courses. I simply absorbed it all. I also read voraciously. I devoured books on positive attitude, personal power, financial success, business organizational skills, and personal development. Although I was distracted by operating my small business, I remained in university and finished my first year of studies with a reasonable grade point average. Then I left university to build my business full-time.

I met my husband, Mike, through this company when we were on a trip to the Bahamas, where we went every four months. I first caught a glimpse of him at a seminar called "Secrets of Success," where the speaker presented Mike with an award. I remember looking at Mike and thinking, *He's got an incredible amount of energy.* He was almost bouncing off the walls, like the Tasmanian Devil! I remember the speaker commenting that he was single and available. That was all that happened for the moment. On the next trip to the Bahamas, we officially met.

We started to date and worked as a team to develop our business together. We continued to travel to the Bahamas, Jamaica, Hawaii, and Florida, and then later to Europe, Russia, and Africa. I'd say, "Put me on a plane and send me anywhere." I just loved to fly, mostly the takeoff and landing and travelling to any destination I could manage to arrange. I was fascinated and curious about the way other cultures lived. I saw my travel adventures as an integral part of my education.

Cathy and Mike formally-dressed at the head table
on a Bestline company trip in Freeport, Bahamas

I learned much about world history and other cultures from my travel experiences. I also gained an appreciation for life in Canada. I loved to visit castles and ancient ruins and discover the art and history of my destinations. During this time, Mike and I advanced in the company to become regional directors. In this position, we facilitated a variety of training sessions for the sales and management staff. We made excellent money but spent it all to keep up the lifestyle of entertaining, fine dining, and travelling.

We dated for several years, developing our relationship. Throughout this time, we discussed getting married and having a family. Mike was skeptical of marriage, as almost all of his family members had been divorced, and he didn't want that to happen to him. Over the next two years we became more serious and wanted to build our life together as husband and wife and talked about having children together. We seemed to have similar dreams and directions in life. After a business trip to Paris, he proposed, I accepted, and we were married on July 11, 1981. I was twenty-four years old. Two years prior to our wedding, Bestline went out of business. We were left with experience, memories, no income, and a mountain of debts.

In spite of the financial burdens, we planned and I organized a beautiful wedding celebration. Two hundred and sixty friends and family attended. We had the Catholic ceremony at St. Mary's church in Maidstone, the same church where my parents wed forty years earlier. We had the reception in a community hall in Woodslee with the ladies' league preparing a delicious home-cooked meal. After paying all the expenses of the wedding we calculated having a $600 budget for our honeymoon. Due to our financial restraints we had traded in our fully-loaded, metallic black Lincoln Continental for an orange Pinto hatchback.

Well our two-week honeymoon was still on—a road trip through the states making our way to New Orleans. Having a hatchback that turned into our sleeping space was innovative. Mike, being the brilliant mathematician he is, had figured our daily spending budget. Seven days in he admitted to having made an error, and we were out of money. As the adventure continued we chose to get jobs for the weekend to support the remainder of our trip. In Oklahoma we discovered Frontier City. They had a sign advertising a need for staff. Mike went in to offer his services. They needed a female saloon maid. You guessed it, I dressed up in the costume, including mesh stockings, and slung beers for the weekend. Mike got to play cowboy. It was a blast and I made enough money to continue our travels.

Kotow Clan gathering the night before my wedding at our farm, 1981

Cathy and Mike's wedding

Mom, Dad and five siblings at my wedding

Eileen, John, and Dockman siblings at our wedding

Cathy and sister Beth, my maid of honour

Cathy

On our honeymoon in Frontier City, Oklahoma dressed in western wear

Cathy on honeymoon working as a saloon maid

After the business closed, we both worked two jobs to get ourselves out of the financial hole we had dug. We returned to the real world of the working class and trying to live within our means. By the time we were married, we had cleared our debt by hard work and determination, and we had started our own express courier business.

I had achieved my goal of travelling and seeing various parts of the world. I learned much about myself and how other cultures lived as my eyes were opened to a much broader world. This new perspective was valuable and helped me to move from focusing on myself to seeing other people's views. I was growing up!

I worked hard in business and achieved reasonable success. From the ages of nineteen to twenty-four, I matured and grew personally, building a healthy self-confidence and more balanced worldview. Those years provided more knowledge and experience to prepare me for being a parent and moving into motherhood. So I began another phase of my life as a married woman and entrepreneur. It was an exciting time with much hope for our future.

# CHAPTER 2

## *Conception and Pregnancy*

During the last five years of working in business, I felt that I had fulfilled my travel and adventure goals. I was satisfied with my life's path and ready to settle down, have children, and start our family.

I stopped taking the birth control pill for six months to let my body adjust to its natural cycle before we started trying to conceive. After the six-month body cleanse, I was eager to get on with getting pregnant and having a baby. I was ready mentally, emotionally, and physically. One, two, three months went by, and I wasn't pregnant. I thought conceiving should happen naturally, and I was getting impatient. Why was it taking so long? I was disappointed each month when I found out I wasn't pregnant.

I began reading about conception, blocks to pregnancy, and fertility. I figured out which part of the month I was ovulating and developed a plan for those four fertile days. It was simple—have sex every eight hours during those days! Crazy single-mindedness! It took three months of doing this for me to conceive. It worked. I was ecstatic! Now, what next?

I wanted to learn as much as I could about what was happening to my body and the development of the baby. I started to gather books on fetal development, nutrition during pregnancy, and emotional and physical changes. I studied all the information I could gather about this miracle growing within me. I thought, *Hey, more questions! Here I go again on another information-gathering quest.* I looked for answers to questions like: Can I communicate with the baby inside of me? Do my moods affect the child? How can I make these nine months the best for this baby's development?

I read *The Secret Life of the Unborn Child* (Dr. T. Verny, 1981),[1] a book about the baby's development in the womb. I was fascinated to know when the heart, brain, fingernails, and other parts were developing. I also read *Dare*

31

*to Discipline* by Dr. J. Dobson (1992),[2] which gave me interesting food for thought. I didn't agree with many of his ideas, but I gained some knowledge from the read. Another book I found useful was *Children: The Challenge* by R. Dreikurs (1990).[3] Some of the content is old-style now, but I took valuable information about respect and cooperation from the book. One idea I embraced was family council meetings as a way to deal with troublesome problems in a democratic manner (p. 301). I used this idea when my children were older. We called them "magical meetings," where everyone had a right to speak their mind without interruption. I gained much knowledge from my research and reading.

I also read *Parents* magazine[4] and books about different forms of childbirth. From that research, I learned that the baby does feel the moods of the mother. The mother and child are united totally during the gestation period. The baby is affected by whatever the mother puts into her body, whether that is drugs, alcohol, food, or other substances. Healthy living, eating right, and getting exercise was the ticket, although occasionally I'd have a wee little wine. Moderation was the key. At that time research had not shown the negative effects of alcohol on the developing fetus. The medical evidence now shows any amount of alcohol during pregnancy is unsafe, another example of how science and evolution can change the landscape of motherhood.

My research also revealed that the baby recognizes voices and music while in the womb, so a calm environment has a positive effect on the baby's development. My mood, emotions, and attitudes would directly affect the growing fetus. Studies also suggested that drug-free childbirth was best. A spinal epidural freezes the mother's body but also the baby to some degree and it stifles the mother's urge to push and deliver the baby naturally. I was open to considering much of this information, but some of the ideas were too "out there" for me.

I decided that I wanted the baby born in a hospital, as I was too nervous about possible complications of a home birth. But I wanted a hospital that believed in natural childbirth, and I wanted to avoid the use of any drugs if I could. I wanted more of a home-birth atmosphere but with surgical equipment and doctors handy if there were any serious problems. I had too much fear of the unknown to give birth in water or with a midwife at home.

I kept active and worked throughout my pregnancy, seeing my doctor regularly and eating well—very well, in fact! I took being pregnant as a license to eat. I had struggled with 15 to 30 pounds of extra weight since my teenage years, and now I was able to eat for two for the health of the baby. So I ate and ate all the time. It seemed I was constantly in a state of hunger. I gained 55 pounds during that pregnancy. My doctor checked for any problems the extra weight might create and said that as long as I was active and experienced no negative side effects, he didn't see the weight gain as a problem. Even though I was self-conscious sometimes, I felt that the weight gain was okay, so I grew very large! Although my huge midsection slowed me down, I was still doing most things right up to the birth. Thank God!

I remember the day I weighed the same as my husband. I almost went into shock when I saw 182 pounds on the scale! I'd weighed 135 pounds when I became pregnant. We laughed about it, but I was horrified for a while. Since I still felt healthy and mobile, and my doctor said the babe was fine, I relaxed about the weight gain.

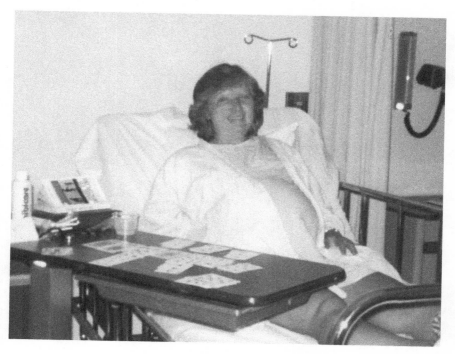

Cathy slow-labouring with childbirth

It was exciting to see the ultrasound images, to hear the baby's heartbeat, and to see the baby's physical formations. The visual proof in the ultrasound made the baby seem more real. When the baby started to kick and move inside of me, I was startled and fascinated. It was hard to imagine that this was a real person moving around! I talked to the baby, and Mike sang to my middle section. The baby had a calm nine months growing in my uterus. We didn't know its gender, but I secretly wanted a girl first, and Mike wanted a boy. Typical!

My dream of being a mother was becoming a reality, and my due date was coming closer. On the one hand, I was thrilled and anticipating our baby's arrival, but on the other hand, I was worried about the massive responsibility of caring for a child twenty-four seven. It can be overwhelming. I also had moments of doubt regarding my ability to be a good mother. Gathering knowledge was helpful for me when I was worried. Solidifying my views, values, and ideas about parenting kept me busy and free from worry as I clarified the ways I planned to parent.

# CHAPTER 3

## First-Born Child

My doctor had given me an approximate due date for the expected delivery of my first child. Two weeks before that date, I was getting serious nesting instincts. I had her room ready, including clothes, a diaper service set-up, blankets, a musical bear, and all the necessary stuff I could possibly perceive I needed. I had powder, Vaseline, gripe water, salve for diaper rash, wipes, a change table, and a really cool wicker bassinet from Zambia that my sister Cris used for her two children when they'd lived there. My sister-in-law Christine's boyfriend, Alfonzo, built shelves and closets and finished the tiny room that was just off our bedroom/sitting room. The room had been a walk-in closet and was very small, but it would have to do for the baby's room. We painted it a soft, calming mauve colour and securely hung the bassinet from the ceiling so it would swing and rock the baby. Alfonzo and I turned the tiny space into a lovely, cozy baby nook! I called the baby "her" not because I had learned the gender of my child but because my instincts told me I was carrying a female.

I was very anxious about the upcoming delivery of my child, particularly about the pain, possible complications, and possible health problems for me or the baby. I was moving slower and expecting her to come any day. She didn't.

When the due date came, I went to see my doctor. The baby had dropped, but my cervix hadn't started to dilate. The doctor said the baby was full-term, developed, and safe to be born, so I had to wait and be patient. Ohhh, the anticipation and fear were terrible! I wanted her to be born now!

Four days later, Mike was at work and the mucus plug came out, so I thought my water had broken. I had no idea! All excited, I called Mike and told him to come home and take me to the hospital. Then I called Chris, my sister-in-law, to tell her what had happened and that I was going to drive myself the hospital.

African bassinet, lent from Cris and John, hanging in Lisa's nursery

"Cathy," she said, a bit exasperated, "you may be in labour. You can't drive yourself!"

*Okay, I guess I could let her help me.* She picked me up with her year-and-a-half-old daughter and drove me to the hospital.

Mike met us at the admissions office, where we filled out all the paperwork. The doctor examined me and said I was three centimetres dilated, but my water hadn't broken. They put me in a room and we waited. That was a Friday. By Saturday afternoon, nothing more had happened, so they said I was in false labour and sent me home. Really? OMG! It sure felt real to me. Off we went to wait and fill in time until labour started again.

Mike and I went out for a steak dinner at the Ponderosa restaurant, where they had a "two can dine for $9.99" deal. After that we went to watch a movie, *Mr. Mom.*[5] It was funny and appropriate to our situation. I was still having the odd contraction during the movie, but the pain was manageable. When we got home, I was so uncomfortable that I couldn't sleep at all. At 2 a.m., contractions started again, five to seven minutes apart for the rest of the night and into early morning. At 6 a.m. I woke Mike and asked him to take me back to the hospital. I really didn't know what to expect, and I didn't want to deliver at home. Let's face it, my first child was about to be born, and I was skittish, nervous, and afraid of the unknown.

Mike was skeptical as to whether I was really in labour. I didn't know either, but I wasn't taking any chances. The hospital checked me in again. I was five centimetres dilated and the cervix had softened. I was in real labour this time. Yes, finally! The nurse brought us to a labour room that was furnished like a living room. It was comfortable and cozy, so I could relax and continue with the labour process.

I labored all day with little progress. The doctor was concerned about the slow progress and at 5 p.m. he decided to break my water to speed up the delivery. The contractions kept coming five to seven minutes apart. At 6 p.m., my doctor was starting to get worried, because the cervix hadn't dilated any more since morning. She decided to induce labour further with an intravenous drip of Oxytocin. I was so exhausted. They also gave me a shot of Demerol in my hip to relax the muscles and lessen the pain. I fell into a dead sleep for three hours! Any kind of medication generally hits me hard, and the Demerol knocked me out. Right in the middle of labour, I slept. Totally amazing!

While I slept, Mike paced the floor, thinking something was extremely wrong. I was still having contractions, but I slept through them all. The baby was being monitored, and she was fine. In hindsight, I guess that due to my fear I was holding back and not relaxing enough to let the baby be born. Also, she was in no hurry to exit her warm, safe cocoon. As I discovered later, she was a very inquisitive yet laid-back baby. Her personality showed through even during the delivery.

After being in a deep sleep for at least three hours due to the Demerol and with no conscious awareness of the consistent contractions I woke up with a start and scared Mike half out of his wits. I sat up in the bed and exclaimed, "The baby is coming. . . now!" Mike called the nurse, who told me not to push. I looked at her like she was crazy. Every cell in my body was pushing. I couldn't stop! Even if I tried, the urge to push was there instinctively. My body had taken over my mind. The nurse rushed the doctor in, and she checked me as they moved me to the delivery room bed. By then I was ten centimetres dilated, and the baby's head was showing. I had slept through transition labour—pretty unbelievable. They gave Mike sterilized scrubs and a hat and booties to wear. Everything happened so fast. Just a few more contractions and the baby's head came out. I used laughing gas (nitrous oxide) for the last contractions to dull the pain. The doctor performed an episiotomy, but I still tore. I was frozen from a local anesthetic and not aware of that pain. The rest of the baby's body was delivered smoothly and with little effort. It was a girl! Yippee! I saw and felt her come out of me. Incredible!

At that moment, something unbelievable happened. Unfathomable! If I hadn't felt it, I would say it was crap and wouldn't believe it was true, but it was miraculous! I forgot about the stress, the worry, and the incredible pain. It all vanished, only to be replaced with awe, love, joy, and gratitude! Literally, I forgot the pain and only saw her—this beautiful, healthy baby. In reality, she was swollen, bloody, and had a conehead. I checked, and she had ten fingers and toes. She had the most serene look on her face, with a slight smile. It was like she was thinking, *I made it. I got out!* Conehead and all, I thought she was the most beautiful thing I'd seen in my entire life! WOW!

Her head was almost pointed, with steps of bone layers formed by the pressure and force exerted during her time in the birth canal. The doctor explained that the head changing shape was normal and that the bone plates in her head would move and adjust back to their normal, rounded shape. I accepted her explanation and didn't worry about the shape of the head. I simply reveled in the joy and contentment I felt from feeling and seeing her birth.

I was so consumed with looking at her that I forgot about the placenta. The afterbirth still had to come out, and I had to push again to expel it. I was flabbergasted at how massive an organ the placenta was. Wow! It was like a mammoth liver that had sustained her life throughout the pregnancy. I stared at the placenta in amazement and wonder.

The doctor stitched me up while the two nurses cleaned up our little girl. . . well, not so little. She was 9 lbs. 12 oz. Her size was part of the reason why she took so long to arrive. She had a little contented, serene smile on her face, and she didn't fuss at all. Mike and I held her for a bit.

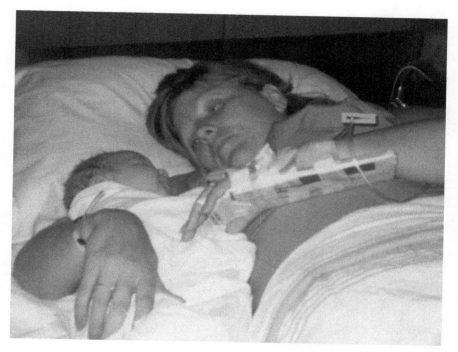

Annalisa with Mom, shortly after her birth

Eventually, the nurses took her to the nursery to check all her vitals and brought me back to my room to rest. Baby and I were both exhausted and slept for three hours. Then they brought her to me to breastfeed. The nurse assisted me, and it took a bit of encouragement before the baby latched on. After several tries, we got the whole nipple in her mouth and she sucked. We were on our way! The regular milk wasn't coming yet, so she just had the first milk, called colostrum, which was yellow and packed with nutrients. It was a lighter substance that got her body adjusted to the changed form of nutrition. The regular breast milk would come in approximately three days. Mike and I had previously decided to call her Lynn, but after she was born, I changed my mind.

"Why?" Mike asked.

"She just doesn't look like a Lynn," I said.

Of course, he couldn't understand. I think it was some kind of mother's instinct that told me Lynn was not the right name for this little girl. We called her Baby Dockman for her first month of life, because Mike and I couldn't agree on another name.

We had thirty days to register her name. Finally, in desperation, Mike started going through the alphabet. Through much time and deliberation, we settled on naming her Annalisa Dawn, partly from our family history of names. My mother's name is Elizabeth, and my grandmother was Anna. We also chose it because of the Christian meanings. Ann meant "full of grace, mercy and prayer" and was originally from the Hebrew "Hannah." Elizabeth meant "consecrated to God" (Hebrew), and Dawn meant "the break of day." Plus, we simply liked the name. I knew it suited her, but I don't know how I knew that at the time. Intuition? A sixth sense? Maybe her character that I was already picking up on? Spiritual messages? Well, maybe all of the above and more that we simply don't understand. But there she was—a beautiful, healthy, happy baby girl. Annalisa Dawn Dockman had arrived. I was relieved, scared as hell, and elated all at once!

I had a fairly straightforward pregnancy with very few health issues or problems. Even though I'd done a substantial amount of research through reading and taking classes, the birthing process was shockingly difficult. I'm a mostly optimistic person, and my expectations were very different from the reality. Endurance, physical help and encouragement from Mike, and the medical staff's support and explanations of various options and medications all contributed to my first child's safe arrival. It can be a complicated process, but women have been carrying and bearing offspring throughout human history. My choice, my body, and the challenges and risks did not outweigh the benefits of having a child and becoming a mother.

If being a mother turned out to be as difficult as childbirth I was in for years of challenges, learning and having to ask for and accept help. Now I had successfully given birth. It was time to begin my motherhood duties. I assumed difficulties would arise. Challenge embraced!

# CHAPTER 4

## *Bringing Baby Home*

I spent five days in the hospital after Annalisa's birth. I was anemic, therefore I was extremely tired and needed rest. I was given an iron supplements intravenously to build up my red blood cell count and hemoglobin levels. The doctor also wanted my stitches to heal before she let me go home. The nurses would cleanse me, give me a bed bath, and then put my legs in the stirrups. I had to lie in this very awkward position for fifteen minutes under a heat lamp they'd set on the bed. The heat enhanced the healing of the incision and helped to prevent infection. Thankfully, I had no infection or any complications after the birth. Both the episiotomy and the torn skin healed well. We began shortening the baby's name to Lisa, for simplicity I guess. She had a bit of jaundice on her second day, and the doctor wanted the jaundice cleared up before she was released.

On the fifth day, we were released from the hospital. I dressed Annalisa in a beautiful, crocheted, handmade outfit that Grandma Kotow, my mom, had made for her. I wore a loose- fitting, pretty pink dress I'd made myself. I'd lost 28 to 29 pounds through the birth but was still swollen, sore, and felt heavy with extra weight. We put Lisa into the car seat and headed home.

In 1983, baby car seats were a new concept, and we had no idea how to use one. Mike had bought one while I was in the hospital, as it was the law. All right, no problem. We loaded Annalisa into the car seat in the back of our car. I sat in the front passenger seat, Mike secured the new baby into the multitude of straps and buckles, and we were on our way home. Mike drove. Our new family unit!

My emotions were working overtime. I think my hormone activity brought on some postpartum depression and worry, which converted me into an emotional, irrational wreck. I was turned around and watching the baby through tear-filled eyes from the front seat. When Mike turned the first corner, I watched the car seat roll over and land upside down between the front and back seats!

"Oh my God! Mike, stop the car," I yelled.

He pulled over. What had we done to this child already, only a few minutes from the hospital? All my fears had manifested themselves; I was a terrible mother! Awwwk!

Thankfully, she was well-strapped into the car seat and hung there quietly, looking around. In hindsight, I believe she was quite comfortable with being upside down after floating for nine months in the amniotic fluid in my uterus. To her, it wasn't unusual. To me, it was a major parental catastrophe, especially considering my turbulent emotional state. The sides and top of the car seat were built up and protected her, so she was undamaged. What a relief. How stupid did we feel, not putting the seat belt around the car seat!

Being ignorant about child car seats did not improve my insecurities about my parenting abilities! I cried uncontrollably all the way home. I was on an emotional rollercoaster and had no idea why I was so emotional and out of control with tears. I guess there were lots of valid reasons for it. I was sore, and it hurt to sit. I was tired and had been through labour and delivery and many days of nursing the baby every three hours with only short naps between feeds. I was also an excited new parent with a new baby. I was afraid and uncertain. Could I really be a good mother and look after this little being? Now that I'd left the hospital, she was all my responsibility. I wouldn't have the hospital staff to help me. The total weight of the responsibility I held for the life of another human being came crashing down hard on me, and I was petrified.

Thank God that my mother, father, mother-in-law, and sister-in-law were all there at the house to help and support me during the first few weeks. I seriously needed them. I had to rest, eat, and then feed Lisa every three to four hours. My family looked after the meals, laundry, cleaning, and abso-lutely everything else so I could regain my strength physically, mentally, and emotionally. That was it. I basically ate, slept, and nursed her during the first week. Soon I began to get stronger in body and mind. My parents left after my first week at home. I couldn't have managed without their generous and loving help. I was very appreciative and grateful that they had foreseen the need when I did not.

Cathy's emotional arrival home with our first child, Annalisa

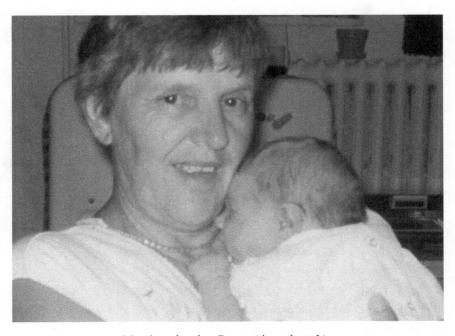

Mom/grandmother, Betty, with newborn Lisa

Mike and Annalisa and I lived in a one-bedroom basement apartment of a large country home owned by my mother-in-law, Eileen. She and my father-in-law, John, had been divorced since Mike was fourteen years old. They bought the acreage after moving from England after the second world war and John had built on additional space, turning the small cottage into a five-bedroom multilevel home. The space accommodated separate living arrangements for our three families. My sister-in-law Christine and her daughter, Giselle, lived in the top floor apartment. Eileen lived on the main level and we lived in the basement suite.

Family group hug saying goodbye with Nana and
Uncle Harry in front of their home in Brampton, Ontario

After my parents returned home to their farm in Maidstone, I still had Eileen and Christine as additional support in our home. I soon realized that I could look after the baby and take care of all her needs, but knowing I had support close by was very comforting. My family support was invaluable, and I learned from their experiences. Caring for my first child, I erred on the side of caution, asked lots of questions, and was most definitely overprotective! My confidence and strength grew with time, experience, and support.

Annalisa was a calm and contented baby. She cried when she was hungry or needed her diaper changed; otherwise, she was curious, wide-eyed, and enjoyable. She also slept well from the beginning. We cuddled her, talked, sang, and played. She was unafraid of other family members and fell asleep on many of them when they rocked her or sang to her. I carried her around in a sling on my chest called a Snugli. With it, I could carry her on my front or back, like a backpack. She fit into the Snugli comfortably, and I had my hands free. She could sleep or watch her environment while feeling my warmth and heartbeat and hearing my voice. She was content to be close to me much of the day, and we were rarely separated. Sometimes she'd sleep for a few hours in her bassinet while I rested, cooked, or tidied up. I found this time to be both exhausting and fascinating.

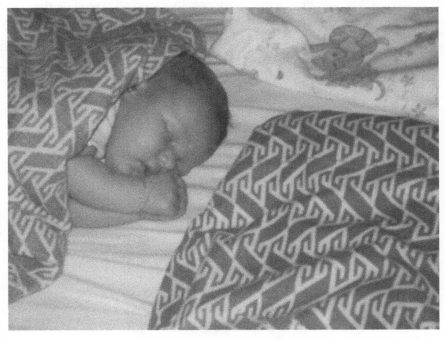

Beautiful and calm sleeping Lisa

Nursing Annalisa was an intimate bonding experience. I especially loved the middle of the night feedings when our entire world was quiet and only Annalisa and I were awake together. While nursing we became one again. She was totally trusting and dependent on me. It was overwhelming at times but also an incredibly nurturing experience for both of us, physically and emotionally.

I found joy in every little progression she made. I'd survived the first week, then the first month, and I knew I'd be fine. Lisa and I became attuned to each other. We grew to know the meaning of each other's sounds and communication clues, and we became more connected with one another as time passed. She and I would be more than fine—we would thrive!

Becoming a competent and confident mother takes time and experience. I had some fairy-tale ideas about motherhood coming naturally, with the maternal instincts just kicking in. That was not the case for me. It took practice, work, and trial and error to figure out what the baby needed and to decipher her noisy vocabulary. With observation and patience, I learned how to mother this child. I talked with mothers in my family and asked questions and read about child development whenever I could. As I became more confident in my skills, I was able to relax and find joy in the experience of motherhood.

Lisa happy in her one-year birthday present,
a rocking chair from Grandma and Grandpa Kotow

# CHAPTER 5

## *Extended Family and Travel Adventures*

I consider myself very fortunate and blessed because of the extensive amount of family support I had, especially during my children's baby and early childhood years. When Lisa was born, not only did I have family living in the same home, Lisa had her cousin Giselle living upstairs. The home was situated on a hill, and behind it was a valley filled with mature trees, lush greenery, and a creek meandering through the bottom. It was a beautiful and peaceful setting.

The best part of living in Eileen's home was that we were surrounded by family. Although I was sad when my mom and dad left after the first week I was home with the baby, I didn't feel alone, because my husband's family was living in the same home and available to help when I needed them. They made me feel secure and supported. Giselle, my niece, was a year and a half old and very curious about Lisa, her new cousin.

It was August in Ontario, and the weather was sunny and very hot. I regularly brought Lisa outside to the back patio in the shade or on the grassy area, where we would bask in the sunshine of the beautiful summer days. I'd let the sun heal her diaper rash. She enjoyed the warm nakedness. I was feeling stronger every day and week that passed. I was still ravenously hungry all the time, and I continued to eat well, but thankfully I was losing the pregnancy weight. Nursing Lisa helped to tighten the muscles, which shrank my uterus and tummy. The stitches also healed well. I wasn't sleeping as much or as long as I needed. My sleep was fragmented into smaller naps between waking to breastfeed Lisa.

During Lisa's first three months of life, every little sound she made woke me, and I'd get up to see if she was okay and still breathing. Sometimes I'd check randomly, even when she was sound asleep. I was worried about

47

"sudden infant death syndrome" (SIDS) and was definitely hyper-vigilant about her health. My worry was a waste of time, though, because Lisa was healthy and thriving.

I had an abundance of milk, and my breasts had gone from an A cup to a D. I'd stand in the shower, start the hot water and the milk would squirt out about three feet. Incredible! We would joke that I had so much milk, I should bottle and sell it. I did express milk with a breast pump, which was a funny looking glass contraption with a funnel on one end and a rubber ball on the other. It worked! I put the milk into glass baby bottles and froze it. When we went out for an evening, Chris (Christine) or Eileen would warm up the bottle and feed Lisa my breast milk.

Occasionally we did go out without bringing Lisa, but usually I took her with me in the Snugli or the car seat. I'd nurse her wherever I was. This wasn't a problem in most places, as I would be discreet. One time I was at Zellers department store, and it was time for a feeding. I went to the cafeteria and covered her and myself with a receiving blanket and nursed her. I was told by the staff that I had to leave the cafeteria! They said that I could not do "that" (referring to me breastfeeding my baby) there. I was shocked! I tried to explain that it was totally natural, but they said I had to leave. I was very upset by the archaic thinking. At that time, many people weren't used to women nursing their children in public. It was sad.

Nursing is such a beautiful and natural thing. When my mother gave birth to me and my siblings in the 1950s and 60s, breastfeeding was taboo. It was out of vogue. My mother nursed us, as it was naturally done in her family, but the medical profession and baby food companies stressed that baby formula was a healthier alternative. They convinced parents not to breastfeed but to use this new formula instead. Many new parents chose the store-bought formula and mixed it in sterilized baby bottles to feed their babies. Somehow breastfeeding had taken on a sexual connotation during those years instead of being seen as a nurturing and natural way to feed infants. It was slow to change that societal thinking when women began to breastfeed again.

The books and studies I read explained that natural immunities are passed on to the child through the mother's milk—not to mention the emotional feelings the mother and child experience while connecting in this most intimate way. It made sense to me. Cow's milk is for cows. Human milk is for humans. It's warm, nutritious, and ready anytime, anywhere! Breastfeeding is much more convenient than using bottles that have to be sterilized, filled, and heated to body temperature. It also makes travelling with a young child so much simpler. The planes in those days had a bassinet that hung on the front wall of the first row of seats for a baby to sleep in. I'd feed her when needed, like during takeoff and landing to help with the air pressure changes in her ears. Travelling was a breeze.

Speaking of travelling, my sister Cris and her husband, John, lived in Zambia, Africa, and we had many relatives living in England. In 1984, we combined the trip to see Grandma and Grandpa Fursey and other family in England with a trip to see my sister in Zambia. I got a good deal on flights for the three of us from a British travel bureau, so the cost was actually half the price of what the North American airlines quoted. The catch was we had to fly with Aeroflot, the Russian airline. We had to go through Moscow and stay there for three days. *What a bonus!* I thought I could handle this hardship! Ha ha!

We took advantage of the unique opportunity and travelled to London, England and then to visit with Lisa's great-grandmother and great-grandfather in Staffordshire, Stone. They were in their eighties and still living in their own home. They were absolutely delighted to see us. Great-Grandma had been in bed for some time suffering from ill health, but she got up before we arrived and made a full English tea, as was her British tradition. They were wonderful hosts. When she saw Lisa, Great-Grandmother was so delighted, she came to life and got out of bed to visit with us and enjoy tea together. It was a thrill to meet and visit with Mike's family in England.

After visiting aunts, uncles, and cousins in Manchester and several other smaller towns in England, we travelled from London to Moscow on Aeroflot airlines. The plane stopped in Budapest, where the airline staff took out eight seats and brought in a wounded man on a stretcher, who was apparently a war casualty. Doctors and military men also boarded the plane with this obviously seriously injured person. The hospital bed was right across the aisle from us, but the airline staff put up a curtain between us for the injured man's privacy.

Cathy visiting Eileen's parents, Grandpa and Grandma Fursey, in England

The plane didn't seem to be up to our normal safety codes. It seemed mechanically sound, but it looked much older than any plane I'd ever flown in. It was quite an experience— somewhat frightening but at the same time an interesting adventure! I had been used to flying to Canada, the US, and the Caribbean. Despite the airplane's questionable state of repair, we successfully made it to Moscow.

At that time, the Cold War was going on, and Russia was still known as the United Soviet Socialist Republic (USSR), existing under a communist regime. When we landed at the Moscow airport, we saw military men with machine guns everywhere. That was a shock to us as Canadians. I'd never been to a communist country before. I'd only seen that kind of military surveillance on TV. Most of the airport was closed; dozens of commercial airplanes were on blocks and full of snow. Dozens of military planes were on blocks as well. The lights were turned off in more than half the airport, and only one restaurant was open. I was obviously entering a different world than I was familiar with.

A military customs officer asked to see my identification and passport as we entered the airport. He was a scary, formal, serious man in a uniform and with a machine gun. He was clearly suspicious of us. He looked at my passport photo and then at me. He looked at my photo again, studied it, and then looked back at me. Silence. It seemed like forever as he waited for approximately thirty seconds. I was terribly frightened about what he was going do with me. Then he pointed to my picture on my passport and asked, "Is this you?"

In fear, I said yes. I thought they were going to search me and not let me into their country—or worse, put me in jail for something. Wow! What an awakening!

After much deliberation and skepticism, the customs soldier let us into Russia with what seemed like much reticence. Aeroflot put us up in a hotel close to the airport for three nights. We had three days to explore Moscow. I was excited! My husband and child were tired, and they wanted to sleep, but I hadn't travelled all that way just to waste my time sleeping. I was going to use every moment wisely and explore.

On the way to our motel room, we saw security cameras everywhere—in the lobby, the elevators, and the hallways. There didn't seem to be any cameras in our room, though. Naively, I went out of the motel to try to exchange some US dollars for Russian rubles. I had heard that I could get thirty rubles to one US dollar on the street. Then we could shop and get souvenirs and clothing with the rubles. Sounded good to me!

I went onto the street alone to find someone with whom I could exchange money. I met one fellow, whose friend joined us in the conversation. I told them what I wanted to do, and they shook their heads yes, as if they understood what I was saying. We walked back to the hotel lobby. I said I would give him $100 US to exchange for rubles, and he nodded his head, so I figured it was a done deal. They followed me to my hotel room, and at the door I again offered $100 US for rubles. This time, he said no, the $100 US was for me, and he pointed to the floor in our motel room. Awwwk! The light went on in my brain. *Oh swear!* I realized that what they were really after was sex, right there on the floor of my hotel room. Fear crawled over my skin in a cold sweat. *What trouble did I get myself into?*

I had the door open halfway and said, "No, husband, child there," as I motioned with my hand. He pointed to the floor beside him in the entrance-way of our room, indicating that there was good. I was scared. I said no, jumped into the room, and slammed the door and locked it. I couldn't believe it. How could I have been so stupid, so naive? I leaned against the door, breathing hard and trying to calm my frantic heart. The two men left and did not persist in their request. That was too close for comfort. I'd managed to escape unharmed, but so much worse could have happened. Maybe it was good that the cameras were there to watch me, because they could have protected me by alerting someone to the incident. I didn't dare go out alone again. I learned that lesson quickly. In the morning we exchanged the money in the hotel restaurant at eight rubles to one US dollar. We got fewer rubles, but the transaction was done legally and safely!

After that whole fiasco, I was shaken but not stopped. Off we went to explore and discover Moscow together. First, we went to Red Square. Such a famous place! It was exciting just to stand in the square where there had been so much history and horror. It was an awesome moment, but I also had an eerie, chilled feeling come over me. The square certainly had a powerful, historical, nostalgic feel to it, but there was also a feeling of darkness and sorrow surrounding it, as if the energy of past souls lurked in the crevices and shadows, waiting for redemption. I could feel the intense power and the deafening pain and was startled by the depth and vividness of the sensations. It was powerful. I felt I was walking on sacred ground.

St. Basil's Cathedral resembled a lone sentinel watching over the square, like it was frozen in a time long past. It was a beautiful church with incredible architecture. Unfortunately, the cathedral was closed, and no one was allowed inside, visitors or locals. We weren't allowed to enter any of the churches in Moscow, as religious teachings or ceremonies were not permitted under the country's political regime.

We went looking for places to shop and buy some souvenirs. There was a long line down the sidewalk, maybe fifty to sixty people waiting to shop at the grocery store near Red Square. Inside the store were basic foods for the locals to buy, but there were mostly empty shelves. The stock they kept on the shelves was a small fraction of the amount of food we would find at a small grocery store in Canada. We waited in line to check out their grocery store but didn't buy anything once we got inside. The shelves were mostly bare, with only basic staples for purchase. We bought some silk scarves and Russian Matryoshka nesting dolls at the store in our motel.

On the second day, we got on the local Moscow transit bus to do some touring around the city. As soon as we got on the bus, a fellow overheard us speaking English and began to talk with us. He was a local with a wife and small baby, like us. He offered to show us around Moscow, and we accepted his offer with gratitude. Our own personal tour guide! It was great. We toured a whirlwind of churches, historic buildings, government buildings, KGB buildings, and other interesting sites. I remember little, only that it was fascinating. In some areas he warned us not to talk, for fear of being caught together speaking English. He said his father was a Russian ambassador who travelled frequently and knew the ways of other cultures. He invited us to his place to meet his wife and child.

We went to their apartment at dinnertime. They lived in a very small flat and were as intrigued with us as we were with them. We all asked a lot of questions and were very curious about each other's lives. They cooked us eggs and toast for dinner. We ate and exchanged stories. He asked us to look at a plastic package his father had brought for them from the West. It was a box of disposable diapers. They were confused, as it was totally foreign to them that anyone would use anything other than cloth diapers. They thought it was some kind of food napkin. When we explained, they were perplexed. They lived a totally different life than we did in Canada. We were on the lower to middle end of the economic scale for Canadians, but we were not living nearly as poorly as they were.

They were mostly closed off from other cultures of the world, with only Russian- monitored and -produced radio and TV. It was like they were on the edge, wanting to know, yet afraid to know. I couldn't help but think that if I'd been born in Moscow and them in Canada, I could be in their shoes. Learning about this young family living in Moscow was a huge eye-opening experience for us and a humbling encounter. They invited us to his mother's place to meet the rest of the family and visit with them, so we went.

We were like a novelty to them—our child, our clothes, our way of doing things. They were extremely hospitable, feeding us and giving us gifts. They looked at our money with awe and curiosity. We left some US dollar bills for them, and they were thrilled. The man escorted us back to the bus to ensure our safety. He talked about exporting electronics from Moscow and us doing business with him, but we weren't interested. After the interrogation we'd had at the airport, we felt that doing business with him would just be too dangerous. We exchanged names, phone numbers, and addresses. He said that for everyone's safety, none of the information could be written down, we could only commit it to memory. We parted company with the man and got back on the bus. Interesting!

We visited a freestanding communications tower in Moscow, somewhat like the CN Tower in Toronto. The tower was not a tourist attraction but was for communications and was full of security people. We weren't allowed to take any pictures of the structure, but we did check out the tower and the view. There was a simple restaurant at the top, just below the radio tower. It was a very secure military location. Life was so different in Russia than what we were used to in Canada. It was really unbelievable. We take our freedom of mobility, speech, and travel for granted. When I saw that our way of living was not the norm for many people in the world, I became more appreciative of my privileged life in Canada.

We had no trouble with the customs officers on the way out of Russia. Their only concern seemed to be about how much money we'd spent while in Moscow. All of our spending had to be documented and reported. We did this and had no difficulty leaving the country. Wow, what an amazing time we had in those few days! It was a small amount of time filled with lots of varied adventures and eye-opening experiences. It was a once in a lifetime opportunity, and I cherish the memories.

From Moscow we flew to Zambia on another Aeroflot plane. The plane was leaking water above my head from lose screws, and there were chickens in wire crates on the plane with us. It was again of a lower maintenance standard than we were accustomed to in Canada. Mechanically it appeared to be sound enough to get us to our destination safely, but it was quite the experience travelling with the livestock on a rickety plane. Fortunately, we arrived without incident at the Lusaka airport.

My sister Cris, her husband, John, and my niece and nephew, Clare and Francis, met us at the airport. The kids had both been born in Lusaka. Being able to spend time with my sister and her family was the reason we'd travelled so far. I'd gone on my own five years earlier just after Clare had been born, but I hadn't met Francis. Annalisa was only eight months old, so none of them had met her either. We had quite a family reunion. They brought us to their home in a compound surrounding a school, where the Jesuit priests who taught at the school lived. As missionaries, Cris and John taught English and other subjects to the local children.

Cathy carrying eight-month-old Lisa in an African cloth, with Clare in Zambia, 1984

We stayed with them in their home and were immersed in the local culture. Lubinda, a local girl who worked for them and helped with the children, cooking, cleaning, and laundry became like a part of the family. We even went to her family home for dinner. Lubinda's family lived in a two-room building. Her father was seventy-two years old and a fairly wealthy man. He had two wives, which was common in their tribe, as polygamy was a way of life for them. One of his wives was thirty-two and the other thirty-four years old. One was Lubinda's mother, and Lubinda had twenty-three siblings. The two mothers worked together preparing the meals and helping each other raise the children. Their father was often off working. The experience was a fascinating cultural education about the differences in marriage traditions.

We had a lovely meal of "inshema," which was made of cornmeal dough. This was a traditional meal that we ate with our hands; we picked up a piece of inshema and dipped it into the vegetable dish, sauce, or chicken. We ate inside one of the rooms with the adults, and the children were outside playing and being looked after by the older siblings. They were full of life, content, and very happy to meet us. Lisa was eight months old, and they loved babies. They each took turns holding her and cooing and smiling at her. Experiencing their lifestyle was another eye-opening adventure. Really amazing. They had lived that way for generations. It was very practical, and the two moms were supportive of each other and appeared to be friends. It worked well for them.

As the world became smaller because of technology and faster communication between cultures, sharing information globally became available to all of us. Lubinda was exposed to other cultures by being with Cris, John, and the family. She began to see how other cultures treated women and was educated about birth control. She saw alternative choices to her family traditions and began to question her parents' choices and rethink her own values. Lubinda acquired further education and got a job in a government office. This was a huge step for her to go outside of her history and traditions. Lubinda travelled to Canada as well, which was a great adventure. She chose to get married and have a monogamous relationship.

During our visit, we travelled to the country of Malawi, to Victoria Falls in Zambia, and experienced an incredible lion safari. At that time, the political climate in Zambia was unsettled. We were travelling by car to Malawi when we were stopped by a bus full of uniformed men armed with machine guns. They questioned us about where we were from, where we were going, and for what reason. They also checked our identification, passports, and travel documents. Thankfully, these soldiers let us proceed after being reassured we were not a threat.

We regularly heard bombs exploding as we sat outside the Jesuit priests' house in Lusaka. There were military troops fighting around the city, and military armed men all over the country. It was very unnerving. Gunfire and exploding bombs seemed like an everyday occurrence to the people living there, and they continued their daily routines without disruption. They'd become accustomed to the actions of war. As a Canadian, I was unfamiliar with civil unrest or any type of war, and the bombings and military people frightened me. Fortunately, none of us were injured or threatened by the military activity around us. It was such a paradox going from the war zones to the beauty of the landscape at the game reserve and Victoria Falls.

Victoria Falls was brilliant! We travelled by car to Livingstone to see them. We were able to walk right to the edge of the cliff and observe the escarpment, which fell some three hundred feet down, where we could see the falls on the opposite side. There were no fences or rails or warning signs to keep people away from the dangerous edges. The whole area was open and natural. It wasn't commercialized like many of the tourist attractions in Canada. We stood on the opposite side of the cliff looking at Victoria Falls. They were incredible, magnificent— not in width, like Niagara Falls, but in height.

The thundering sound of rushing water pounding on the rock below beckoned us forward. The water tumbled some three hundred feet over the rock cliff, directly in front of us. The depth that the water plummeted magnified the power of nature. I felt small, vulnerable, and insignificant in comparison. It was very frightening, but also glorious!

We were in this beautiful wonder of the world, enjoying its magnificence, yet we had not escaped the human dangers. We were on the border of the country of Rhodesia, and there were snipers and other military men in the woods on the Rhodesian side of the falls. Yes, snipers with machine guns and such. We were warned not to take our cameras out, because it would be a security issue for the soldiers. In Canada, I was never exposed to any war-related events, but in Zambia, the war was happening in our midst and in most places we visited. War was a way of life there. After a month, I became somewhat acclimatized to the war activities happening around me, but I was still surprised when I'd hear a bomb explode.

We visited a hospital for lepers in a small, remote area near Malawi. I felt acutely emotional throughout the experience. Many of the patients had lost their arms or legs because of the illness. I found this very disturbing to see. Again, I grew more appreciative of my own health and home country.

Encountering the wars, suffering, and diseases the people in these countries experienced was enlightening but also heartbreaking.

We also explored a game park in South Luangwa National Park in Zambia. This was an exciting adventure! The game reserve was massive two hundred kilometres long! We didn't observe wildlife that was contained safely in cages, like we see in zoos in Canada where we're not in danger of the animals attacking us. In the game reserve, the animals ran free in their natural habitat. The tide was turned—we were trespassing in their territory, their home. Since many of the animals were natural predators and carnivores, and they outnumbered us humans, it was an unusual experience—scary but exciting at the same time.

While visiting the game reserve we stayed in a grass hut. The people there warned us not to leave the children alone on the porch or outside unattended. They explained that the monkeys or baboons would come and snatch the children away and carry them up into the trees, and we would have great difficulty catching them and getting the children back. Of course, we held on to our kids tightly and kept them attached to us. The baboons came right up onto the porches. They were not afraid of humans. They seemed curious about us as we watched and were curious about them.

Off we went one day in an open Land Rover to go game viewing. How exciting! It was also scary, for there was no protection for us in the open-topped Jeep. Our guide carried a shotgun, which gave us some comfort, but we were at the mercy of the wildlife. As we drove along the dirt lanes, we saw kudu and gazelles by the dozens, a cobra, and lots of elephants and giraffes. It was just like you see on TV. . . really wonderful. I felt like such an awesome adventurer, with Lisa in the Snugli on my chest. I found the whole setting of the wildlife in their natural habitat breathtaking. It was a dream experience for me and something I definitely checked off my bucket list.

That evening we went night viewing. If I enjoyed the day safari, I was blown away by the night viewing. It was pitch-black, and we couldn't see a thing except for a few feet in front of us. We were at the mercy of our guide and his wisdom of the animals and the area. Again we went out with the guide in the same open Land Rover. I hadn't noticed earlier, but there was a spotlight near the front of the jeep attached to a pole several feet above the driver that he'd move around to search for wildlife. All we could see when the light shone on an animal was a flash of red eyes in the distance. The guide would guess the animal by the size of the eyes, its height from the ground, and his own experience. As the Land Rover got closer, the guide said they were probably kudu. There was dead silence, only the rumble of the engine. We were searching in every direction to see animals. Our guide stopped the truck and turned off the engine. The air crackled with expectation, the heat hung like a curtain around us, and my skin prickled with anticipation.

We sat frozen on the edge of our seats in hope, fear, and excitement. Then the animals appeared right in front of us, maybe eight feet away from where we sat. They weren't kudu— they were lions! I held my breath as one by one the lionesses walked across the road directly in front of us, like we didn't exist. It was a pride of female lions, ten in all, and they were stalking their prey. They were focused on the kill, and we were irrelevant. Lisa felt the tension from me and started to fuss and whimper. I tried to settle her for fear that the lions would turn on us. From our vantage point, we could see the lions spreading out, circling the herd of kudu we could not see. From the darkness to our left came a loud hissing, a sort of coughing snort. The prey, probably kudu, had sensed or smelled the lions and was warning each other of the imminent danger.

Immediately following the kudu's warning sound, the lionesses rushed in for the kill. The entire scene disappeared into the trees and darkness. We only heard the noise of rustling leaves, grunts, and crushing sounds. In the hushed darkness the lionesses fed. My heart still pounds erratically when I recall that scene and those few moments with the lions, watching them stalk their prey. Wow, what a thrill! Exhilarating beyond belief! The Land Rover started to move forward again, and we began to breathe. Apparently we weren't in any danger. I felt super-charged, as the danger seemed potently real to me. I take a deep breath to calm myself down even now.

That same night we slept under mosquito nets in the grass hut, and John slept in a tent near the Zambezi River. We had seen signs of hippopotamuses that day, their footprints tracking along the water's edge and around our hut. On the water we saw the tops of their heads. In the middle of the shadowy, muted night, John crept out of his tent to relieve himself. Within seconds he came face to face with a hippopotamus. The massive, bulky beast shocked John, and he startled the hippo. John screamed, and the hippo made a loud, harsh snort. Man and beast ran off in opposite directions. We laugh about it now, but it was terrifying for John at the time.

Sister Cris, Francis, Clare, and John while living in
Zambia, Africa. elephant and hippo crossing!

The fear of sizeable wild animals wasn't our only concern. We had to sleep under bug nets to protect us from the smaller critters, lizards, mosquitoes, spiders, and other creatures. Mike woke up the next morning with peculiar rows of blisters covering his back. I'm talking about a string of blisters an inch wide and three or four inches long each. It was appalling. Cris had a man from the game park come to look at Mike's back. He was familiar with the blisters and said they were the result of bites from a blister beetle. The beetles and their bites were harmless, and the blisters would dry up and go away without any other side effects. Such a totally different world—one that we were learning about firsthand in leaps and bounds. What a great education!

Our travel adventures coincided with visiting relatives while we explored the countries in which they resided. This was a great way to see everyday life and get a feel for their cultures. We also got to know members of our immediate and extended families. I felt it was important for my children to know their roots by getting to know their relatives. Grandma and Grandpa Fursey were in their eighties at the time and told us wonderful stories about life in England during the First and Second World Wars and wonderful tidbits of family history. These family connections gave us a feeling of belonging to something larger and linked us to the past.

I find travel fascinating. One of the most interesting parts of experiencing various cultures is seeing how families interact with each other and their children. I was able to observe various methods and views of motherhood. From that trip alone I was able to share time with great-grandparents in England who glowed with pride upon meeting Annalisa. I met young parents with a little baby and witnessed the love and bond they felt for their child. I met Lubinda's two mothers, who had twenty-three children between them and were in love with life and full of the joys of motherhood. When they met Lisa, they crooned and were thrilled to see another baby! Incredible. Reuniting with my sister and her husband and two young children was a thrill. Their parenting skills were epic, and I saw them as mentors. The value and importance of families and children was a theme of this trip that was not lost on me.

The families we visited ranged in economic status from being comfortable financially to being economically poor. What struck me the hardest and taught me the most was the realization that financial wealth did not equal happiness. Those families were all happy regardless of their economic status. This verified my view about being happy. Happiness is not about what you have, as in materialism, but about whom you have, meaning family.

# CHAPTER 6

## *Arrival of our Second Child*

We returned safely from our adventure overseas with no other snags or travel blunders. I was struck by an overwhelming and deep sense of gratitude for that unique travel opportunity. I felt I had grown up by many years in my understanding of life and the ways of the world. I now observed my homeland through a broader lens. My travels helped me to appreciate more fully the safety, security, and excellent quality of life we enjoy as Canadians. I was grateful and proud to call myself a Canadian.

I settled down from my travelling adventures and resumed my focus on motherhood. I began to introduce soft foods to Annalisa, and she started eating rice cereal and mashed fruit and vegetables. I purchased a food processor to prepare baby food for her in larger amounts and freeze single portions for use later. I chose not to purchase premade baby food unless it was something like pure apples. Many of the baby foods had added sugar, salt, and other items, like preservatives. I didn't want to introduce these things to Lisa yet. She began to nurse less often and relied more on other foods for her sustenance. She slept through the night at about nine months, which allowed me to actually get a full night's sleep—sleep I needed and for which I was most grateful.

Throughout our trip, I nursed Annalisa less often, so I guess the natural birth control of nursing couldn't be relied upon. As I was tapering off the frequency of nursing, I became pregnant again somewhere in England, Russia, or Africa. So this second child was truly an international baby! I weaned Lisa off the breast milk at one year because I was pregnant with child number two. I was extremely tired, and the extra food energy I needed to support the new child growing inside of me took priority over nursing my first child. It was a tough choice.

I felt I'd given Annalisa a healthy start in life physically and emotionally through nursing her, but I didn't have the energy to both nurse and be pregnant. I gave Lisa goat's milk, which I researched and found, was nearer to human milk and easier to digest than cow's milk. I gradually introduced new foods to her to make sure she didn't have any allergies or reactions to the new food. Now she was eating a variety of fruits, vegetables, meats, and cereals.

I was excited and happy to have my first two children so close together in age. I hoped that they would become friends and playmates. Lisa and Giselle had started spending more time together and entertaining one other. Giselle was like an older sister to Lisa. I was a stay-at-home mom, as was Christine, Giselle's mother. The two girls loved to be together. I had to keep the door to our apartment closed and locked or Lisa would try to escape and crawl up the four flights of stairs to visit her cousin.

One time I caught her too late when the door had been left unlocked. I ran up to catch her and saw her falling down the stairs. She fell down one flight, about seven carpeted stairs. It was very frightening to see and be out of reach to help. She rolled down in such a way that she wasn't hurt, only scared. We were even more careful to put the gate up or close and lock the door after this scare.

Lisa was very reflective and analytical, even at this young age. She looked at her surroundings intensely and would touch objects gently with rapt interest. She made very little sound and just pointed to what she wanted. Giselle would talk and run around and get whatever Lisa wanted, so Lisa didn't have to talk. They developed their own communication system—non-verbal from Lisa and both verbal and non-verbal from Giselle. It was fascinating to watch the two of them play in synchronization. I was comfortable and happy with a little girl, so now I hoped I was carrying a boy.

I started to expand in size again. I was within 5 pounds of my pre-pregnancy weight when I got pregnant the second time, and I was happy with that because I'd gained so many pounds with Annalisa. However, now I was pregnant and gaining weight again.

I wondered what kind of child would be produced when it was conceived halfway across the world. Would that overseas experience affect his/her personality? My reading was much more limited during my second pregnancy, as I had less time to devote to it. I was happy that I'd spent so much time reading about pregnancy, childbirth, and child rearing before Lisa was born, because I suspected I wouldn't have the time to read and do much research with two children. I spent my days looking after Lisa, playing with and feeding her, cooking, and napping when she slept. I was so tired, and I was hungry all the time. I had a reserve of bottles of breast milk in the freezer that I fed to Lisa to give her the added nutrition and immunities after I stopped breastfeeding her.

Lisa would suck her thumb while holding her favourite pink baby blanket with a satin ribbon edge. She would cuddle the blanket and rub the satin on her face to comfort herself. She was quiet and curious and liked to explore, but her exploration was limited to being within visual range of me. Very rarely would she wander out of my sight, or her sight of me. She liked to stay within the security of Mom. She crawled around with her thumb and pointer finger pursed, like lobster pincers, ready to pick up things and investigate them. It was fun to watch her trying to decipher her surroundings. She was perpetually staring at things, touching them, and investigating her environment. Her intense curiosity enthralled me.

I would have loved to know what was going on inside her brain. It was like she was absorbing information like a sponge throughout her waking hours. She wasn't discerning good, bad, or otherwise—no, she was simply recording data with all her senses. Like a little scientist, her world was her laboratory. I'd watch her observing, tasting, feeling, listening, and smelling. She was tireless in her persistence and repetition, and she seemed fascinated in her pursuit to observe and understand. She would eat, drink, play, and explore non-stop. Then she'd sleep, only to wake up bright-eyed and ready to learn more. I was constantly amazed and intrigued by her behaviours.

I began to read about birth order in a book by Dr. Kevin Leman called *The Birth Order Book* (1985)[6] and was fascinated by the common personality traits shared by children from similar positions in the family. I recognized many of these birth order personality traits were present in me and my siblings. I read this material to gain awareness and guidelines I could use when mothering multiple children.

I spent much of my time with Lisa with little distraction, as I was at home full-time. I wondered how she would handle the change when her sibling was born and how she would react when my time was taken by another child. I researched and thought about how I would handle conflicts and jealousy. I wanted to have strategies ready, preventative measures to minimize the sibling rivalry as much as possible. For example, I could have someone look after the new baby while I focused some attention on Lisa at least part of the time.

As a middle child, I thought about how my position in the family had affected my personality. I'm a peacemaker, a mediator. I like life to run as smoothly as possible without conflict. I'm also creative and can entertain myself. I'm independent and can make decisions and take action without prodding from others. On the negative side, as a child I was quiet and often didn't speak my mind or let my thoughts and opinions be known. Certainly if my thoughts differed from those of others I would be silent. I learned later in life that this behaviour is called "passive-aggression." I think I was simply less confident in my opinions at that stage and was afraid to express myself and my views.

I could be manipulative in subtle ways to get what I needed. I did this to avoid conflict. Mike was like an only child, as his next sibling was nine years older than him. He was strong-minded and independent but also tended to look after his own needs first. I concluded that birth order did have an effect on our personalities, so I read more about it to try to understand the concept better and help Lisa adjust well when her sibling arrived. I was preparing myself mentally and physically for the birth of my second child.

Christmas 1984 I was eight months pregnant with child number two. Lisa was a year and five months old. I was very large in the abdomen area (and everywhere else) and had gained another fifty lbs. so far, with still a month to go! Mike and Lisa and I drove down to Windsor for Christmas Eve Ukrainian dinner and celebrations with my family. Christmas morning, we drove three and a half hours back to Brampton for Christmas Day stockings and dinner with Mike's family. We had a fun time in spite of the fact that my physical activity was limited by my size and protruding stomach, but I was still mobile and doing my regular routines.

Mike, Lisa, and Cathy, eight months pregnant with John, at Christmas, 1984

Family Christmas fun at Nana's

I got tired easily and napped whenever I could. I was healthy and excitedly anticipating the arrival of my second child, but I was also nervous about the pain of childbirth and another long labour. Medical evidence indicated that delivery would be faster for the second child. It made sense. Judging by the size of my stomach and the doctor's measurements, this child would likely be larger than Lisa, and that concerned me as well. All I could do was wait. I hung in there pretty well until January. My due date was January 11, 1985.

I'd been having labour pains on and off for a month, so again I thought the baby would come early. That was wishful thinking! I was happy that the birth wasn't going to be too close to Christmas for the child's sake. This would allow birthday celebrations to be separate from the Christmas festivities.

I was getting tired and anxious to have the baby ASAP. When I went to my doctor the first week of January, she said that the baby was full-term and completely developed, so I could go into labour anytime. On January 6 and 7 I went into false labour. I was learning that this was really preparatory labour, contractions that were getting my body ready for delivery. We went to the hospital, where I was checked and then sent home. Not real labour yet.

On the evening of January 7, we went back to the hospital. By 11 p.m. I was three to four centimetres dilated, so the doctor broke my water sac and then he went home. I stayed in the hospital, but I guess he didn't think I was going to deliver quickly. By midnight, I was losing control because of the pain and difficult contractions. The nurse brought nitrous oxide, laughing gas, for me to self-administer. I breathed it in by an oxygen mask; it eased the pain and helped me relax through the contractions. The gas also left me lightheaded, and it wore off in a few minutes. But I was so happy to have it, as it really eased the pressure. I decided against the epidural spinal freezing and wanted to go as natural as possible.

I was seven centimetres dilated at my next examination, and then came long, strong, and erratic contractions. I was mentally and emotionally at my wits' end and feeling distraught. My control was dwindling, and I fought not to panic. It would have been unbearable without the laughing gas. Suddenly, at 12:30 a.m., I wanted to push. . . badly. Again the nurses said not to push. That was quite impossible, as my body's instincts had taken over control. My body was pushing automatically. I knew the baby was ready. They checked me, and I was nine centimetres dilated.

Mike got dressed in hospital wear and they moved me to the delivery room. Dr. Dobson arrived at 12:40 a.m. The head was just showing. They froze my cervix with a needle injection in preparation for a possible episiotomy. I had another three or four contractions and the baby's head was out, a very large head. Then the baby's shoulders and the rest of his body came out. It was a boy—a very large baby boy!—born at 12:53 a.m. Thank God! What a relief! The nurses cleaned him up, and I pushed out the placenta, which again amazed me. Upon glancing around, I noticed that we'd made quite a mess in the delivery room. It was like a gory horror movie scene; there was blood everywhere. Incredible! Unbelievable! I was so glad and relieved that it was over and my baby boy was born.

After all the time, pain, growth, and change, this precious little boy had finally arrived. I was in awe of the whole process and the wonderful miracle of his birth. We sat and stared at him, speechless. We simply held him, admiring him and murmuring endearments. He was very peaceful after birth and just lay in my arms quietly.

His size had made for a difficult passage, which caused his face to be bruised, red, and puffy. My cervix tore again, even though the doctor did an episiotomy. The baby was 10 lbs. 6.5 oz! He was comparable to the size of a six month old. He had big cheeks and was chunky, but he was oh so precious. I thought he was beautiful. I thanked God again for this miracle of life and that all had gone well through the pregnancy and delivery.

I was thankful, joyful, in pain, and completely exhausted. The nurses cleaned us both up and brought the baby to the nursery for further examination and me to my room to rest. We both slept for three hours. I was out like a light and slept without moving. At 5:30 a.m., the nurse brought him to me to begin nursing. He was hungry and latched on to the nipple immediately, with rapture. He enjoyed nursing from the start. Such a sweetie. They kept us both in the hospital for five days to make sure I healed well enough to be mobile and to ensure that the baby was healthy.

The nurses set up the same interesting procedure for cleaning, airing, and drying the incision as they did when I had Lisa. They also gave me a cloth wipe bath on the bed. Daily they put the heater on the bed and then my legs in stirrups for drying the stitches to avoid infection. This worked well. I healed quickly, and the heat was extremely soothing. I appreciated the extra care and attention the nurses took to ensure our health and get us prepared to go home.

We decided to call the baby Johnathan Andrew. John was the name of his paternal grandpa and great-grandpa. It is a very traditional name with a modern twist, making it Johnathan. Andrew was my father's name. History, family, and tradition all came into play when choosing his name. We also considered the meaning of the names. John came from the Hebrew, meaning "gracious" and "gift of God." Many saints and significant people in history had the name John. *Jonathan Livingston Seagull,* by Richard Bach, (1970)[7] was a favourite book of mine about freedom, independent thought, and levels of consciousness. We also took into consideration a favourite movie of Mike's, *Rollerball*[8], which had a hero named Jonathon played by James Caan. It seemed to be a very powerful name, the name of people who did great things in their lives and cared for people. He had just been born. How could we tell any of this from him? Maybe this was wishful thinking, intuition, or a sixth sense. Whatever it was, I had that feeling about him.

Lisa and Mike came to visit while I was nursing John. (His name became shortened as well.) Lisa wanted to be close to me and to nurse too. She looked at John with her usual curious, questioning look. What is this thing? Why is he here? Are we actually taking him home with us? I gave John to Mike to hold while I cuddled and played with Lisa. I was conscious that I needed to spend as much time as I could with her to ease her through the transition. Tired or not, I had to make the extra effort for Annalisa's benefit.

All was well with John and me. We were released from the hospital and went home with our new family of four. I wasn't so afraid this time. I felt stronger mentally and emotionally, and I felt much wiser from my experience of caring for Lisa. Thankfully my parents came to help for a week after I got home from the hospital. They are saints, as they cooked, cleaned, did laundry, and entertained Lisa for hours on end. I was able to rest and take care of myself and John.

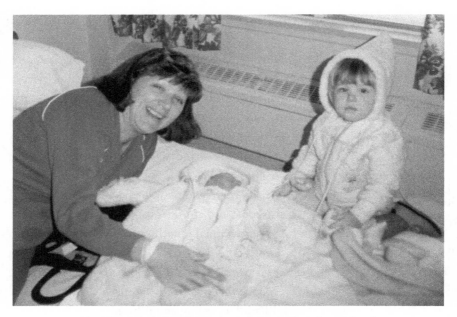

Ready to leave the hospital—Cathy with Lisa and newborn Johnathan

Andy and Betty, loving grandparents, with newborn John

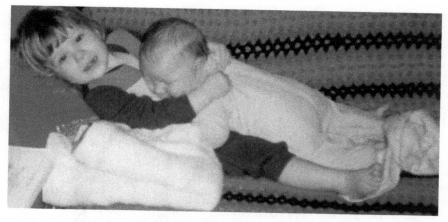

Lisa: *I think I like my baby brother.*

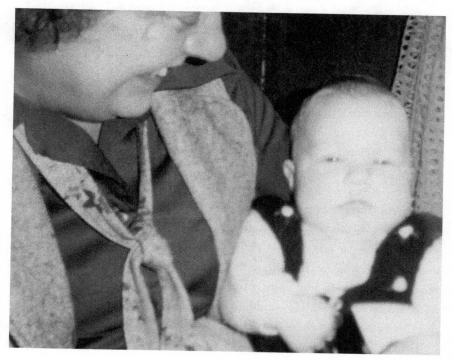

Nana showing love to John

Aunt Beth and grumpy farmer John

John was not a happy guy. He cried and was unsettled continuously, like he was in great pain. We had the doctors check him, but nothing was wrong physically that they could find. It seemed like gas or abdominal pain. Some people called this colic. We'd give him gripe water to soothe him as much as possible. Movement and constant motion seemed to be the only things that helped him and stopped him from crying. I'd walk around with him, put him in the Swing-O-Matic, or take him in the car for a drive. He'd sleep in the car seat while the car was moving. When the movement stopped, he'd awaken and start to cry again. The discomfort seemed to only go away with constant movement. I'd walk him until I was too exhausted to continue, and then Mike would take over. He would do the same while I spent time with Lisa, did chores, or slept. Eileen or my sister Beth would help and comfort John.

For the first three months of his life, John had this vague, faraway look is his eyes. It seemed to me he was in pain, or maybe it was anger or frustration. It was as though someone had put him in this immobile body and he felt trapped and didn't like it. He was like a stranger to this body and this planet. He seemed angry, frustrated, and far beyond my reach. It was frustrating for me, because I could do little to comfort him. Christine said later that she'd felt the unsettled spirit in him as well, and it frightened her. She had a hard time holding or being near him because of that look in his eyes. Almost evil! I know I felt this sometimes as well, but I loved him and tried to comfort him always.

At times John would be so exhausted from crying, he'd fall asleep on my chest and stomach and we'd both sleep for a time. It was also difficult emotionally, because I didn't want him to be unhappy. I felt somewhat responsible for his suffering. Maybe he had an upset stomach, or was colicky, or possibly had an unhappy soul. We don't have any conclusive evidence either way.

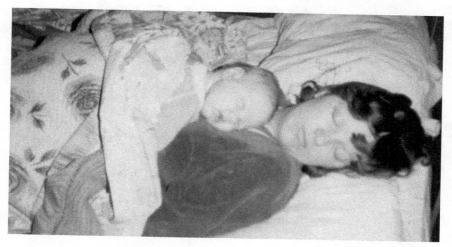

Never enough sleep! Mom and John finally napping together

Lisa was not happy with John either. He was too noisy! He also intruded on her space. She would sit on him or cover him with a blanket to try and hide him or to get rid of him. Her needs were not being met as they had been before he came into her life. It was his fault. It wasn't simple or easy, as a large concentration of my time and energy went into trying to help John feel better. It was a real struggle.

Then, like a miracle, John changed. The difference in him was like night and day. At three months old, it was like the unhappy soul left and a new one blew in. He smiled, joked, and teased. His eyes changed, and they began to sparkle and shine with a zest for life. It was a total transformation. Occasionally he would pee on me while I was changing his diaper, and he would laugh at this "joke." He was only five or six months old. I did not find this amusing until I saw him chortle and laugh at my reaction. What a card! He was so funny. He knew what he was doing, and he was being mischievous. At about nine months he would bite my nipple on purpose while I was nursing him and then look up to see my reaction. Then he'd giggle. It was like he'd suddenly found life extremely amusing. It was a welcome and refreshing change.

Cousin joy!

Grandpa John Sr. and John Jr.

He would watch Lisa's activities and smile and laugh at her. He became a real joy to be with. I could tell he was itching to become mobile as his eyes followed all the actions around him before he started to move. He badly wanted to move and explore, and soon his body did as well. He began to sit up and soon learned to shuffle himself around on his butt. As he began to move, his body thickness started to dissolve. He still had round, chunky cheeks, but now they were framing a fantastic, glowing grin that filled his face, and eyes that twinkled with joy and energy.

At about nine months old, John climbed out of his crib unexpectedly. This shocked me, as I didn't think he could get out that soon. Nothing was safe from him anymore. He was no longer confined by the walls of his crib, which was great for him but nerve-wracking for me. He finally had some mobility and control of his surroundings. My crystal stemware, glass, ornamental things, and really anything breakable were at risk. I had left these items out on display since Lisa was born, so they were within his reach. Lisa had never bothered touching any of those things. She would point and very gently touch the "pretty things." I watched John take one crystal stemware in each hand, clearly wondering what would happen if he hit them together. I was within arm's reach and took them from him. I then proceeded to clear all the breakables away.

Oh my, Lisa and John were such different personalities and opposing characters. It was hard to believe! Whatever John got his hands on he would hit against something or try to eat. Good Lord, it was all dangerous to him now. I had to clear the lower deck and put possible dangerous items up high or away and out of sight. He was fast. Once he started crawling, he quickly developed climbing abilities. Nothing was safe. It was a challenge for me to keep up and try to think ahead of him, and it didn't always work. I'd be talking or playing with Lisa, and John would suddenly disappear. I'd find him crawling at high speed, or climbing on something. He thought it was just hilarious that he could get away! He became a non-stop travelling machine. Movement and discovery were his quests, his missions in life, and he loved every single minute of it.

John also loved the outdoors. I took him outside to larger spaces in the backyard and beyond, where he had room to run. There he explored in relative safety, as long as I kept a close eye on him so that he didn't wander off too far, like to the hill or creek. I would shake my head in wonder as I watched him. He had unbelievable energy and endurance. At night, between six and seven, he'd eat and fall asleep, sometimes mid-action. He'd be half-standing and sleeping at the same time. He'd be out like a light for eleven or twelve hours, only to wake up at 6 or 6:30 a.m., energized, refuelled, and ready to run again.

Andy, my dad, with his treasured flower display, with Lisa and John at our farm

John exploring the creek at our Cambridge home

John cared not if his diaper was dirty, wet, or hanging down his legs to his knees. He was too busy to notice. He had important life discoveries to make! With time, as I figured this out, I got good at changing his diaper on the fly, with him standing or walking. I'd remove the old diaper and reload him with another while he was in action. That was amusing! How could something so little have so much energy, vibrancy, and enthusiasm for life? He would eat things whether they were edible or not. Any kind of substance, whether glass, metal, or plants—like a human computer he tested his environment and filed away all the information. He didn't necessarily see or use the items in their traditional way; he tried various angles, uses, and alternatives. It was mind-blowing.

For example, I was taking his temperature by mouth one day. What was I thinking voluntarily putting a glass object into his mouth? He chewed the thermometer. He just chomped right down on the glass and crushed it! My God! I was freaking out. He constantly surprised me. Who does this stuff? I called the poison control centre while I put all the pieces of glass together to make sure nothing was missing that he may have swallowed. The poison control centre said that the mercury inside the thermometer was the bigger problem. Well, of course it was! He'd swallowed mercury, even worse than glass. But they said the small amount of mercury in a thermometer wasn't dangerous. It looked like he hadn't swallowed any glass, but he may have swallowed some mercury. I took him to the doctor. They checked him out, said he was fine, and sent us home. If he could chew glass, then I guess a little mercury wouldn't hurt him. Ha! What a relief. I tied to pre-empt his thoughts and plans and cut him off at the pass.

John was 100% different from Lisa. She was calm, pensive, and curious in a quiet and thoughtful way. He was physical, active, and always moving. John didn't care if I was in sight of him or if he could see me. Lisa remained close and within sight of me always, but John knew no boundaries and had no fear! That was scary. If I built a fence to keep him in, he'd climb it. Lisa would play with him and be rough, and he would snicker. I'd have to watch her and keep her busy doing other activities so she wouldn't hurt him. She was jealous of the times John took me away from her.

Lisa loved books, and I read to her often. John would sit for a while so I could read to them both. At night, especially when I was tired, reading was a restful and quiet thing to do. John would fall asleep, and then Lisa and I would have some time together. We'd draw, play with blocks or games, or read some more. She loved to hear the same books over and over again. I'd put her in her crib, and she'd play and talk and comfort herself until she fell asleep, which was usually late, between 9 and 10 p.m.

John always woke up early, and Lisa would sleep until around 10 a.m. Their different sleep patterns afforded me individual time to focus my attention on one child for a few hours each day. I'd spend the early mornings with John. He ate with enthusiasm, like it was his first meal in life, with ravenous hunger and enjoyment. He loved to build stuff, anything, with blocks, wood shapes, and items he could pile on top of each other.

At eleven months, he was trying to walk with amusing persistence, smiling all the way. He was such a ham and such a little actor. He'd take a step and then grin and clap for himself, so funny. That charming, I-can't-do-anything-wrong kind of grin would light up his whole face. He tried to charm me all the time. If it wasn't a safety issue, I'd let him. His mind was absorbed in his surrounding, as Lisa's had been, trying to master it. He wanted to test it, challenge it, and try to overcome it. I never knew if this was normal for boys or just for him to be so active. I accepted him for being like he was and tried my best to keep him safe in his learning and the environment.

So there you go—my first year of motherhood with two children as I learned to adapt to having the second child. They were very much the opposite of each other, but both were unique and wonderful little human beings, each with their own way of viewing and interpreting their world. My challenge as a mother was dealing with sibling rivalry and trying to divide my attention equitably. I took the time to get to know each developing personality and watched them grow with fascination and wonder. I learned how to be a mother with them as they developed through childhood. I didn't know if I was doing the right things or not, so I tried my best to be thoughtful of my actions and consciously aware of interactions and feelings as they happened. I constantly reviewed and assessed my beliefs and values to become a better mother for my children.

John is on the move. *Look at me walking!*

# CHAPTER 7

## *Christmas, Birthdays, and Holidays*

In December 1986, Johnathan was eleven months old and Annalisa was almost two and a half years old. We celebrated another Christmas together with all of our family members and were still living in the basement suite in Eileen's country home in Brampton. As was our tradition, we travelled to my parents' house in Windsor for my family Ukrainian Christmas Eve dinner. We had perogies, cabbage rolls, pickled herring, and kolach, beautiful, braided homemade bread. The house was getting too small for our growing family, as more grandchildren were born each year.

Making do with our Charlie Brown Christmas tree and leotard Christmas stocking

My two sisters, two brothers, and their children all came. It was a joyful time with funny stories being retold as we reminisced about past Christmases and other activities we'd shared. We talked about the times when we were farming and the mischief we got into as children.

That year there were seven grandchildren. We enjoyed plenty of excitement over the gifts and toys exchanged. The house roared with noise and laughter. We all played with and enjoyed each other's children. Of course, the kids enjoyed each other too. It was fun getting to know their newest cousins. It was a pleasure for me to see the beginnings of bonding between my children and their cousins. Four of my siblings were having children at the same time, so the cousins were very close in age; therefore, they could all grow up together. New memories and cherished stories of this next generation were being created.

Andy and Betty with seven grandchildren

After the evening's festivities, the company left and we put my children to bed, as we were staying overnight. The adults stayed awake to visit and wrap gifts to be ready for the morning stockings and gift exchange. In the early morning, it was clear that Santa had arrived at the Kotow house. Lisa and John ripped open their gifts. Lisa was old enough to grasp the events somewhat, and John looked on with uncertainty and delight. The ultimate was relishing the homemade perogies, fried with onions and smothered in sour cream that we ate for our Christmas breakfast. Oh, they tasted yummy.

We prepared for our departure mid-morning, as we had a three and a half hour drive to Nana's, which is what they called their grandmother Eileen, house in Brampton. Upon arriving there, I had to finish wrapping the stocking stuffers and then sort them and fill the stockings. Opening the stocking gifts was always first on the agenda at Nana's house, and we had to get redressed into our pajamas to do it. We always opened them on Nana's bed, so Nana, Harry (Eileen's long-time partner), Christine, Giselle, Mike, me, Lisa, and John all piled on and around the bed. Opening our stockings was a part of Christmas that Nana Eileen loved. She was surrounded by family, and she simply purred with joy. The stockings brimmed with treats and small gifts, which we opened one at a time. It would take us up to three hours to open all the goodies. We laughed, munched, drank champagne and orange juice, and took our turns around the circle. There were always silly gag gifts, which were such fun! Often we laughed until our stomachs hurt. I loved this tradition!

Christmas stockings with Nana, Uncle Harry, Lisa, John, and cousin Giselle

Harry and any willing helpers would go and cut down a fresh fir tree, and it would be shaped to perfection by cutting off branches and wiring them to the tree trunk to fill in any bare spots. Harry was an artist and had an eye for creating beautiful things, so the tree became quite a creative work of art. It looked amazingly balanced when their rebuilding work was done.

Eileen's living room had lovely high ceilings and was classically decorated in greens and browns, in a British style. The furniture was old but well-kept and had seating for eight to ten people comfortably. The tree would be magnificent at 11 to 12 feet high, with a width of 6 to 7 feet in diameter at the bottom. It would be the kind of Christmas tree you'd see in classic movies with stately mansions, giving the air a feel of nostalgia and old-world charm. We would start the decorating with the strings of flashing coloured lights. Decorating the tree was a family effort, and all participated in some way.

Special decorations had been collected for decades, and each ornament held precious memories and contained a story. For example, the burnt orange and green glass carrot decoration Eileen received as a gift from her father in the 1920s was like a piece of history, a cherished reminder of the extraordinary bond Eileen shared with him. Many other significant ornaments and handmade or purchased gifts had been collected over the years and held individual snippets of historical tales. This narrative was like a thread that wove links between past and present and stitched an eclectic pattern of family that gave us a feeling of belonging. These legends had a life of their own, bursting to be told and retold!

When our decorating was completed, our tree was as spectacular as the showcase trees you'd see in the large department stores like the Eaton's showcase windows downtown. We all gathered together to celebrate the completion of the tree decorating and watch as the lights were turned on.

When the tree lights were on, the fire in the fireplace was blazing, and the candles were lit on the mantle, the room magically transformed into a supernatural Christmas fairyland. I felt like I was inside Clara's home in *The Nutcracker*[9] ballet. The view from the picture window showed a winter wonderland of snow and trees in the valley behind the home. All life outside that room ceased to exist. Eileen's living room was as enchanted as if we were living within the *Nutcracker*'s mists. We were all swept up in its spell, enjoying our own cocoon of love and family.

Nana in her glory with the Christmas tree and gifts

On Lisa's first Christmas, when she was only five months old, we joined Eileen and Harry in a tree-finding adventure. Nana had recommended cutting down our own Christmas tree at a farm that raised money for handicapped people. Of course, we agreed to participate. The place was out in the country and had dense woods behind it. There was hot apple cider and treats to enjoy inside the building, which added to the cozy, festive spirit. A horse-drawn wagon took us out to the bush, where we wandered around to pick and cut our own special tree. Talk about going back in time! I was very excited to live this experience.

The weather was frigidly cold that day, around -30 degrees Fahrenheit, the transition to Celsius was in process in Canada. Only in Canada, eh? There were 6 to 7 inches of snow on the ground, which created the winter wonderland image. We were well-dressed and prepared to brave the cold weather in search of our perfect Christmas tree. I had Lisa bundled up well enough, I thought, but it was colder than I expected in the forest. I had sewn a tote bag that looked like a dog, which I called the Diaper Dog. It was a brown quilted duffle bag that had long, floppy dog ears and a cute face sewn at one end, and a tail at the other end. It was a unique and useful diaper bag and carryall. Well, I found an interesting and alternate use for the bag that day.

We put Lisa right into the diaper bag and zipped it up most of the way, so I could just see her eyes peeking out at the end of the zipper. She was surrounded by cloth diapers, clothes, and blankets that kept her toasty warm. We thought this was humorous and cute, but the idea was an excellent unconventional way to keep Lisa protected from the elements.

We sang Christmas carols along the ride on the wagon. Nana swore Lisa was singing along with us, at five months. Hmmm. . . That was questionable. She was making little noises, though. It was hilarious! This confirmed to Nana just how clever Lisa wasJ. Maybe she was joining in, in baby language. The whole tree-finding quest became another precious memory.

With some deliberation, because Harry is a perfectionist, we found the perfect tree. Mike and Harry proceeded to cut the huge tree down. It was to become another epic Dockman family Christmas tree. It was about 14 feet high, so we'd have to trim it to size when we got it home. We hauled it back with much effort and warmed up by the fire with hot cocoa for the kids and hot toddies for the adults. Nana called the hot toddies her tea and sympathy—tea with Grand Marnier liqueur. This was a special Christmas treat with a blend of Cognac brandy and bitter orange flavours.

Uncle Harry and Nana

After much group consideration and debate, standing and straightening and turning the tree to find the absolute best-looking side, it was secured in the stand. Harry had a trick; he would wire the tree on two sides to the wall and add branches to fill in gaps. Intriguing! Finally we could begin the process of decorating. Picking, cutting, adjusting, and decorating the tree was a full day's activity, and some years it took two days. The process was most enjoyable as the group of us worked together to create an artistic masterpiece that became our central focal point of all the celebrations to come over the following weeks.

When the decorating was complete, we put the mountain of gifts under and around the incredible Christmas tree. The surprise gifts and the special ones were hidden behind the tree so that the recipient couldn't peek or shake to guess its contents. Surprises, secrets, and mysteries abound! The secrecy escalated the excitement, and mystery piqued our curiosity. We took much care and thought when choosing and packaging the gifts.

Each year we had an appointed Santa's Elf, who wore the Santa hat. This person was in charge of doling out the gifts. That year it was Mike. He sorted the gifts into a pile for each person so the distribution was evenly done. We all had drinks, snacks, and lots of chocolates. We took our time and shared stories about our lives now and about past Christmas celebrations as we watched and opened our gifts. The giving was as thrilling as the receiving when we saw the reactions of each person when they discovered the contents of their package. I thoroughly enjoyed the entire process and cared not that it was a week's worth of celebrations. It was well worth the time and energy, because we had a fantastic time.

One of my favourite stories was one Eileen told about a Christmas she had as a child in England. Eileen's father put the first electric lights to be displayed in their town on their Christmas tree. Certainly it was a piece of history and an amazing technological development some sixty-odd years before. Eileen told us about how fascinated and mesmerized she was when she saw the tree light up. Prior to the introduction of electricity, candles were placed on the tree! Having the first electric tree lights in their town was magical. Eileen noted how thrilled and proud she was of her father. That Christmas was a very special moment in Eileen's life, and she remembered it vividly. She would get a faraway look in her eyes and stare into space, and we knew she had the vision of that memory in her mind. That special childhood memory of a wonderful moment between her and her father made Eileen's Christmas tree extra special.

We would delightedly open the gifts one at a time and pass them around like they were precious jewels for all to admire with "ooohhhhs" and "ahhhs". Then we'd thank and hug each other. A fire would be blazing in the fireplace, candles glowing on the mantelpiece, and lights sparkling brightly on the tree to create an atmosphere of warmth, gratitude, and security. I bathed in the love that surrounded me.

At Eileen's home we would have a traditional English turkey dinner with trifle for dessert. Another feast! We'd open more gifts for the children before they went to sleep, and then the adults would stay up and continue the celebration into the wee hours of the morning. There would be lots of reminiscing and stories told about family members here and in other parts of the world.

Cathy and Dave enjoying Christmas at Nana's

Boxing Day at Eileen's home was traditionally an open house for neighbours and extended family members to drop in and visit. Another fifteen to twenty-five people would arrive for a buffet dinner, drinks, a gift exchange, and more visiting. Add that number to the ten to fifteen of us already there and you've got quit a rambunctious crowd. Aunts and uncles, cousins, nieces and nephews—lots of people we rarely saw. This day was for catching up with each other's lives. Mike's brother Jack, his wife, Esther, and their five children would come on Boxing Day. Lisa and John were quite taken with their older cousins. Jack was twelve years older than Mike, so his children were teenagers. I thought it was great that my children were able to spend time with their cousins and build the beginning bonds of these new relationships.

The week of Christmas was hectic. There was much activity, food preparation, gift wrapping, eating, drinking, and visiting with relatives and friends, not to mention the small task of looking after two small children. When it was all over, I was exhausted. I made a feeble attempt to rest and catch up on sleep, but it didn't happen. The experience was well worth it to miss a little shut eye. I just accepted the fact that being well-rested was not a part of motherhood! When I fell asleep at the dinner table one night, I knew something was wrong—or perhaps right! I went to see my doctor. Yes, I was pregnant again. That's why I was feeling so tired. . . all the time. . . again.

I was pregnant with child number three! It was so soon, I wasn't quite prepared for being pregnant and having another baby quite yet. But I had to agree, it was good news. I had always wanted four children. They were just being born closer together in age than I had planned. Could I manage three? Really, it wasn't my plan that was being played out. There was a larger picture in the big scheme of things that I wasn't aware of and had no control over. God had other plans for how my life was going to play out. I soon accepted his plan and let go of my expectations and control. When I did this, I got excited about being pregnant again.

In January 1986, John turned one. My mom and dad came to our home in Cambridge, Ontario, for his first birthday party. I baked a chocolate cake with chocolate icing for him. As was our tradition, on each first birthday the child got the cake put in front of him or her. John devoured the cake with his hands. He had a blast! It was hilarious. There was chocolate everywhere. I laughed so hard, my stomach hurt and tears rolled down my cheeks. There were enough bits of cake left intact for us to enjoy a piece with our vanilla ice cream. Here we celebrated another milestone in our family.

At Easter we celebrated with our traditional Easter breakfast. When I was a child, I joined my Grandmother Kotow, Babka, at the Russian Orthodox church in Windsor on Easter Saturday. We brought a basket full of food, including boiled eggs, fish, kielbasa, and braided "paska" homemade bread.

Some people stayed for an all-night service followed by the blessing of our baskets of food. On Easter morning we went home to celebrate Jesus rising from the dead. I continued many of the traditions I learned from my Babka with the meal menu and preparations. We added homemade perogies to the Easter breakfast menu, because we all loved perogies, and Easter seemed like a valid excuse to make and enjoy them.

Traditional Ukrainian Easter dinner

On Easter morning, the Easter Bunny came with gifts and chocolate treats. After breakfast we had a scavenger hunt and a candy hunt. I made up simple clues for the kids to solve to find their goodies in hidden places. This tradition grew over the years and became an annual event. The hunt expanded and became more complex as my children grew older and smarter, but it was always humorous, with silly and gross clues. We all participated with enthusiasm and energy.

We made traditional Ukrainian dyed Easter eggs, which was an intricate and pleasurable creative activity. I taught my children how to decorate these eggs in the old traditional way. It was quite a complicated process, but I simplified it depending on my kids' ages and skill levels at the time. The eggs are decorated by using melted wax and coloured dyes applied with a special stylus called a kistka. I tried to do this every year so I could give the decorated eggs away as gifts and have some for decorating our table. Making these eggs was a part of our heritage that was important to me to pass on to the next generation.

Our usual Easter dinner would include our family, my sister Mary Beth, and friends who may not have a family dinner to attend. We often had a few extra guests join us at our dinner table, especially on holidays. I would hate to be alone during those special celebrations, so I wanted to welcome people who otherwise would have been alone. We had an open-door policy at our dinner table any day of the year, but particularly on holidays.

I always made an effort to make holidays special. I'd incorporate the family traditions from my family using the Ukrainian and French ethnic foods and traditions, as well as the English culture from Mike's side of the family. Our own traditions became personalized with a wonderful mix of the past with modern, new ideas blended in. Dinner time was our family social time, with lots of yummy food and drinks. I love all the holidays, but my favourite has always been Christmas.

I was at church the other day (in 2009, while I'm writing this chapter of my book). The minister was talking about the judgment day and how God chooses if we go to heaven or hell. The bottom-line question seems to be, "Do we show compassion for all of our fellow humans?" He was preaching from Matthew 25:31–46, *The Bible, New Testament*.[10] Two parts of the passage struck me and brought back another memory.

I believe in treating all humans equally. Since our family meals were such crucial gathering times in our lives, I simply wanted to share the time, joy, and love with whoever wanted to join us. Sharing food seemed like an appropriate way to join in friendship and fellowship. As the passage says, "For I was hungry and you gave me something to eat, I was thirsty and you gave me something to drink, I was a stranger and you invited me in. I needed clothes and you clothed me, I was sick and you looked after me, I was in prison and you came to visit me." Later he says, "I tell you the truth, whatever you did for one of the least of these brothers of mine, you did for me." (*Quest Study*

*Bible).*[11] I tried to be non-judgmental about people's circumstances and just accept them for who they are. I would help them if I could, whether by lending a hand or an encouraging word. I shared this value with my children, the golden rule. Treat others as you would like to be treated, because what you hand out comes back to you.

This idea of treating all humans with respect and dignity brought to mind a Ukrainian tradition we had at Christmas of placing a lit candle on the windowsill for passersby to see. The candle was a symbol of an open-house policy that any stranger who had no place to go for Christmas dinner was welcome to dine with us. As my children were who they were, they called me out on my belief in this concept as they grew older. "Would you really let a stranger in to join us for Christmas or Easter Dinner?" they asked. We often had friends or acquaintances over who otherwise would have been alone. But a stranger? If they didn't have family around, they were welcome for any holiday with our special traditions, family dinner, and activities. I felt it was important to share and be with family at holiday times in particular and to open our doors to travelers from our own as well as other countries.

We've housed and supported exchange students from Quebec, Australia, Nepal, and Sweden over the years who joined us for these festive gatherings. Mary Beth was always in attendance, since she was often living with us. She's my children's aunt but is also like a second mother to them. Grandpa Dockman was with us many times, especially later when he lived with us in Alberta. When we were in Ontario, we celebrated with Eileen and Harry and Mike's extended family, or with my parents and family in Windsor.

My son David's friend Eddy had gone to school with Dave (David is my third child but he is not born in this book until Chapter 9J) since they were in kindergarten together. He became a regular guest. . . well, more like a family member. . . at our holiday dinner celebrations. Dave was very thoughtful and gentlemanly, so he would always ask, "Is it okay with you, Mom, if Eddy comes for dinner?" I always said yes and that it wouldn't be the same without him. I appreciated being asked, so that we could be prepared with enough food. Sometimes he'd come and help us prepare the bread or perogies. Eddy was grateful to be included and became like a third son to me. He was an important facet of all our celebrations, especially Christmas. This is all fine and good, as these people weren't strangers to me or my children! So what about strangers?

One afternoon I was driving home from work at a hospital in Calgary. It was Christmas Eve, and my four kids were eighteen to twenty-three years old. Mary Beth and the four of them were preparing the food for Ukrainian Christmas Eve dinner. I was stopped at a light at a main intersection in Calgary when I noticed a young man with a sign that said "We are homeless. We would appreciate any donation and any coin would help us. Thank you!" I drove by. I had no money to give! I drove about a mile, thought about him, reconsidered, and turned around. I had something to give—a warm home and a lovely hot Christmas Eve dinner. I stopped at the side of the road and offered accommodation and dinner for the evening with myself and my family.

He was a young man of about twenty years old with warm but well-worn clothing. His wife held a similar sign and was waving at traffic on the opposite end of the same intersection. He said they were students and had recently moved to the area. They lived in a tent year-round and were panhandlers by profession. "Thank you for your kind offer," he said. Any other day they would have accepted, but being Christmas Eve, it would be a very prosperous day for them. People were generous that time of the year. I stared at him with my mouth gaping open. I was shocked.

I drove away, leaving the couple behind to panhandle their earnings. By his admission, the money they received that one night would be enough for them to live on for the next few months. I felt happy with myself for offering what I could, but I was shaking my head in bewilderment because they'd said no. But when I thought about their circumstances, I understood that the money they'd get that day was more valuable to them than the offer of a meal. Wow, accepting them and their choices brought great awareness to me. What a gift!

I went home and told my kids and Mary Beth the story. They were intrigued by my attempt to reach out and proud of me for offering to share our home and meal. I was practicing what I preached and sticking to my values.

"Where would they have slept?" my kids asked.

*We have a full house already*, I thought. *Wouldn't it be better to sleep in a sleeping bag on the floor of a warm home with a full belly than to sleep outside in the middle of the winter? Oh, course it would!* Well, that was my view of the situation, but not from the panhandlers' perspective. As far as my children and I were concerned, my actions spoke louder than my words. We had quite a discussion about different perspectives in life and how our way of seeing things isn't the only way to look at life.

As we lit our candle in the window that night, we were very thoughtful and pensive. This experience brought our tradition into a whole new light. No pun intended! Gratitude overwhelmed me! We did not live a high life, and often struggled financially. We had comfortable shelter, heat, an abundance of food, and a loving family surrounding us. I radiated with joy that Christmas because of the gratitude the experience brought more strongly to my awareness. Those two young adults were homeless by choice. My family's needs were being met with abundance. Most importantly, we were healthy and together. Lesson learned. I counted my blessings!

The holidays and our family traditions were important and special to me, and I made every effort to pass my enthusiasm on to my children. As a mother, I felt it was my responsibility to mentor and teach my children our family history and traditions. I believed that creating strong connections to family through shared time and memories would build a strong foundation of trust and security for their life and future. Whatever we did during holidays, the most important thing was that we were all together as a family. We were blessed to have a large and closely connected family who made the effort to share holiday times together.

# CHAPTER 8

## *Our First Home*

I believe I get signs and messages from people, spirits, and circumstances around me, and I choose to be open to these messages. Sometimes they come in the form of a feeling or intuition. I've learned to listen to my intuition.

Our family had definitely outgrown our current living arrangements, and I was thinking of moving to larger accommodations and having ownership of a home, which I hoped would bring peace of mind and economic security. I began scanning the real estate papers for possible home purchases. Housing costs were high in or around Toronto and were quite frankly out of our financial reach.

After the third time I came across the same advertisement for large brick home in a well-established, older section of Cambridge, I called the realtor and made an appointment to go and view the property. It was located on a main road with good accessibility to Highway 401 for Mike to get to work. The home was certainly below the standard for the area, which meant there was great potential for growth in value. It contained three separate apartments, with a basement, main floor, and upstairs units. Each unit had its own entrance. I was already calculating my renovation and rental plan as we walked through the home. Here was a way we could create income so I could be a stay-at-home mom. It needed lots of TLC, and I was willing and available to do the work in exchange for the reward of having the flexibility of remaining home with my children. I began to get excited about the possibilities. I could make an income from fixing up the place while I was at home full-time, creating more value and equity in the home.

The house was eighty-six years old and had loads of character. It kind of looked like it had been plopped down from the sky in that spot, like Dorothy's house in the *Wizard of Oz*—a little out of place. It needed a sprinkle of magic to transform it into its original beauty and elegance. There you go—I had a vision to restore the home. It was on a large lot with a separate garage, and it backed onto a park with a creek.

We could walk through our fenced backyard directly into green space. From the kitchen window at the back of the home, I had a panoramic view that felt like I was standing in a castle overlooking an immaculately-tended garden and lawn, and it was tended and maintained by the city! I could enjoy it without the work involved. Meandering through the greenery was a stream that seemed to invite me to rest on its lush grasses and relax by its meditative flow. The trees stood watch, like sentinels protecting their wards. There were mature and massive maples and majestic oaks, which I love, and flowing weeping willows. The whole scene was inviting, and I was drawn to join in. I had a strong sense of home, of rightness. The home was ours. We simply had to figure out how to make it so. I knew this location was a wonderful place to raise children in the city, but with nature and freedom at our back door. Wonderful!

The sellers were asking $56,000 and change. We made an offer and purchased the home for $52,000. Such a deal! We managed the small down payment and arranged for the mortgage. The decision was a no-brainer. They accepted the offer, and we bought our first home. I was ecstatic!

Finally, we would have all the space we needed for our growing family. We would have the three levels inside the house, the garage, and the backyard. The kids and I would have space for a playroom, and we'd have our own kitchen and living room. It was a mansion compared to the basement suite we'd been living in for the last four or five years. We could rent out two levels and use that income pay the mortgage. This income would also allow me to continue as a stay-at-home mom. My "job" would be mother, landlady, and renovator. I could stay at home with the children and work on the house while enjoying our new home and the natural beauty surrounding it. It was a perfect set-up.

We thought that we could expand our space as needed and as our finances improved. We could take over the basement or upstairs and use the whole house ourselves over time. It was very exciting to move from Brampton to Cambridge into our own home as first-time property owners. The downside of the location was the forty-five-minute commute each way to Mike's work at our courier business by the Toronto airport. That was a compromise we felt was worth doing compared to all the positives of ownership and the advantages of the location for raising our family, not to mention the positive financial gains we could make over the next few years as we improved the property.

We moved while I was pregnant with our third child. Mike started to commute, and I began my multiple duties. We all began to settle in. We rented the upstairs apartment to a single young woman, and the downstairs suite to a single young man. The rental income covered out mortgage payment, so I could relax about our finances and prepare for the impending birth.

We fully enjoyed the warmth of the summer. It proved to be as beautiful and peaceful as I'd expected. I used my large, old-style perambulator to transport the two children around and walk to the park to explore and soak in the beauty of our natural environment. We bought a swing set and built a sandbox in the backyard. I built two picnic tables, one adult-sized and one kid-sized. We spend much time in the backyard playing and picnicking.

I arranged for someone to finish one section of fence with a gate so that the yard was completely fenced in for the children's safety. Not that a mere fence was going to stop John, but I was trying. A ten-minute walk along the stream brought us to an escarpment that ended with a bridge overlooking a waterfall. The view was absolutely breathtaking and nearly at our doorstep. I loved it! The pathways through the park led from behind our house, across the street, and through another park to the river and the escarpment. I often took advantage of the nearness of this paradise.

Lisa and John playing in our Cambridge backyard

98

The park was lined with mature trees, like towering weeping willows with tendrils seeking the sky and then plummeting toward the earth in their sweeping, flowing, lazy manner. I found relaxation simply by watching the tendrils flow in the gentle breeze as we wandered daily through their paths. Sometimes we sat under the willow and absorbed its power. The mature maple trees were magnificent, and the oaks in their majesty took ownership of the park by right of their seniority. These grand trees lined and guarded the paths and beckoned one to explore or rest at their shady feet. And explore we did, every day. We played in the stream, searched for and collected pretty and interesting rocks, lay on blankets and watched the cloud formations, and brought picnics and ate heartily as the outdoor activities enhanced our appetites. Every day was like an adventure. I was happy and grateful to have bought the home and to have this opportunity with the children with all this nature at our immediate disposal. It was a delightful and a peaceful place. I loved it! That serene environment nurtured peace within me, which gave my child within a calm beginning and the two children without some wonderful spaces to explore.

I was growing larger again, and the summer was flying by. My sister Mary Beth moved in with us, and I felt more secure having a family member so close, especially when it got closer to my delivery time. If Mike was at work in Toronto, it would be easier to get hold of Beth (she'd dropped the Mary and went by Beth) if I needed help getting to the hospital. Beth settled in and was able to help me through the summer as my delivery date in August approached.

Here we go again! I gained over 50 lbs. with that pregnancy. I was still amazingly mobile for my size, but I had a huge protruding stomach! Near the end of the pregnancy I began to get sluggish in mind and body as I dragged myself around. It was summer in Ontario with its hot, humid weather, generally 80 degrees Fahrenheit and sometimes in the 90s. Normally I love the heat and savour the warmth because I'm often cold. But not that summer, since I was eight to nine months pregnant. Being full-on pregnant in that muggy weather was tiring, so I was mentally and physically ready for the new baby to arrive. Buying the house was a great family-building step, and the timing worked out to be excellent.

The house was organized with space for everything. My mom and dad planned to visit for a week after the baby was born to help me out with the house and the children. All was in place and ready for the next big change in our lives. My mothering instincts had been satisfied by the purchase of the home I'd found in which to make a nest and nurture my offspring. Adjusting and decorating the house prepared us to welcome our new child into our home and family. Owning our home took the stress off my need to work outside of the home and allowed me to relax and focus on my children and the pregnancy. I felt I had the space, time, and energy to welcome our third child and give him the mothering he needed.

First time homeowners, our Cambridge, Ontario triplex

# CHAPTER 9

## *Arrival of Our Third Child*

My third pregnancy progressed, and I grew larger. I found myself a new doctor in Cambridge to prepare for the baby's birth. This doctor and the hospital seemed to be more in touch with the latest research and practices that led to more natural and home-like birthing techniques and environments. Technology had advanced since my other two children were born, and we were able to get pictures of the ultrasound at my four-month examination. The ultrasound image clearly showed details of the baby. It was very exciting to see this child's development in my uterus. I saved the two pictures and put them into the baby book.

The summer flew by. Beth was around, and we spent time talking and sharing meals as a family. I felt secure, content, and happy. Although I gained over 50 pounds, I was still reasonably mobile. This was necessary, as I had two babies to attend to and move with constantly. But with the extra pounds, I was sluggish and felt like a whale by the end of the pregnancy.

On Saturday August 23, my contractions started. Was this real labour or only Braxton Hicks contractions again? They sure didn't feel like practice contractions! By the next morning, the frequency of the contractions had slowed down to one every thirty to forty-five minutes. I tried to relax and rest between them, but it was difficult. I rested as much as was physically possible to relax when the worry and pain overtook my body! By 11 p.m., my contractions were coming consistently at six to ten minutes apart. They felt strong and painful. At midnight, I yelled for Mikes' help, although he wasn't at home. I was cold, sweaty, shaky, and apprehensive about the speed and intensity of the contractions. My behaviour and lack of control scared Beth half to death. Mike was at work, so I phoned him and he came home to take me to the hospital. Beth was extremely worried about me and the baby when we left for the hospital. She rarely saw me in such distress.

My pains continued hard and fast. I thought I had already started into the transition phase of labour. I could barely breathe through the contractions because of their strength and length. The fact that this was my third birth made me concerned that the baby would come relatively quickly. From what I'd heard, and my mother's own experience with me, I had reason to be anxious. I was the fourth child, and Mom almost didn't make it to the hospital when I was born. I was delivered shortly after she arrived.

I feared having the baby at home or in the car on the way to the hospital! My first two babies were so large. I imagined the difficulty and danger of delivering anywhere but at the hospital with the medical team's technical and medical expertise. But because of the size of my babies, it was illogical to think that this one would come quickly. Still, I wasn't taking any chances. I wanted to go to the hospital, even if it was another false alarm. I'd rather be safe than sorry.

At 1 a.m. I was admitted to the hospital. It was August 24, 1988. The doctor examined me, and my cervix was dilated five to six centimetres. My water sac was bulging. It seemed I was in real labour after all. Yes! The doctor broke the amniotic sac to speed up the delivery, and by 2:30 a.m. I wanted help with the pain. They gave me Entonox, the laughing gas, self-administered again. They moved me to the birthing room at 3:15 a.m. I'd about had it with the intensity of the pain. It was beginning to feel unbearable and difficult to handle. I just wanted the horrible spasms to stop!

The birthing room was not a traditional delivery room. It had all the medical equipment that might be necessary for the delivery easily available, yet it also had a home-like atmosphere. The walls were colourfully painted, and the room was decorated like a living room. It was cozy. There was a birthing chair for me to deliver in, designed to use gravity by being in a sitting position rather than lying down on my back. This totally made sense to me. At 3:45 a.m., I wanted to push. Again, it was that incredible, uncontrollable urge. Instinctively my body knew what to do. At least they didn't tell me not to push this time! Thankfully, I could go with my body's natural response instead of against it.

At 3:54 a.m., I gave birth to a baby boy! He seemed so small to me. He had a tiny head and almost no fat. After John, this one seemed little, but he was 9 lbs. 4 oz. He was still a strapping-sized baby.

The doctor put him on my stomach. He looked so fine and so beautiful. I couldn't believe that he was a boy and had arrived! Hallelujah! I wanted to shout with joy. He was all bloody, with red and purple skin, yet he was ever so wonderful. I pushed again to dispel the placenta. Then I was done. Awk! Labouring is hard work. Mike got to clamp and cut the umbilical cord, and then the nurses wrapped the baby in blankets, and Mike held him while the doctor stitched me up. Then I held him again, carefully examining his tiny face, which I found most fascinating! He was so sweet and pale and quiet and perfect. Already he felt like a very contented baby. I was extremely relieved and excited that he had arrived safely and in good health. We'd experienced no complications. I felt intensely comforted and grateful.

The hospital was very busy with deliveries, so they needed the room immediately following the birth of my son. Some medical staff were trying to hurry us out of the delivery room to make room for the next person to give birth, as it was imminent. My doctor did not hurry and told them to wait until she was finished. She was calm and patient as she concentrated on stitching my tears. She had done an episiotomy, but with the size of the baby, my cervix tore also. She focused carefully and didn't let the pressure rush her work. I appreciated her professionalism. She took excellent care of me.

Mike and I spent about an hour with our new little boy, holding him, admiring him, and getting acquainted. At 5 a.m., I nursed him for the first time. He was calm, quiet, and nursed easily. At 6 a.m., after we were both cleaned up and checked, I was taken to my room, and the baby to the nursery. I slept a blackout, unconscious kind of sleep only found in exhaustion. I was emotionally and physically spent. The nurses woke me up every fifteen minutes to check my blood pressure and my uterus. I'd wake up groggily, let the nurse do her thing, and then immediately plunge back into a coma-like sleep.

At 11:30 a.m. I nursed the baby with no problems, and we were off again! He slept well and was a very peaceful little guy. During his examination, the hospital staff made ink footprints of his little feet and gave us a copy. His feet were so tiny and adorable. I also put this print into his baby book. I was so excited with his arrival. I was thankful, in pain, and full of joy.

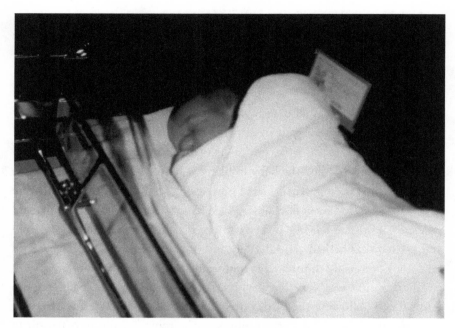

Newborn Dave peacefully sleeping in the bassinet at the hospital

Again, Mike and I had not come to a consensus about a name for him, nor did we have any strong feelings about it. We had many discussions and scoured baby name books without success. Mike's father visited and suggested we name him David. I don't recall why or from where Grandpa Dockman got this name, but we liked the name very much and it seemed to suit him. We decided to use Michael for his second name, after his father. We looked up the names later and found that David was from a Hebrew name, "Dawid," meaning "beloved." David was also the name of the second and greatest of the kings of Israel, ruling in the tenth century BC. In the Old Testament, we see David and Goliath, and in the New Testament, we read that Jesus was a descendent of David.

Michael comes from the Hebrew name meaning "Who is like God?" But that's a rhetorical question, as no one is like God. Michael is the name of an archangel who is portrayed as the leader of heaven's armies. All cool stuff. For all of this depth of reasoning and our sense of this child, David Michael it was.

Baby David and I remained in the hospital for five days, as I had with my first two children after their births. Having five days to rest and recuperate was an awesome luxury, particularly as I had two children at home and would have to attend to them full-on when I arrived. Those five days gave time for the incision to heal and for me to recover from the exhaustion of childbirth. I could regain my energy and go home to hopefully manage successfully with three children. At that time, funding was available for mothers to stay in the hospital as long as needed for health care and support in the transition into motherhood.

Within the five days, my stitches had healed well. I was able to enjoy being taken care of and bonding with David. I was able to focus all my attention on him at the beginning of his life. What an exceptional opportunity. David had a bit of jaundice on his third day, and the doctor wanted the jaundice to be gone before we left the hospital.

Soon, home I went with this newest bundle of joy. My second baby boy! I was nervous and worried about my ability and energy level to look after three children well. I thank God again that my mom and dad came to my rescue and were able to stay for a week after I got out of the hospital. They were so helpful and simply wonderful! They cooked and cleaned and looked after Lisa and John much of the time. I could eat, sleep, and feed David as needed. We enjoyed meals together and reminisced about us as children. I also was able to learn more mothering ideas that only seemed to come from experience and verbal transmission. I could ease into my daily routines without feeling overwhelmed, and I napped whenever I needed to. Oh, what a luxury!

It was also a blessing that David was a relaxed and happy baby. He ate, slept, and enjoyed just being. He was never fussy or demanding, but he disliked having a dirty or wet diaper. He would get a displeased look on his face and an uncomfortable, squirming motion with his body. I would clean him up and he'd smile and be good to go again. He was easy to please. He'd spend hour's just watching Lisa and John play and absorbing all the activities surrounding him. He would follow them with his eyes, and later with his movements, because he wanted to do what his brother and sister were doing. When he could talk, he often said, "Me too! Me too!" He wanted to be involved with them in whatever they did.

And now there were three

Dave cuddling with mom

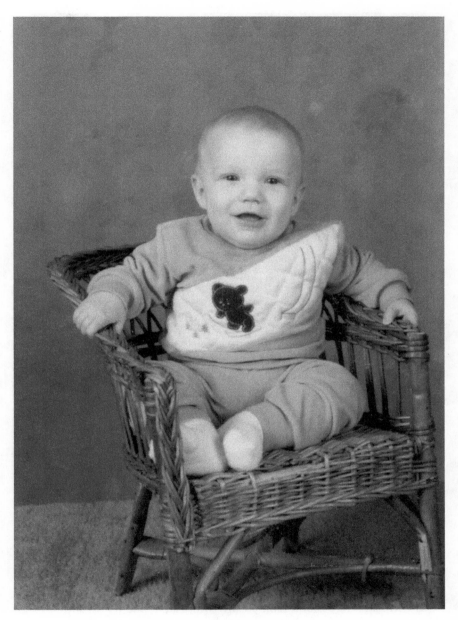

Five-month-old Dave's cheery disposition in his baby photo

Dave's baby photo with Lisa and John

David had white-blond hair, creamy white skin, and a grin so full of joy that his smile lit up his face. He was the cutest baby you ever saw! Of course, I thought all of my babies were cute! I had a biased opinion—it's a mother thing. He liked peace and calmness. David thrived as the newest member of our family. I was proud and happy to be mothering him.

And here I found myself rather quickly a mother of three! I was still concerned about my ability to care for them, but I was a more confident mother this time having successfully managed the first two children. I had systems in place, space for them, family support, and time. I would say I was the most prepared mentally and emotionally for this baby's arrival. I was growing more comfortable and knowledgeable with motherhood.

Dave outside for a walk in the perambulator (pram),
he always liked his soother in his mouth upside-down

Smiley, joyful Dave

# CHAPTER 10

## *Discipline: Saying "NO!" and Alternatives?*

I started reading literature again regarding child rearing and raising healthy children. There were tons of books on the subject, so I had to discern what was relevant and useful to me. I desired to help my children be healthy in all ways—physically, mentally, emotionally, and spiritually. I was eager to develop my own philosophy of parenting, a philosophy that included old traditions incorporated with new ideas that I felt were sound and backed up by evidence.

One book about discipline I read was written by Dr. James Dobson. It was called *Dare to Discipline*[12] and was first published in 1969. A newer version was published in 1996, so it was still older information when I read it. It gave me some excellent ideas about discipline. I also read an article in a parenting magazine that said by the time a child reaches age five, they've heard the word "no" five thousand times. A UCLA study done in 2005 reported that the average one-year-old hears the word "no" more than four hundred times a day! I was determined to use alternatives to avoid saying no too frequently to my children. I wished to practice and learn new techniques that would significantly reduce the number of times I said this word to them.

One of the ideas I read about was to give the child alternatives, or to rephrase and make a positive statement. I could also ask them what they thought the answer was. Distraction was another idea I used, along with keeping the child occupied and doing something fun or interesting to keep them out of things they shouldn't be doing. Being intentional and coming up with creative alternatives took a concentrated effort. Sometimes my first reaction was to simply say no without thought. My brain had been taught and wired to respond as such, but I didn't want to react with always saying no. I wanted to be a conscious parent.

This took much more of my energy than I had anticipated. I tried to think about a positive statement or another alternative rather than simply saying no. My intention was to be thoughtful and active as opposed to reactive. So I would ask myself, *Is this a safety issue? Or a moral issue? Does it really matter if he/she tries this? Is it doing anyone harm?* I would think about my reaction before I made a comment. I didn't want to stifle their creativity, but to encourage alternative thinking. By giving my children a little more freedom and letting them have a voice in early decisions, I hoped to teach them how to make decisions. It was safe to learn how to make small decisions that had few consequences but gave them some power. My goal was to help build their self-esteem and confidence in their everyday abilities and activities.

I encouraged my children to make small choices, like picking what clothing they wore, from a very young age. Often the colours they chose clashed, or stripes were put with flowers, but they weren't going to die or be picked up by the fashion police for alternatively matching their clothing. My kids laugh now at the pictures of the outfits they wore and the hairstyles that happened through their creativity and off-the-wall fashion experiments. They laughed and said to me later, "Mom! What were you thinking?" I was thinking and fully aware of the choices I made with my children most of the time. There was a purpose to my actions, which was to develop their independence and build their thinking power.

I didn't believe in spanking. I had been occasionally threatened with a spanking as a child, but mostly the loud voice scared me enough to behave— or at least I was clever enough not to get caught! With Lisa and David, using a stern voice was enough to get them to stop and listen. They were more easily reasoned with than John in the early stages of development during the first five years. John was a whole other story. He simply never stopped moving! He didn't seem to care or even notice how far he was away from me. He seemed to have no fear and didn't appear to consider the consequences of his actions. He did things without analyzing the risk, and many times he got into trouble physically. But since he was so fit and agile, he usually figured out how to get himself out of the danger or predicament.

When John was about three years old, my four children, myself, and Nana were walking through the park in Cambridge. It was a lovely, sunshiny summer's day. We walked on a path beside the stream, maybe four blocks away from our home that led to the escarpment and waterfall. The kids were enjoying playing in the stream and were excited to show Nana everything. We got closer to the walking bridge that led to the escarpment and the beautiful view of the river below. I got distracted with one of the children at the beginning of the bridge, and Nana followed John over the bridge. John was quick. When I looked up, I saw Nana waving me to her in horror. There was a fence along all sides of the bridge, but somehow John had squeezed through the end of the fence and was perched on top of a rock directly over the waterfall. The falls below were a 60-foot drop.

Nana froze, not wanting to scare him, and then silently crept forward. She slowly reached in and pulled John back out of danger. I saw the whole scene unfold and held my breath, my heart racing with fear, yet I was making sure the other three children were at a safe distance. It was terrifying for Eileen and me. We had visions of him falling to his death. He was unafraid, curious, and fascinated. I had a stern talk with him afterwards about keeping behind the fence and staying nearer to me. I knew he was oblivious to the danger, and that scared me. I thank God Eileen was on the ball and acted quickly. I had to be super vigilant with John and aware of my surroundings and the possible dangers he could get into.

One time when John was about three years old, I was at my wits' end with his challenging behaviour. He wasn't listening, and I was extremely tired, frustrated, and angry. My patience ran out, and I spanked him. I gave him one hard slap on the butt with the palm of my hand. He looked at me startled and with much confusion, but he did not cry. Really, he had no reaction at all. I could see by his facial features that he was trying to figure out why I would hit him. He had a red handprint on his bum, and my hand stung. The spanking seemed to make as little sense to him as it had to me. Obviously it had no deterring affect on him. He had a very high pain tolerance and just continued on like nothing had happened. I began to cry. *How could I do this? What was the point?*

I felt guilty and remorseful for hitting him. Spanking was not an option, because it didn't work. I believe that violence breeds violence. If I hit my children, I only taught them that it was okay to hit someone if you were angry or wanted to teach them a lesson. I didn't believe that. Violence fosters fear, which may stop the behaviour when the risk of punishment is present, but it's not a sustainable solution. When the punisher is not present, the undesirable behaviour is likely to continue.

I knew I didn't want to use violence as a form of behaviour control with any of my children, so I chose to come up with alternative ways to deal with them. For example, if I took away a toy John really liked, or made him stay in his room while the others played or watched TV, this consequence resonated with him. What worked best was taking away privileges that he loved and activities that he enjoyed, like food. John enjoyed eating. Of course, I still fed him, but I learned that if I delayed food delivery, things got done rather quickly. Ha ha! Seriously, I never threatened not to feed them. . . only to delay the meal until the particular chore was completed. If they were hungry, the chore was done quickly, and the place tidied up lickety-split. We would then enjoy dinner or lunch together! I could also enjoy the meal in a less chaotic environment.

I knew John well and had deduced that he needed to be hands-on and the consequence had to be related to the action. In other words, the consequences needed to be logical; they had to make sense. He desired to be physical and moving all the time. He wanted to be building something, running, or climbing, and the more strenuous the activity, the better he liked it. He had incredible physical endurance, much like a long-distance runner. Keeping him busy and giving him physical activities to do focused and funneled his energy and he rarely misbehaved. He would look at me with his sly grin, as if to say, "Will I get into trouble if I do this?" He was charming!

Not to say John wasn't a handful, because he was. I had the time and energy to work with him, and I learned ways to utilize his unbelievable energy. I tried to be a step ahead of him to keep him out of danger or to talk him down from wherever he had climbed and managed to get himself stuck.

He'd often get himself up on top of something and yell "Tuck! Tuck!" to get my attention to come and rescue him. It was humorous. "Tuck" meant he thought he was stuck. I'd smile at his antics and the precariousness of the new situation he'd gotten into. Then I'd stand and look at him from below his perch and say very calmly, "John, you got yourself up there, so you can get yourself down." He didn't always believe me. He wanted me to get him down, to save him. I didn't. He was a capable climber from a very young age, and I knew he would have to learn to do it himself. What if I wasn't there to help him down? I couldn't always be there watching him. He needed to learn to get himself out of the stuck places. So I would convince him to carefully and slowly climb down, talking to him and giving him ideas. He would cry and whine and beg me to help him, but I'd simply continue to tell him in a calm and matter-of-fact voice how to climb down. I was there to catch him if he fell, but he could get himself down. And he did get himself down every time. The only obstacle was fear.

These scenarios were not without worry on both our parts, but my tactic did work. He never fell. His physical expertise grew as he pursued his multitude of climbing apparatus. His ability to climb and descend was skill-fully developed. He learned to be careful and assessed his surroundings and vantage points before he climbed. He became strong and agile and able to climb up and down the most unusual places. I knew his physical capabilities, and this gave me some peace of mind.

For example, when John was about five years old, we attended a wedding in Calgary. I sewed new outfits, little suits with funky buttons for the boys, and satin and chiffon dresses for the girls. We all wore stylish matching hats and dress shoes. I loved to dress up and wear hats, so why not dress up my children as well? A wedding was a great excuse to go formal and be extravagant in our costumes (attire). John donned a dapper pale green linen suit, Dave a grey and white striped suit, and Lisa and Rachel beautiful long dresses, all with hats and caps to match.

While we were milling about outside the church after the ceremony, John scaled the brick wall. Yes, I'm telling you, I would not have believed it if I hadn't seen him with my own eyes—a five-year-old climbing a wall like he was an experienced rock climber. He used his little hands and the toes of his shoes to grasp into the small mortar crevices between the bricks. Like Spiderman with some finesse, he clambered up the wall. We all stopped in silence as we watched him climb, our mouths gaping as he hung like he was attached to the wall with suction cups. He was some 14 feet above the ground, unaware of his audience. He then looked down as if to say, "Look, Mom!" He climbed down safely and appeared quite proud of himself.

All dressed up for a friend's wedding in Calgary. Cathy loves hats!

John playing Spiderman, scaling the brick wall, with Dad and Dave watching

Another time, we were visiting my parents at the homestead farm in southern Ontario. Although my parents no longer farmed the land or raised animals, several of the outbuildings and the silo still stood. The silo was a circular cement block structure about 15 feet in diameter and 40 to 50 feet high. There was a ladder attached to the silo that started at about 12 feet from the ground for safety reasons. A portable ladder was needed to reach the bottom of the attached ladder. Steel rebar rings ran horizontally at intervals of approximately 3 to 4 feet from bottom to top that reinforced the cement structure.

A long history of climbers in our family. Another generation scaling our silo!

I found it most interesting that history often repeats itself. I had climbed that same silo often as a young child of five or six. I guess I was a good climber as well, because my father wasn't alarmed at the time, but I remember my mother and Uncle Bill being frantic about the danger I was in. Obviously, Dad and I didn't think so. John was also about five or six years old when he discovered the ladder. He scaled the cement wall using the 3/4-inch steel rebar to shimmy himself up to the ladder. I was called by my dad when he found John at the top of the silo looking down with great satisfaction.

Of course, I had some natural fear of the danger he could be in, but then my logical mind kicked in and lessened my fear, because I knew he was an excellent climber. I asked him to come down so my family could calm down about his safety. I knew any ladder John saw was like a magnet to him. Curiosity would get the best of him, and he would ascend with grace and anticipation of the thrill of climbing and the success of seeing the world from above. I can't guess all that was swirling around in his mind, but he loved climbing.

I found that if I minimized the need for discipline in my children's lives, our enjoyment increased. I attempted to narrow my discipline efforts to safety and major issues and didn't sweat the minor stuff. The main way I avoided undesirable behaviour was to keep my children involved and engaged in a variety of activities. I regularly engaged all of my children in creative projects like drawing, painting, and sculpting. I loved these types of activities and found them most rewarding and fun for all of us.

Lisa, Dave, and John: wintertime fun at Nana's, in her river valley

Mike and the four kids on summer vacation in British Columbia

Cousins pool time with Lisa, John, Dave, Vicki, and Crystal

Dad, Mike giving swimming instructions to Dave, Lisa, and John

John and Lisa playing a birthday party coin toss game

Personalities developing

I found an edible, non-toxic play dough recipe, just in case they decided to eat it. I coloured the play dough with food colouring, and it made for lots of creative play. We would make figures and shapes and then tell stories about them. Our imaginations ran wild. I chose to use these creative projects to exercise the kids' minds, teach them skills, and keep them busy with constructive pastimes. Therefore, I rarely needed to use any form of discipline.

I began to read books by Maria Montessori, including *Discovery of the Child, (1973),*[13] about her philosophy of teaching young children by using all of their senses. Studies have shown that children aged birth to seven use both sides of their brain simultaneously. This means they use their logical brain and creative brain together. I could see this was happening with my children, as they seemed to absorb all of their surroundings like sponges. Research also showed that children learn differently. Each individual child tends to use one or two senses predominantly. The challenge is to learn which senses each child learns with best, and then utilize that information to help them learn and grow by using their unique strengths.

For example, Lisa was very visual. She loved to look at picture books and to draw and colour pictures. She would observe her surroundings fully before cautiously moving forward to try it out tangibly. Her method and approach showed from a young age her analytical mind. This balance between the logical and the creative was distinctive to her personality. She could formulate conclusions and apply them in a visually creative way. I found this aspect of Lisa's personality captivating. It was an unusual blend.

David was very auditory. He could hear the slightest, softest sounds in his environment. He also had a keenly-developed memory and could remember things with great accuracy. When David connected his auditory skills with his keen ability to remember information, he was awesome and learned optimally. Through this combination, he also developed a sixth sense and could read people and predict situations very well. I believe David's sixth sense, his intuition, grew out of his quiet nature and keen observational skills. This may be linked to being a third child. He carefully watched and remembered minute details. I think he could observe and appraise a situation and make complex conclusions at a young age.

His acute hearing helped him in all sorts of life situations, because I'm sure he heard things that most of us didn't. His logical mind combined with his uncanny intuition continually surprised me. It was like he understood the undercurrents of how life and people worked. It seemed natural for him to see abstract things clearly and pick up on feelings when drawing his conclusions—which often weren't obvious to the rest of us until David explained his deductions. I would look at him and say, "Of course!" He was right! It was fascinating to watch him in action.

David's uncanny intuitions often appeared on his birthdays or Christmas when he would predict the contents of gifts. We would wrap them to conceal what was inside, and he would shake it, look at it, and guess correctly. He had seen all the signs, heard the comments, and assessed the clues. He saw and heard the whole story about things and then could predict the "logical" outcome. "Oh, it's probably a CD," he'd guess, even when the CD was wrapped with weights in a shoebox. We would laugh and continually wonder how his prediction abilities were so accurate.

John was physical. If he could touch it and feel it, he could figure it out. If it came in a three-dimensional form, that was the ticket! Then he could comprehend the concept. At the Montessori school he attended when he was three years old, they had the Pythagorean theorem in three-dimensional block/puzzle form. John played with the cube, masterfully disassembling then reassembling the blocks that represented the complicated theory. He could understand the concept because he could physically manipulate it. He could see and feel the theory, the formula, in three dimensions. The problem then became logical. A three-year-old could understand the concept of the theory without knowing the formula! Amazing!

Three children, and all three were different types of learners. I had thought that the two boys might be more similar, but they were very different in how they approached life. They actually complemented each other. One would compensate for the other's lack or weakness. Now isn't that an ideal partnership? I read more about different styles of learning and birth order and how children fit into certain roles. This all helped me to be a more effective parent, to encourage and discipline each child according to their personality, learning style, and birth order in our family.

Part of the solution to keeping them happy was to keep their minds occupied with interesting things to do and fun activities that fit with their style and personality. There were no cookie cutter solutions to parenting and motherhood. I had to be flexible and live and learn along with them. That was part of the adventure and the challenge!

When my kids' minds and bodies were occupied with an activity they each loved, they simply couldn't misbehave. They were too enraptured with creating, building, or solving some problem that captured their attention and focused their energies. They were in the "zone." Cooking became one of these creative and all-encompassing learning experiences for me and my children. They all wanted to do it themselves, and there were enough parts to cooking that I could get each of them doing something they liked. That was always intriguing to me. They wanted to try everything! They were eager to forge through the unknown with vigour and verve. Why would I want to discourage that kind of enthusiasm? I wanted them to try and learn and try something different if it didn't work the first time. Even though the kitchen might end up in a huge mess, which it often did, that was a small price to pay for the immense rewards. We all loved cooking together and then eating what we'd cooked.

When my mom and dad came to visit, the first thing they'd do was attack the mess in the kitchen. They did the dishes and pots and pans, cleared and cleaned the floors, and sorted out and filled the refrigerator with food. I didn't have a dishwasher, and the cleaning up was neither high on my list of priorities nor within my energy level. Mom and Dad would happily see to setting the kitchen straight and then get a meal going. They also prepared meals and desserts to freeze for us to eat after they'd gone home. My mother is a great cook and baker. She'd have a huge pot of lentil soup on the stove with loads of fresh vegetables. We would all eat our fill and then freeze the leftovers. It was yummy and healthy. My parents were such a great help to me as a mother.

I always enjoyed my parents' company, our conversations, and their advice when they answered my questions about child rearing and life in general. They were a blessing and a joy to have around not only for all the valuable help they gave us but also for their support and company. I think it's most important for children to know their grandparents, cousins, aunts and uncles, and other extended family. The whole family network was a critical part of building the feelings of belonging, well-being, connectedness, and stability for my children.

Mom and Dad, Grandma and Grandpa Kotow,
visiting and taking such good care of us, with Lisa

Lisa and cousin Clare hugging

Children don't misbehave without a reason. If they feel secure, loved, and wanted by their caregivers, they'll behave from a feeling of attachment and the fulfilling of their needs. Therefore, they won't need to misbehave to get attention. I used my energy, knowledge, open affection, and family supports to fulfill my children's needs a much as possible to avoid the need to discipline them.

When discipline was needed, I tried to gear the consequences to the action. I prioritized safety first and wasn't as concerned with exploratory actions that showed alternative thinking. I encouraged alternative thoughts that could lead to different solutions, and I made a conscious effort to minimize how often I said no. I engaged the help of family members with care and affection to increase my children's feelings of belonging and attachment, and I made attempts to give them attention and food prior to them needing either form of nourishment.

Part of my experiential learning and growth into motherhood was realizing the depth of emotional and mental work and energy it took. To make an effort to change my thought patterns and habits took awareness and creative thinking to come up with alternative ideas, and then to conjure up the courage to try a different strategy. When it came to discipline, taking the approach of a "can do" instead of a "can't do" was important. Positive reinforcement I liked.

1986

Family photo: Balzac, Alberta, home

Hey, we are all smiling, *eh viola!*

*Do we have to get another picture taken? Really?*

Maybe Christmas cheer?

# CHAPTER 11

## *Family of Origin*

Details of my family of origin have always been of interest to me. My curiosity grew stronger the older I got. Recently I've been studying the genealogy of my family and researching our history for details about names, dates, marriages, deaths, and health issues. I developed a heightened sense of urgency because my parents' generation is growing older and many are dying. I felt time slipping away for the chance to get the information directly from the horse's mouth and knew I needed to speak with the older members of my family to gather information and documents about our history while they were alive.

Family members recently organized a ninetieth birthday party for my mother-in-law, Eileen. It was a wonderful celebration of her numerous successes in life. Many of these elderly family members attended, so I set up a family history gathering table. I asked members of each family unit to write down the names of their family, and the dates of births, marriages, and deaths. Also, I asked them to note the causes of death and any diseases they suffered from during their life. I brought a large Bristol board with circles and lines and information I already knew. By the end of the party, I had gathered an incredible amount of detail, which filled in most of the blank spaces. I was extremely happy that I'd taken the opportunity to gather this valuable information. Relatives were eager to give their input and share their family history.

California wedding finery, Cathy and Eileen

Our "adopted" sister Lorraine, with Beth, and Cathy. We named ourselves
"The Twisted Sisters". Visiting Grandpa Dockman in his nursing home.

That same holiday in Ontario, I went to visit my mom for a few days, and she helped me fill in information on the family tree from both the Malenfant and Kotow sides. While we talked, Mom remembered some dates and names and was able to look up information she didn't remember in a record book she kept. I wasn't even aware that record book existed. I'm glad we spent the time finding those documents, dates, and stories. We also looked through a large box of pictures, some of which had information written on the back. Mom also had a massive old Bible. In the past, people had written important dates in it, such as baptisms, first communions, marriages, and deaths.

Dad joking and teasing Mom, again

The whole process of researching and documenting the information was more time-consuming than I had imagined, but it was also more informative and full of enjoyment and surprises. We had such fun looking at the pictures, and I loved it when Mom reminisced about each person and event she remembered. The pictures jogged her memory, and many interesting stories followed. Without her help, I could not have gathered, or known where to find, this information.

What I found most fun about my search for family history was the stories Mom and Eileen told me about different members of the family. Many stories I had not heard prior to beginning this project. Mom told me about her Aunt Corinne and Aunt Adelle while we were adding their names and details to my family tree. My Great Aunt Corinne was my mother's father's (whose name was Ferman) sister, and one of nine siblings. Aunt Corinne had been married three times; her first two husbands had died. Aunt Adelle was apparently extremely opinionated and vocal with her opinions to her family.

As my mom was recalling stories, she called them both "bitches." You have to understand, my mother rarely swears. I was shocked. I had to laugh at her words and expressions and how she used her hands to emphasize her points. It was amazing to hear her talk so frankly about these past relationships and characters in her family. We laughed at the audacity of those two aunts; it was just like in the movies. Unbelievable!

When Mom announced that she was getting married to Dad, Aunt Adelle was horrified, as she'd heard that Dad came from Russian/Ukrainian descent. She proceeded to give my mother a lecture and dire warnings about marrying a communist. According to Aunt Adelle, there was conniving and plotting going on. Dad could not be trusted because of his country of origin. He must be involved in some undermining scheme to overthrow democracy and our government. She basically told my mother to cancel the wedding. Fortunately, my mom didn't listen to Aunt Adelle. She married the Russian/ Ukrainian, handsome, dark-haired man, Andrew George Kotow. As it turned out, Dad was not involved in any conspiracy or communist plot to take over Canada, or any other nefarious activity. He was a lovely man with whom my mother fell in love and remained married to all of his life.

Another story concerned my Great Aunt Adelle and finances. Apparently, she was a miser and what they called an "old maid" in those times, because she didn't marry until after she was forty years old. This was unheard of at the turn of the century. Aunt Adelle was born in 1889. My grandparents, Ferman and Rosemarie (Rose), were cattle and grain farmers. They ran a farming operation in McGregor, Ontario. There were lean times in the farming business, and cash money was often short.

During one of these particularly difficult times financially, my grandparents were compelled to ask Aunt Adelle for financial help to save the farm from ruin. Aunt Adelle, with apparent reluctance, lent my grandparents an infusion of cash to keep them afloat. This family loan turned out to be a hands-on investment that Aunt Adelle was adamant about protecting. Her impudent nosing around the farm weekly to collect her funds and make a return on her investment was annoying and embarrassing for my grandparents. Aunt Adelle was shrewd and nasty about the whole deal. I could see why mom called her the "B" word! Aunt Adelle lived to a ripe old age of eighty-nine and never changed her character. She remained a meddling, opinionated bitka!

I found the process of gathering the family history enlightening. I began to see established patterns of disease, addictions, and mental illness through the years and generations. The age at which people died gave me insights into longevity and the diseases that shorted the lives of some. Something interesting I noticed was that many names reoccurred in various versions over time. Francis, Joseph, Andrew, Alfred, Catherine, Annie, John (Jack), Mary, Rachel, and Peter were common on both sides of our families, as were versions of Elizabeth, such as Lisa, Beth, and Betty.

I have a theory about how names and personalities match. I've taken note of people with the same names and seen how their character and behaviours are similar. This is partly why I had such difficulty choosing names for my children. I had a friend in my youth whose name was Lynn, and there were parts of her personality I didn't like. For example, she seemed to be inauthentic to me. She often acted superior to us, and although I was friends with her, I was inferior. Because of my belief in character connections, I couldn't see naming our first child Lynn. That's why it took so long to decide on Annalisa's name. I needed to feel that the name complemented the child and feel positive about the name/character match.

I could also see patterns of prevalent diseases, like diabetes, mental health problems, and common causes of death. I also saw the alcoholism that was linked through the generations. I could see the genetic and social determinations toward these lifestyles that affected social and physical health. I was able to view the larger picture historically, which was informative and fascinating.

Putting together my family tree started as a University of Lethbridge class project when I was studying family dynamics and using genograms (family trees) to help clients see how their family history affected and shaped who they were. The assignment was the catalyst that started me on the journey of discovery, and I became fascinated and committed to its completion. The project turned out to be much larger than I had anticipated. I got so involved in it that I worked on it for months after I'd handed in the actual paper. It was personal, and I realized that my history not only affected me, but my entire family, including my children.

Researching and analyzing the information I'd collected was valuable to learning about the destructive cycles within our family. Knowledge is power, but as Napoleon Hill says in his book *Think and Grow Rich*,[14] "Knowledge is potential power." Anyone can have the knowledge, but if you don't use it, it's useless. I intended to use this knowledge to learn how to break yet another cycle of destructive behaviour and study preventative measures to reduce disease in my family as best I could. Also, I wished to share my learning with other family members for their awareness and growth. Having the knowledge of those illnesses and behaviours was critical to building my awareness. With awareness, I could proceed with changing behaviours and forging alternative paths in my health and that of my family.

Researching the family tree took a massive amount of time and energy. Thankfully, other historians in the family had done prior research, and I was able to gather their documents and photocopy them, which saved me time. Mike's sister Maureen had a file 2 inches thick filled with pictures, documents, newspaper articles, and other interesting family paraphernalia. She was a family historian and had been collecting information for years. One Christmas, while I was visiting the family at Eileen's home in Brampton, Maureen was there with this file. I was able to photocopy the whole file.

The entire project was time well-spent, as I felt the information was invaluable. A huge side benefit was the wonderful stories I heard from many family members that I otherwise would not have heard. To put the icing on the cake, I was able to spend all that time with Mom and Eileen, which created new memories of its own. I cherish the time with both of these women whom I love and admire. Both have been strong and positive role models and mentors for me throughout my life.

The gene pools from my mother and mother-in-law are in my four children. Their genetic makeup came through my ancestors throughout history. A specific combination of genes was distributed to each my children, making them unique. Everything is designed in the genes, from the quality of their health to their physical size and hair and eye colour. The genes hold a massive amount of information that formulates a blueprint of how this new human child will develop. Nature, in its orderly way of operating, miraculously puts together a unique and complicated set of traits that creates each child. I believe God had a hand in it too. All these aspects of nature affect who we are and who we can become—our potential. So what do I know about my ancestry that affects my children and who they are?

Recreation Vehicle trip to Alaska with Nana and Uncle Harry

Soul Sister Christine Dockman and Cathy on an Alaskan Cruise with all our glam and glitter

My father's parents came from the "old country," as they called it—Eastern Europe. They were of Russian and Ukrainian descent and came from a small town near Kiev, Ukraine. Both of Dad's parents, Feodor (Fred) and Annie, spoke Russian and Ukrainian. They came to Canada in 1929 in search of a better life. They spoke no English. My dad's parents and uncle, Grandma's brother, travelled across much of Canada and settled in Redcliff, Saskatchewan, in a small farming community. A few years later they moved to southern Ontario and bought a farm on a quarter section of land 20 miles outside of Windsor.

My father's parents began a farming operation of growing grain and vegetable crops and raising cows, chickens, and horses. They began slowly and gradually to build up their livestock. They sold the crops and raised the livestock for milk and meat. The big positive aspect of being farmers was that we always had food. We had an orchard of fruit trees, which grew apples, pears, plums, and walnuts. We had a large vegetable garden with herbs, leafy greens, carrots, cucumbers, tomatoes, peppers, and potatoes. I remember growing and picking monster zucchinis the size of small watermelons. We also had strawberry plants and raspberry bushes. We canned and pickled for days when one vegetable became ripe, preserving our food for the winter season.

We made dill pickles that were to die for. They were tart, juicy, and delicious. In addition to dozens of jars, we would have a five-gallon crock in the pump house filled with small cucumbers in the dill, vinegar, and salt brine. It had a plate with a rock on it to stop the cucumbers from floating. My brother and I would sneak in to test the pickles to see if they were done. We'd get in trouble if we got caught. I remember one year my mother pickling three hundred quart jars of dill pickles from our garden cucumbers! That's an amazing amount of work and dedication. We loved dill pickles and still do.

We also made jams and canned fruit. We had an abundance of fresh fruits and vegetables and meats readily available in the long summer season. In the winter, we ate frozen meat and vegetables, as well as canned fruit and vegetables we had put away from our fresh produce. We had an excellent, healthy diet.

The downside of farming was that we had limited cash. The money was tied up in the land ownership and the many costs of running a farm, from buying seed, to machinery, to labour. That was the challenge of farming: the year, the weather, and the health of the crop decided if there was money to buy seed for the next year's planting. Sometimes there was a need to borrow money to buy tomato plants, or wheat or corn seeds. Crops were rotated to preserve the topsoil and nutrients in the soil. Each year a different seed or crop was planted in each field for better crop yield in the future. My family worked hard, and all of us helped from a young age.

I remember driving the tractor that pulled the tomato planter when I was ten or eleven years old, or riding on the back of the tomato planter, where two metal seats faced backward, one on each side. We'd place one tomato plant at a time on the revolving machine that stuck the plants into the earth. My father was up at 5:30 a.m. to milk the cows, feed them, clean the stalls, and then work in the fields, ploughing, tilling, planting, weeding, or harvesting, usually until late in the evening. He would eat lunch in the field as well to reduce the down time. My mom would bring food to the field he was working in. He'd come into the house for dinner with us and then go back to the barn or the field to work until sundown.

My dad enjoyed working with his hands and felt a sense of pleasure and reward from his hard work. It was labour-intensive and hard on the body, but it was a good life. We all enjoyed the fruits of our labour by eating well and working together toward a common purpose. Although my parents were stressed at times from financial difficulties, as children we did not feel affected. I thoroughly enjoyed my childhood and growing up on the farm.

My mother's families were Quebec and Ontario French for many generations. My mother spoke no English, only French, until she went to school and learned English in Grade 1. My four siblings and I grew up on my dad's family homestead. My mother and father spoke only English to us, so we didn't learn either of their native tongues.

Mike's parents came from England in the late 1940s, after the Second World War. They lived and worked in Toronto, Ontario, and shortly thereafter bought some land with a small house 15 miles north of Brampton. Their roots were English on Nana's side of the family and Estonian and German on Grandpa's side. John Karl Dockman was Mike's father's dad.

Mom, Betty and her five adult children

Andy and Betty's fortieth wedding anniversary celebration

Cathy communicating with Grandpa Dockman,
who was almost completely deaf, through the written word

Mike's grandparents on his mother's side were John Peter and Emily Ivy Fursey, who lived in England. In fact, all of Eileen's family lived in England. She was the only member of her family who emigrated, whereas Mike's dad's family immigrated to Canada shortly after he came. We travelled to England often to visit family. My children were born and raised as Canadians, but I felt it was important to know about their European heritage.

When I was married at twenty-four years old, there was no divorce in my family, but Mike had experienced broken marriages in his family. His sister Maureen had been married a long time, but she and her husband split up the year after we were married, so Mike was very leery of the institution of marriage. His parents had separated and divorced when he was a young teenager. Although his father was still somewhat involved in his life, Mike's mother had been primarily responsible for his care from when he was fourteen years old on. Our attitudes toward marriage differed. I was more traditional and probably more idealistic with my thoughts of how marriage would be. We each learned those values from our respective families.

We also learned about keeping ourselves active and healthy from our families. My family had its share of heart disease, cancer, and diabetes, which can be caused by genetics in combination with lifestyle choices like smoking cigarettes, drinking excessive alcohol, keeping an unhealthy diet, and failing to exercise. Preventative measures could be taken to prolong a healthier life. Mike's family suffered from deafness, tuberculosis, and circulatory problems. On the positive side, my family consisted of hard-working farmers and blue-collar workers. Their intelligence came not so much from education in traditional school settings but mostly through life experiences. Mike's family had intelligence through schooling and experience, and they tended to be white-collar workers. They also had longevity, as his grandparents lived to ninety-two and ninety-three years old. There's a mix of genes and environmental factors that promote health or disintegrate it. I believe that making healthy life choices tips the balance toward better physical, mental, and emotional health.

Emotionally speaking, my parents' generation was too busy making a living and trying to survive in a new country to evaluate and understand their emotions. They had dealt with two world wars, the economic crash of 1929, and the great depression. All survival issues! They were busy with farming, working, and raising many children, with little money available. Emotional and mental health was not a priority through those hard times—putting food on the table and keeping everyone safe was.

My generation in Canada, my cousins, siblings, and I hadn't been touched by war, economic disaster, or depression. Illnesses and disabilities like dyslexia, bipolar disorder, schizophrenia, and addictions ran through the generations and touched many of us. Although in the past two generations these aliments may not have been acknowledged or discussed, they affected our families' lives significantly.

As far as we can figure, my paternal grandmother was an alcoholic. When she drank, she became angry and violent. I was told she was constantly picking fights with one or another of her four children, or trying to cause rifts between them. I heard she was always mad at someone. My impression of Babka was that she was a nice old woman who'd lived a hard life. She took me shopping with her and to the market and her church. I was young and didn't understand these family problems. I loved her. She died when I was twelve years old, and I was sad and missed her.

Looking back on her behaviour, I can see the destructive acts and how she used alcohol to cope with being alone, my paternal grandfather's death by a heart attack in 1951, and running a farm on her own in a new country. She had a mickey of whiskey hidden in her kitchen and in the barn. That's how she coped. At times she became out of control from stress and over-drinking. I believe she had an alcohol problem. My father and one of my brothers were also alcoholic. Because of my grandmother's violence when she drank, my father swore he would not act like her. So when dad drank and got angry, he would leave and hide those emotions.

Thankfully, when I was nineteen and away from home attending university, my dad quit drinking and went into a recovery centre. The beginning of dad's recovery from alcoholism started over thirty years ago. Now my father has passed on, God bless his soul. Dad had thirty some years of sobriety. He never drank alcohol again after the age of forty-nine. One year after dad started his recovery and stopped drinking, my brother Frank did the same. My brother is still in recovery and turned his life around because of quitting drinking and changing his attitudes and behaviours. It's amazing how the fabric of our family, the very fibre, has changed since Dad made the decision to seek help. By admitting and getting help for his alcoholism, he started a positive ripple of acceptance, healing, and recovery for our entire family. One of my cousins in Michigan, Ed, chose not to have children because of these physical diseases and emotional and mental disorders that were prevalent in our family. He didn't want children who would be susceptible to this trauma and be potential carriers of these illnesses to future generations. I took a different view. I chose to have children and to try to break this cycle. I began to heal myself by dealing with some of the ghosts of the past that had been swept under the carpet. I learned about alcoholism and mental health and tried to create a healthier lifestyle though education, knowledge, and awareness. I was optimistic that change could happen over time.

I had faith that maybe we could become better as people and as a society. Awareness and acceptance of our past was the first step, and then discovering what we could do about these problems to create a different outcome and hopefully a better future! I had hope and vision. What's life without hope? What's life without faith in our future? It would only be depressing. Hope carried me through many difficult and seemingly closed situations in my life. One of my all time favourite poems describes how hope feels to me. It was written by Emily Dickinson: *Final Harvest, Emily Dickinson Poems* (1961).[15] It goes like this:

CATHY KOTOW-DOCKMAN

"Hope" is the thing with feathers -
That perches in the soul -
And sings the tune without the words -
And never stops - at all -

And sweetest - in the Gale - is heard -
And sore must be the storm -
That could abash the little Bird
That kept so many warm -

I've heard it in the chilliest land-
And on the strangest Sea -
Yet, never, in Extremity,
It asked a crumb - of Me.

This poem is a gift to young and old. Hope suggests possibilities! There were many occasions in my life where I had lost myself, when my sight of the future was clouded and seemed to darken. Reflecting on those times, I recall that hope was the key to pulling me through them. When I read this poem, I can visualize a small, grey, vulnerable bird being bashed by nature's cruel elements but perched proudly, dripping wet with soggy wings, and belting out its song. The bird sings only for singing, no other purpose, with no expectations. Because he is a bird, singing is what he does. It's so simple, it's beautiful! Hope gave me the vision that motivated me to find the strengths I used to overcome the tough times. I used my vision of how I wanted life and our future to look like to empower me to find my voice, to speak up and lift myself above and through my challenges.

The image this poem creates in my mind makes my heart sing! It moves me to gather my deep inner strengths. It inspires me to take a deep breath, pull my shoulders back, and let my voice be heard through my fear. Hope gives me vision to see the future as bright, and the motivation to try to change myself and the world for the better. I had hope for my marriage. I had hope for my children, and I still have hope for all our futures. At twenty-four, when I began my marriage, my goal was to build a better life for me and my family. I fully intended to make a valiant effort to change the negative family cycles for our future generations. I had hope that the changes I made would make a difference.

# CHAPTER 12

## *Arrival of Child Number Four*

David was coming up to one year old. He continued to be a social and happy baby. He was small compared to John, even skinny, but he was also healthy and strong. Dave was still as cute as a button with white-blond hair and a beaming, happy grin for all. He was eating a variety of foods now, including cereals and fruit and vegetables. I was nursing him less and should have learned from the other two times and taken better precautions.

I discovered I was pregnant again, and I felt like a baby-making machine. I was prolific and fertile, and my body was doing what it was made to do! I was shocked and surprised, but mostly afraid. Tears came. How could I do this? I would have four children in less than five years! Did I have it in me to take care of another child? I felt overwhelmed.

I got the news of this pregnancy when I was visiting at my mother-in-law's home. My sister-in-law, Christine, was with me as well. I had gone to see my doctor for a regular check up for myself and David. She took blood work to check for a few things, like anemia. I thought I was so tired because of low iron and all the running around I did, taking care of three young children. But that was not the only reason I was tired—far from it. No, I was pregnant! Oh my God! Christine and Eileen heard me on the phone. I sat down and asked the doctor, "Positive? What does that mean?"

"Positive results mean you're pregnant. Congratulations," the nurse said. Pregnant again!

I was in shock and felt emotional. How did this happen? I was already extremely busy with three babies. How could I take care of another child? On my God! Christine and Eileen helped me to sit down, put my feet up, and made me a nice cup of hot tea. They sat with me and offered soothing words and comfort. I wanted four children, that wasn't the point. I'd just thought they would be a little more spread out in age. I'd hoped to have time to adjust and prepare for them. I was afraid of being incapable of supporting four children so young and close together in age. I had a very real fear! Getting pregnant again was out of my control, and God had another plan.

With much thought, time, and conversations with supports, I began to accept this new being growing inside of me. It took me about a month to adjust to and accept this news fully. I came to the realization that this little person was meant to be a part of our family. I do believe in fate, and this fourth creation was bound and determined to be here on this earth. I believe things happen for a reason, as my mother often said. Having this child so soon was a part of the larger scheme of things, the bigger picture. This baby was coming. I accepted it and soon actually embraced the idea. So I changed my attitude and started to get excited about her arrival.

As it turned out, she was a very determined little human being and was coming regardless of my plans! When she came, she completed our family and was crucial to the dynamics of our family unit. Since I was pregnant and so tired, I weaned David from breast milk and began to focus again on the mental and physical nurturing of myself and this new baby growing inside of me.

Thank God I never experienced morning sickness, nausea, or other pregnancy-related difficulties. I had three other young children to look after and needed all the energy I could muster to keep them safe, fed, and happy. Fortunately, I had another healthy, active pregnancy. I gained lots of weight again, over 50 pounds, even though I never seemed to stop moving or get enough sleep. I was happy and constantly engaged in small children's activities, cooking, and play. In hindsight, I can't imagine how I coped with everything. It must have been my superpowers! Or maybe it was me constantly running on adrenaline.

I did what I had to do to survive. I'd love to have a video of myself and watch the incredible life as it happened. . . or I should say the crazy life that was happening. That's what it was—a full life with an abundance of energetic souls. We were living at maximum capacity. My life was hectic, chaotic, and messy; if you were looking in from outside, you may have seen a disaster zone and gasped. Yet the pure joy my children brought me through sharing their unconditional love, eyes-wide-open wonder, and shrieking excitement about everything and anything made me enjoy my time in spite of the mad busyness. I believe I rose to the challenge successfully. I prayed that this baby would be a girl. *Oh God, please let it be a girl!* Having a third boy could be more difficult, especially if the fourth one was as active as John. Thus began the story of my fourth child.

It was October 1987. Lisa was four years and two months, John was two years and ten months, and David was one year and two months. My baby bump was beginning to show. In between each pregnancy, I lost the 50–60 pounds of pregnancy weight, which was all I had gained during pregnancy and more. It certainly helped when I had nine- to ten-pound babies, as well as delivering a huge placenta and losing loads of blood. Eee-gawd! I lost 25–30 pounds simply by giving birth! That was a wild fact to me and pretty unbelievable! Nursing each child did wonders for using up calories, as well as flattening my tummy and tightening my abdomen muscles. I ate healthy and was very active with the three children. I got down to my pre-pregnancy weight before I got pregnant each time. So the cycle began again.

I was pregnant, and my insatiable hunger started all over again. I was constantly hungry. I ate well and lots. I seemed to need the food energy to keep up the pace at which I was going and to nourish the growing child inside of me with the proper amount of calories. I got major cravings for chocolate, chips, nuts, milk, and carbohydrates. I ate pasta often and had cereal and milk with bananas any time of the day.

I gained another 55 pounds, from the start of the pregnancy to the delivery. I felt like a yo-yo spinning out of control! Even with all that weight, I didn't feel self-conscious. I felt happy, and people told me I was glowing. That's how I felt—radiantly excited about the miracle growing inside of me. Often I floated around in awe, grace, and joy. I felt grateful to be healthy and blessed to be able to carry a child successfully and give birth to a healthy baby.

At the same time, I wondered how I was going to keep them all safe. I was nervous. Thank goodness I was pregnant over the winter this time, as I didn't have to deal with being huge in the blistering heat of summer in southern Ontario. John had turned three in January, and by April I was ready to deliver the baby as soon as possible. My mom had put her back out and was physically unable to come and help me after this birth, and Dad had to look after Mom. I would miss them and their help and support. I understood, especially since this time I would have four children I needed help with. I was worried. Mary Beth was there, so Beth and Mike looked after the other three children while I was in the hospital giving birth to my fourth.

I thought the fourth child's delivery should be easier and faster than the others. That was the theory. The size of my babies so far left me no guarantee of speed or simplicity with childbirth. I was healthy right to the end. I had no anemia, diabetes, high blood pressure, or other problems. My feet would swell up at the end of the day, but I suppose that could be expected due to the immense belly of baby I carried. During the last month of pregnancy, I waited impatiently for natural labour and delivery to start. I waited and waited. I think time slows down in those situations. In those last few weeks, I felt like I was living inside a movie in slow motion. I waddled around sluggishly at a snail's pace. I think more from mental and emotional exhaustion than physical. I watched my children playing, laughing, and frolicking about as if I was an observer from somewhere else, their laughter and voices subdued like it was being filtered through a thick liquid. I was in a pregnancy daze.

It was a challenge to stay focused on my children and keep my thoughts in the now when my body was obviously getting ready to give birth. I was easily distracted by the activities happening inside me, like the baby moving, a hand hitting my stomach from the inside, my belly moving with the baby, or my muscles contracting involuntarily. I was absorbed in my body shifting, my uterus tightening with contractions, and the baby's almost imperceptible movement down toward the birth canal. I had to concentrate to focus my attention outside. I imagine there was cellular communication between the baby and me, non-verbal cues drawing me into its conversation. That conservation was real and intense. Fascinating! I had to remain vigilant about the care of my other three children, which was a challenge those last few weeks.

On May 26, 1988, I started to have contractions and went to the hospital. The labour room was full, and we had to wait for a space. We waited from 4:30 p.m. to 9 p.m. to be admitted. They took me to the labour ward and into a birthing room, where the doctor checked me. I was four centimetres dilated. The doctor broke my water sac and decided not to use any drugs to induce labour further, but just to let the process develop naturally. My contractions were nine minutes apart, and then they continued for one hour and ten minutes at four to five minutes apart. They became stronger and more painful. Mike was there and dressed for the operating room at 10:50 p.m. I was still only four centimetres dilated.

The doctor suggested using a muscle relaxant, Demerol. They had given me that same drug before Lisa was born. I didn't think I could handle the contractions for another three to five hours without help, so I took the shot. It made me drowsy. The next hour was hazy. At midnight, the doctor checked me again, and I was eight centimetres dilated, and the baby and I were still doing fine. I started to use the nitrous oxide to dull the pain. I was light-headed, moaning, and fed up. I felt exhausted and unable to handle any more pain.

Finally, I felt the urge to push. The nurse called the doctor in, as the baby's head was crowning. The nurse put pillows under my hips in case the baby came out on the bed before they got me into the birthing chair. She almost did arrive in the next contraction. When the contraction stopped, the nurses quickly moved me to the birthing chair. When I was in midair, another contraction started. The contractions were coming very close together, only seconds apart. I wanted to push with everything I had, that instinctual, whole-body urge to expel the child. The doctor and nurses rushed over. The baby was coming out. Her head and shoulders came out simultaneously with the next contraction.

SHE! She came out all in one push. I was moaning and yelling with the pain and excitement of the birth finally happening. No time for nitrous oxide. Ouch! I saw her coming out. She was so purple, I was worried. The doctor cleaned out her mouth and nose, and she started breathing, let out a howl, and cried. What a huge relief. I couldn't believe it. She was a girl. I looked again—a beautiful, healthy girl. Thank God! Perfect. I was truly blessed. I thought I could handle a girl, and God gave me one. I thanked him and felt like the luckiest person alive. My family was complete. I had Lisa, John, David, and now another girl. I was so happy to have two of each gender. She was born at 1:15 a.m. on May 27 and weighed in at 9 pounds 11 ounces. I wasn't surprised to have another sizeable baby. She was beautiful!

The doctor had anticipated her size, I guess from my charts and records, so she did an episiotomy, but I still tore. I delivered the afterbirth with no trouble, and she stitched me up. The baby was healthy, and no visible physical problems were discovered. We stayed in the hospital for five days while I healed and she nursed successfully. She was a quiet and contented baby. She and I bonded during that time. She spent the five days in my room in a bassinet beside my bed. Mike brought the other three children into the hospital to visit me and to meet their new baby sister.

Lisa was happy to have a little sister, and the boys looked at her curiously. I was pleased to have those days in the hospital with just the new baby and no other responsibilities to worry about. I began to recover and regained my strength and energy so that I could cope with all four when I got home. Being healthy and energetic would be important. I could barely walk for the first two days after the birth. I'd lost a lot of blood and was weak. My hemoglobin levels were low, and I was anemic, so I had to increase my iron levels to get my energy up again. Of the 55 pounds I'd gained, I lost thirty from the birth and delivery alone. Nursing helped to shrink the uterus and my stomach and to get me back to pre-pregnancy health. The body is really amazing in how it heals itself and works to return the system to normal health after childbirth.

With much deliberation again, Mike and I debated her name. I felt the name had to fit the child, as I'd learned from Lisa's naming, so choosing the right name was critically important. Her name would affect her throughout her life, and it had to suit the personality and character. Shortly after she was born, the name Rachel came to me. Maybe my children's names came to me from an infinite intelligence or a universal consciousness, or maybe from God, but I got the message each time and I listened to it. I knew in my heart, intuitively, that she was a Rachel. Thank goodness Mike agreed. We used the name Mike wanted previously for Lisa as Rachel's second name, Lynn. My godmother's name was Rachel, and it's also a biblical name. When I looked up its meaning, I saw that it fit. She was definitely a Rachel.

I know it may seem strange, but I listened to my instincts. Rachel, in the Christian sense, means "naive and innocent," like a lamb. Lynn comes from the name Evelyn, meaning "life or living," and Madeline, meaning "a tower of strength." That's quite an interesting mix of innocence and strength. It would be fascinating to see how her character developed according to her name's significance.

Nana with newborn Rachel at her dedication celebration in Cambridge, Ontario

Baby Rachel in a photo session

I came home from my five-day hospital stay to the house on Blair Road to care and nurture these four children, all less than five years old. I was anxious. I was determined. I was ready to take the bull by the horns and meet this challenge. I was purely committed to doing my very best for these four little human beings. I was totally responsible for them and felt the heaviness of that responsibility, but I wasn't immobilized by my fear. I was motivated by it.

The family dynamics changed again. Now I had Lisa, the eldest, the two boys in the middle, and Rachel as the youngest. I was always amazed at just how different they each were. They all had the same two parents, the same history, and the same ethnic background. They shared the same environment, yet each of them had very distinct and individual personalities.

Rachel with Nana at Christmastime, 1989

Rachel was intensely determined and persistent from the very beginning, even to the point of stubbornness. I seemed to spend a lot of time protecting her from the other three until she learned to speak up and defend herself. I understood that was because she was the youngest and wanted to participate in what the others were doing. Rachel also saw herself as her siblings' equal and figured she should be allowed to do anything her three siblings could do. This was a challenge for her and me throughout her growing-up years.

Rachel developed, or simply was born with, an innate sense of fairness. She demanded fairness. She longed to understand. When I would explain the "whys" of a situation, she would simply accept its truth and would be okay, if she understood. Most of the time I was aware of this and gave her explanations. At times when an explanation wasn't timely, or unsuitable or not forthcoming, Rachel became like a bulldog fighting for her rights. This was when the stubbornness came into play. She was immovable during these circumstances. She would hold her ground like a fierce soldier. Incredibly enough, she needed to see the larger picture in order to put her life's pieces together. I got it. I could relate. Why would I agree to anything if it didn't make any sense to me? She was similar. I learned that these characteristics were a part of Rachel's personality. I accepted her and did my best to work with her and help her understand life and her world.

Cathy, Rachel's protector

Rachel and Mum, trying to figure out life

Rachel swinging in the park, not a care in the world

Birthdays are special

Rachel playing Nintendo

Rachel's fifth birthday, with Dave

Sibling love: Rach and Dave

Dave with pet kittens

Rachel had a special ally in David. David had a gentle, caring soul and a deep connection with Rachel from the very beginning. I believe part of this must have been instinctual, because he was only a year and nine months when Rachel was born. He was just a baby himself. Dave made it his job to look after Rachel from those early days. When Rachel cried and I was busy, David would come to get me, saying, "Baby hungy." He would grab my leg and pull me over to Rachel. He was such a sweetie. They formed a powerful bond between them that still exists today. David shared Rachel's belief in equity. He was patient and explained things to her without judgment or emotion. That fairness and want for justice was of crucial importance to both of them. The emotional, physical, and mental bond between them grew through the years.

Rachel had a keen sense of humour and loved to be in the limelight. She loved to play dress-up, dance, and paint. When she laughed, it was a full-out, mouth wide open, belly laugh. When she cried, she would wail and flail dramatically. She was a passionate soul with a creative energy that she pursued with intense fervor. She was also very literal. She took words at face value and sometimes misunderstood jokes or sayings. She would often miss double meanings or slang words. I regularly took her aside to explain what the term meant or the joke implied.

Rachel painting with Uncle Harry

Rachel with Nana all dressed up for a family wedding in California

All in all, Rachel was a joyful baby. She and I spent the majority of our waking hours together. We became acutely attuned with each other's feelings and moods. This unspoken pact served us well, especially when we were faced with difficult future events. This bond was essential when the "bulldog Rachel" came out fighting and I had to deal with her. She knew I cared for her and loved her deeply, and this connection carried us through some difficult disagreements.

John, Dave, and Rachel, it's always special to have brunch at Nana's

We were not a financially secure family. We lived from pay cheque to pay cheque, and often worse, with little money and loads of debt. At this point, Mike was in real estate, so it was feast or famine, large pay cheques far apart. We had adequate living arrangements. I was creative with running the household, from decorating with hand-me-down or second- hand furnishings, to stretching the food budget. I found ways to build healthy meals from scratch. The key to our fulfillment in life was the fact that we had each other and enjoyed our family time together. That was of utmost importance to me. I wished to build lifelong bonds as well as an abundance of loving memories. I chose to be a stay-at-home mom for these reasons.

We received lots of hand-me-down clothing from family and friends, so my children had enough for whatever their activities were. They wore the hand-me-downs, which were beautiful, or I made their clothes. I used my sewing skills to create great outfits for various family events; like weddings. I made Halloween costumes and we used them for play and everyday dress up. I got plenty of girl hand-me-down clothes, including some really elaborate, fancy dresses, like red velvet and lace, satin with beads, or chiffon and lace dresses. They were like princess dresses. The girls liked to wear them anytime, any day. We had an abundance of pretty dresses given to us from cousins Clare and Giselle.

This was not the case for the boys. We received very few hand-me-down boy outfits, and I wondered why. Maybe boys had less clothing, or weren't as interested in shopping or clothes, or maybe they wore them out faster. That was probably it; the clothes got torn and tattered by the boys. Because of the lack of availability and inadequate variety of boys' clothes, and our financial situation, I made them some fun, unique, and classy outfits. The girls had fun and pretty clothes, and I wanted the boys to have a similar experience. I searched for and found funky, boy-style fabrics and sewed cute little suits, vests, and pants with soccer ball buttons or saxophone designs. I made vests in metallic fabrics for Christmas and concerts and plays they attended at school.

Dave in a two-piece suit Cathy made for him, modeling
in a Catwork's Sewing Centre fashion show in Airdrie

162

Rachel modeling mom's creation at the Catwork's fashion show

For every day wear, I found a great pattern for sewing a jumpsuit. It was one piece, slip-on pants with the top attached, and it had a front zipper. Some call them onesies. Very easy for a child to get in and out of, so they could easily dress themselves and remove it simply at potty time. I made this same outfit in denim, with flowers, spaceships, race cars, and other motifs. I also used different fabrics, such as cotton, denim, corduroy, and metallic. I made them for the boys and the girls. David called them their "jumping suits!" Some of the jumpsuits I made with sleeves and some without. The ones without sleeves could be worn in summer by themselves or winter with a turtleneck underneath for warmth. These jumpsuits were durable, washable, and very versatile. Plus, my kids loved to wear them. They were fun clothes.

Rachel was four months old when Mike was offered a job transfer to Calgary, Alberta. We were travelers and had often wistfully discussed living in another part of the world. Alberta was still a part of Canada, but being some 3,000 miles from Ontario, it seemed like another world. It took me all of five seconds to decide: "Yes, let's go!" I had four very young children, yet I was ready to up and relocate just like that, in a snap of my fingers. It would be an adventure. Mike wasn't so sure. He had to think about it and weigh out all the options. It was a very lucrative position with much potential. He was offered a raise in pay and a promotion, and all our moving expenses would be covered. How could he refuse? He took a few days to think about the move and then accepted the offer!

I had fulfilled my goal and dream of having four children, and it was certainly much more difficult and complicated than I ever imagined. I don't believe a person can understand birthing a child until it happens. The rewards of motherhood struck me to the core often and would render me speechless. Beyond my wildest dreams I felt joy, wonder, and gratitude regularly. I was committed to digging deep to collect all my reserves and give motherhood my all.

Rachel, our fourth child, completed our family. I was done with pregnancy and childbirth. Four was enough for me. I had already committed to twenty years of full-time motherhood. I figure these four would fill my time and years sufficiently. I was excited about the move and eager to begin our new life in the West.

# CHAPTER 13

## *Birth Order and Sibling Rivalry*

I found myself in June of 1988 at the age of thirty-one with four small children. Annalisa was four years and ten months old, Johnathan was three years and six months, David was one year and eleven months old, and Rachel was a newborn. I was somewhat aware of how the order of one's birth shaped a person's personality. I concluded the younger children would likely have more difficulty than a child of three years or more with adjusting to a sibling's birth and entrance into the family. I had my fair share of running interference over the years with nasty and unbecoming behaviours due to jealously and sibling rivalry. I hated it when it reared its ugly head. I did research about the effects of and preventions ideas related to sibling rivalry. I found the book *Siblings Without Rivalry*[16] gave me helpful ideas to try.

Lisa had a hard time when John was born, as she'd had all her family's focus on her for a year and a half. Now she not only shared us with John, but he monopolized our time for his first three months. Lisa did not like it! I can't blame her at all. She'd had me all to herself prior to John's birth, so why would she like him at all? He was the reason she lost my attention. Subconsciously, she wanted him to disappear. She'd cover him up with clothes or blankets while he lay in his rocker or car seat. In her mind, if he was out of sight, he didn't exist. I had compassion for her and tried my best to give her attention, even when I was exhausted and probably should have slept. I read to her alone when John slept. I also made every attempt to spend time with her whenever someone else took care of John.

To Lisa's dismay, John did not disappear, and he didn't go back to wherever he'd come from. He stuck around. John had to deal with Lisa competing for our attention constantly. Fortunately, after three months of crying, John became a social, smiling, and humorous baby. I believe his newly acquired easygoing nature saved him from Lisa's wrath, or at least protected him and made his life a little easier. I was now able to give them both my time, together and individually.

Lisa had some typical traits of being the eldest, like having a focused and determined personality. She liked being the "boss." Years later, I recall Rachel often saying to her, "You're not the boss of me!" Those were the times when Rachel and Lisa would clash in yet another of their power struggles. Lisa's strength and conviction was apparent at that early age and fit with her role as the eldest. Interestingly enough, Rachel had the same sort of determination and strength. Sharing similar characteristics caused friction between the two girls.

Size didn't matter to Lisa when she was dealing with John. As John grew and became her equal in size and physical prowess, she never faltered. John's physical power and ability soon surpassed hers, but they played and found joy in each other's company. They did become close friends over time. It appeared that Lisa didn't see John as a threat most of the time. It seemed to me that underlying Lisa's behaviour was her need for power and control. That's not such a bad thing in the overall picture. Her strength and determination have served her well in many ways. It was an ongoing challenge for John in his relationships with females to see potential girlfriends as different from his sister with her domineering personality. We all faced challenges that resulted from Lisa and John's sibling rivalry.

John's birthday with Mom, Dad, and Lisa

Lisa at her birthday party with Nana

When John was about three years old, he was very mobile and had a wickedly awesome sense of humour. One day Lisa was taunting him again. I would observe their interactions unobtrusively from a distance to make sure I was getting the real goods when they later tried to tell me what had happened. I learned plenty about how they treated each other, and filed the information for later learning opportunities. I wanted to be an informed mother and not take sides. I wanted to treat them justly.

It seemed John was observing Lisa's behaviours as well and had developed his own set of strategies for standing his ground with her. One particular time I watched Lisa taunting John. He was bigger and stronger by then, and I guess he decided it was time to take a stand and show his strength. He took a predatory stance in attack mode, with a serious "I'm going to get you" look in his eyes, like an animal ready to pounce. He could be such an actor! This startled Lisa a bit as she watched him carefully. He began very slowly and stoically, pretending he was running after her to "beat her up." He then ran dramatically and intentionally toward her like he was in slow motion. It was his turn for revenge, payback time for her dominant past activities. I remember the stern look on his face, direct eye contact with Lisa, and his determination. He was in pursuit of her.

A glint of fear shot through Lisa's eyes and face. *Oh crap, what is he going to do to me?* I could see her worry. He was stronger and bigger, so he could have hurt her if he wanted. John ran in slow motion, taking exaggerated steps toward Lisa. As it turned out, John was playing with her; it was only a ploy to show her that if he wanted to, he could physically stop her. He stopped suddenly just in front of her, shocked her with a mischievous grin, and started to laugh.

Lisa realized he was playing with her, and she was angry! He'd fooled her. I laughed as well; it was just hilarious. At that moment, I knew John could look after himself and would only be pushed so far. Maybe he would let her take advantage of his good nature sometimes, but he could speak up and stop her if he wanted to. I figured that would be one of his challenges in life—to stand up for himself and not let Lisa, or anyone else, take advantage of his placid nature. He showed he had the strength of character to hold his own. It was a proud and freeing moment for me as a mother.

Now add David, my third-born child, into this equation. He was laid back, curious, smiley, and extremely cute. He absolutely adored and admired his two older siblings. He wanted "in" to their sphere, to be their equal. He wanted peace and harmony in life and acceptance from Lisa and John. At one year old, Dave was crawling around and followed Lisa and John everywhere. He learned and grew and interacted with them continually. He disliked them fighting and would distract them or engage them in fun activities with him to stop them. Baby conflict resolution! It was too funny. These diplomatic aspects of Dave's personality grew to be among his major strengths.

Dave saying "Me Too", gets buried in toys by Lisa and John.

David did have his limits, and he could be very loud. If he was feeling left out or taken advantage of, he'd use his big voice. He would squeal or yell, and it would get everyone's attention instantly or change dynamics of the situation. Marvellously clever he was. As I said before, he had auditory strengths. He loved sound, music, and noise and used his voice to his benefit. For the most part, he was quiet and cooperative, but there were moments of, "Hey, what about me? I'm important, and I need your time and to be recognized. So there, listen to me!" He'd stamp his foot with his voice! That was his way of getting the attention he needed.

David was always aware of his surroundings and picked up on the undercurrents of others' feelings. He could read situations based on what he heard and feelings he picked up, and then he acted on them. Or he would seemingly study the whole scene, think and analyze, and draw his own conclusions. I would watch him plan and methodically make his move, like a chess player. I don't claim to understand how or why complex brain mechanisms work at a young age, but it was fascinating to watch. That was his makeup, his personality, and how he carved out his place in our family. Fairness was always an integral part of his deliberations. Those early experiences, combined with his personality, make him the caring man he is today.

Rachel's arrival initially didn't create any new sibling rivalry. The other three were well established, and it took a year and a half to two years before Rachel began to communicate her desire to be equal and participate in everything the other three were doing. Being the fourth child was difficult for Rachel at times, because she liked getting attention from everyone. In fact, I believe her personality needed more attention than any of the other three. It was an interesting revelation for me. I had always seen equality as equal shares of time, but I was aware that individual perceptions can be different. Rachel's perception of time was different, and I tried to compensate for her needs by giving her the extra time and attention. I think this tactic worked, because for the most part, Rachel saw me as an ally. I was there to explain, protect, and foster inclusion for her.

This task was a major and ongoing challenge for me, as Rachel didn't acknowledge that the age difference between her and her siblings meant anything. If her sister and brothers could do it, she could too. Sometimes I let her, and sometimes I didn't. For this reason I think Rachel learned things before she may have been physically or emotionally ready. She wouldn't settle for anything less, so I tried to guide her through those challenges. For example, there were times when she wasn't physically capable of something, yet she would get extremely frustrated because she couldn't do something her sister and brothers were doing. She was a trooper and she tried very hard.

Most times she did well and became physically capable and mentally strong, but her emotions sometimes took their toll on her. She didn't understand why she wasn't at the same level emotionally as her siblings, and she always seemed to be trying to catch up to them, which was impossible. It appeared her personality demanded this challenge. I believe my guidance and understanding, and David's close bond with and belief in her, gave her the encouragement she needed to maintain her determined stance.

I could see bits of their history and family genetics in each of their personalities, their physical features and their character, attitudes, beliefs, and styles.

It was a foundation set prior to their birth. After birth, the environmental and social aspects would solidify or alter some of those innate characteristics. How could I best serve them to help them to discover who they were and what they were meant to be? How could I best nurture their positive qualities, help enhance their strengths, and guide them to recognize these qualities in themselves? Also, how could I help them to see their weaknesses and learn to acknowledge and accept their flaws without criticism? I wanted to help them discover who they were and love themselves as they were.

Lisa had the challenge of having two brothers who were strong in themselves. She tried to find her identity separate from them but still be a part of them. Isn't that a challenge for all our relationships at any age? She was trying to figure out her anger and frustrations with them and learn how to deal with those feelings—a very difficult task for anyone, let alone a four-year-old. Sometimes, she would get very frustrated and bite or throw something. I would talk to her and try to show her how to deal with that anger and express it appropriately.

Lisa seemed to feel she was in competition with John and that she had to prove herself. I tried to show Lisa her strengths and also stress how important family was, now and in the future. I wanted them to nurture a relationship as children so that as adults they would have a strong base of trust, love, and understanding with each other. I felt that way with my siblings. Sure, we had had disagreements as children and as adults, but my siblings are blood and very important to me. In a pinch or a crisis, my brothers and sisters always have my back. They have supported me through innumerable difficult life phases, and I am confident they will continue to help me in the future.

I wanted my children to get along and support each other. Plus, having siblings of the opposite sex really helps to understand the male/female personality differences, which would assist them with their relationships. I learned a lot from my brothers about how the male gender thinks and why they act in certain ways. Trying to figure out the male species has been an ongoing learning curve for me throughout my life, but having a base of male relationships in childhood was very helpful. I'd say to my kids that sometimes they wouldn't agree, or they might fight about stuff, but in the long run they'd be a sounding board and support for each other throughout their lives. Siblings have known you all your life. They know everything and still love you. That kind of total acceptance is so valuable. I wanted to instill that camaraderie into my children.

Three Sisters! Beth, Cris, and Cathy

Cris's fiftieth birthday party. Cathy sewed a sister surprise: matching dresses!

My brothers, Frank and Joe, suited up

My sister Mary Beth and I enjoy this kind of adult relationship now. We share jokes that are relevant to our age, family, and upbringing. We need few words to explain ourselves. Sometimes just a look suffices, a word, or a "ditty," and we know exactly what the other person is thinking. Sometimes we finish each other's sentences, because we know each other so well. It's comforting to have this kind of friend, support, and family member all in one person. She has helped me through many difficult relationships and life problems, and I have helped her. It's comforting to know she's there to talk to and to have this kind of close relationship with my sister.

Beth and Cath

Special Christmas moment!

I've talked to my siblings on many occasions when I was dealing with different life issues, problems, and successes, and I've received support, suggestions, and often a sounding board to simply listen. I got great comfort from hearing that they had similar problems and what they did to work through them. I wanted my children to see that possibility in their lives and have those family resources available to them, so I did what I could to nurture their relationships. For this reason, I kept Lisa and John in the same bedroom as young children, so they had time to play and be together as long as possible to build a bond and a strong relationship. I figured John and David would bond more naturally as time went on, being male and close in age.

I also kept David and Rachel in the same room as children for the same reason. They got along well and cared deeply for each other. I believe that the enjoyable time my four children spent with each other has built an incredible sense of belonging, care, and love between each of them. Certainly they don't agree on many aspects of life, and they have their own ideas and beliefs, but a common denominator holds them in constant awareness of each other's needs, wants, and desires. They have the ability and means to support and encourage each other in all aspects of life.

David's sleeping habits were similar to Annalisa's. They didn't fall asleep until 9 or 10 p.m. and would wake between 8 and 9 a.m. This allowed me to spend time individually with Lisa and/or Dave after John crashed. I would spend time with John in the early morning hours, since he woke up around 6:30.

Rachel's sleeping habits were similar to John's. She would stay up later in the evening and be up early in the morning. During the day, I usually did activities with all four of my children together. We went to the park to play, cooked meals together, and created a variety of art projects. I had a large pram that I could fit three children in. After Rachel was born, the younger three went in the pram and Lisa would walk. I'd push the pram to the park or stream to play and have a picnic. There was method to my madness; if they were confined to the pram, I could control the whereabouts of all three. This gave me some control and peace of mind about their safety.

All my children loved to play in the water and with the rocks, and explore nature under the wonderful shady trees by the stream behind our home. In the summer, we spent plenty of time in Windsor with my family and on the farm with my parents. We'd have barbeques, and the kids could roam the property and play in the outbuildings. Every summer we'd spend four to six weeks there. We'd stay at Mom and Dad's home on the farm for part of the time and then go to one of my brothers' places, and later to my sister's. Wherever we were staying, we all got together two or three times a week for picnics, barbeques, and baking or canning marathons.

I was able to enjoy these times with my family because I was a stay-at-home mom and wasn't limited to a two- or three-week holiday per year. I could stay all summer if I wished. It was great! It was important to me that my children had the opportunity to know and love their grandparents, aunts, uncles, and cousins. In fact, it was a high priority for me to spend extended amounts of time together with family for that reason.

My brother Frank and his wife lived next door to Mom and Dad's farm, so we spent much time with them. It was only a few minutes' walk across the field to get to Frank's house from Mom's place. Frank and his wife, Bern, had three children, almost the same ages as my four. My brother Joe and his wife, Sandy, had two girls of similar ages as well. Both my brothers had swimming pools in their backyards. We spent many hours sipping icy drinks with the kids cooling off in and around the pools and enjoying the beautiful sunshine and hot, lazy southern Ontario weather.

Grandma Kotow admiring ten of her eleven grandchildren

All Moms' grandchildren, 2004

My sister Mary Beth was single by choice and spent lots of time with my children. She became like a surrogate mother to them. Mary Beth was with us for almost every holiday, birthday, and special event. She and I became close friends over the years, and she built a trusting and loving relationship with my children. Beth had a warped sense of humour, and when she laughed her open-mouthed laugh, her eyes often twinkled with mischief. She could lighten any situation with her humorous observations. This was most helpful and appreciated. There aren't many life relationships in which we feel loved and understood. I am grateful I felt both with Bethius (a nickname my children call their Aunt Beth).

Family New Year's celebration with Aunt Beth

Aunt Bethy: *I'm just trying to read here, guys!*
Rach and Dave using Aunt Beth as a jungle gym. Beth, what a gem!

John and Dave helping Aunt Beth with dinner prep—"sous chefs"

Cathy, Lisa, Beth, and Rachel making our hundreds of yummy perogies

We had a family reunion every year at the farm with Dad's siblings, the Kotows, and their families and we had a Christmas reunion every year with Mom's family, the Malenfants. It was fun to see all the extended families growing as my cousins had children. At these reunions, we'd have a potluck buffet meal where everyone brought prepared food and meat to throw on the barbeque. We organized activities and games that we played on the large manicured yard, which all enjoyed. We set up clothed picnic tables and blankets under the shady trees for eating on and sharing conversations. The reunions were a way to keep in contact with relatives and enjoy the benefits of the homestead.

Kotow farmhouse, 1990s

Poolside Kotow family picnic, early 1990s

Mom, Betty with family, 2000

My sister Cris and her husband, John, were still teaching in a missionary school in Lusaka, Zambia with their two children. Nana lived in Brampton, and we visited her and Harry at their home, where we'd lived when Lisa and John were infants. Eileen is very family oriented, and we often visited together. It was very important to her to build a relationship with her grandchildren.

We also visited Mike's dad, John, and his wife, Helen, one or two times a year in Toronto for dinner, walks, and ice cream cones. All of us being there was a little too much for him and his wife, as they weren't used to small children and their home wasn't child- proofed. We never stayed overnight, only for the afternoon or evening.

Grandpa John came to our home in Cambridge to visit and help me with home renovations. He did the upgrading, and the kids and I assisted whenever possible with set-up and cleanup. He was an engineer and very handy with plumbing, repairs, and building things.

My four children were fortunate to have spent time with their immediate and extended families. I felt it was important for their growth and identity, as well as for support and camaraderie. Since I was less traditional in my child rearing ideas, it was helpful for my children to see other styles of parenting and concepts of discipline. Building these relationships helped to develop love and respect for their elders and for other family members.

Although I can see how birth order affected each of my children, many genetic, social, and environmental factors impacted them as well. My children were no angels; of course they fought and argued. I saw these conflicts as an opportunity to learn to deal with differences in character, and I tried to make those altercations meaningful learning times. After the fight, we would talk out the problem and try to come to a compromise. If no compromise was reached, we agreed to think and revisit the issue at a later date. It was a challenge for me to referee the fights and arguments. A few times I had to separate them physically from each other for their safely and let them cool down before trying to talk and deal with the problem.

I learned. My children learned. Sibling rivalry happened on and off over the years, and I attempted to show them how to resolve their differences. We have philosophical discussions to this day about our relationships and alternative perceptions. We each bring our outlook, argue out points, and try to see the other person's point of view. Because we care so much for each other, we respect the differences and see each other's strengths. As I tried to teach them as children, there are many ways to look at life, and we each have our own perspectives. In order to have peace and get along with each other, we need to have empathy and respect for our differences. I believe this understanding comes with practice, time, and maturity.

# CHAPTER 14

## *Play, Sport, and Activities*

I had three children in diapers for six months! Just imagine that scenario. Wow! Some of you may have experienced this and know how chaotic it can be. It's like being caught in a revolving door of dirty diapers: change one, turn around and change another, only to find another one to be cleaned up. Aawwwk! How unbelievable it was! So much work! I was going non-stop cleaning up dirty baby bottoms. Looking back, I don't know how I managed. I wonder how I had the energy for cooking, play or any other activities with three children so young and needy.

For Lisa and John, I used a diaper service, mostly for environmental reasons. I wanted to use cloth diapers but didn't like the idea of cleaning them every day, but I also didn't want to contribute to landfill sites piled high with disposable diapers. The diaper service provided cotton cloth diapers and rubber pants to cover them. They gave me a rubber-sealed bin to put the dirty diapers in after I rinsed the major feces into the toilet bowl. It's really a nasty business cleaning all that up. Mothers and fathers do it every day, everywhere, but this was not my favourite part of mothering.

Each week the diaper service would pick up the bin of soiled diapers and take them away to be cleaned. They also delivered a large stock of fresh, clean cotton diapers and rubber pants. Good deal! This worked very well when I had two in diapers; I could manage and justify the cost. But when I had three babies in diapers, I could no longer afford the service. Much to my chagrin, I switched to disposables. At two and a half years, Lisa pretty much potty trained herself after being resistant to my efforts up until then. Oh, it was so much easier and less expensive to have only the two boys in diapers, but it still required effort to keep their little bottoms clean and happy. I had less work, and Lisa's potty training was progress in her development.

At the same time, Lisa decided that it was time to talk. Up until then, she had spoken almost no words—zero, nil, nada. She listened, absorbed, and used her receptive ability to file the language, so it seemed she understood what was being said or asked of her. She used non-verbal communication to get her needs met, mostly through her cousin Giselle. Now that we had moved and she didn't have Giselle in the same house, talking became a requirement. Very practical child! She started to express herself verbally.

Just like her Nana had predicted, Lisa had been taking all the vocabulary in, understanding and storing it, and one day she simply started talking in sentences. I was very pleased and relieved as a mother that she was okay. I had worried about her verbal delays, so I was somewhat shocked by the words that started spewing out of her mouth. She didn't miss a beat. She started conversing as if she'd been talking with us all along. Maybe she had been, but inside her head. It seemed that she knew what she was saying, and her replies made sense. She would blurt out a question or statement, and I would be stupefied. I wasn't used to these clear, vocal interactions with her. I soon became accustomed to having conversations with her and thought it was great to be able to communicate so well with her and have her verbalize her needs and thoughts. Her talking was a relief and a joy.

Soon we were having interesting conversations, and Lisa was asking many questions about how things worked and why. It seemed to me she had a list of inquiries in her head and now was ready to ask them as she ticked them off in her brain. She was constantly engaging me in conversations. These discussions were serious information-seeking times to her. A serious look would appear on her face, and she would crinkle up her forehead and purse her lips in concentration as she studied a morsel of new food, a plant, or anything in her environment. She seemed driven to understand. She asked some very serious questions. Some were quite humorous, and I tried to see things through her eyes as she envisioned her world growing around her. I answered as simply as I could or showed her through drawing or doing hands-on activities that visually described the answer. Her growing curiosity was like a compulsion, a need to figure out her world. It was fascinating to watch her put the pieces together for herself.

How did I keep them occupied, have fun with them, keep them safe, and stay sane myself? We did almost everything as a group. We made meals together, cleaned together, and shopped together. Mike had a one-and-a-half-hour commute, unusually in rush hour, each way to work, and he worked long hours; therefore, he was gone much of the time. I took it as my role to develop daily routines and organize outings. I was their major caregiver and nurturer.

I'll start with play. My kids had lots of toys they'd received as gifts or hand-me-downs. Their favourite toys were building blocks made from coloured wood in all sorts of shapes and sizes. We would build castles, bridges, towers, houses, planes, and other structures with these blocks. We also had Lego. . . lots and lots of it. We got the larger ones for younger children to start with for safety reasons. When they were younger, they tended to place everything into their mouths, so these Lego building blocks were big enough that they couldn't eat them and choke! They all loved Lego, and so did I. It's a very creative toy. Lisa, John, and David spent hours building structures and imaginary places with Lego.

We also coloured, painted, and drew pictures. I love art and am a very creative person. I enjoyed these activities immensely. I had a kid-sized easel set up with large jars of water paints in the living room. I had a large-sized paper pad that clipped onto the easel for easy changing from one painting to the next. I positioned a cloth beneath the easel to protect the hardwood floor. Several children's aprons hung on the easel for them to wear to protect their clothing while they created their masterpieces. At any time, Lisa and I might have been painting while the boys were playing with Lego nearby, or vice versa. The painting corner was always set up. Any painting activity was accessible anytime with minimal cleanup required. Often I found my children had short attention spans, so the availability and simplicity of operations was critical to be able to engage them all in activities. Sometimes I got to paint as well, which was a great release and creative outlet for me.

Lisa, John, and David all loved the outdoors in the green space behind our home, or in our fenced backyard with the swing set and sandbox. It was safe for them to play in the yard with the fence, as they couldn't escape. . . at least not yet. John hadn't yet figured out how to climb the fence or unfasten the gate hook. I had some sense of security in that, but I was still careful and watched them from the kitchen window. Most of the time, I was outside with them.

Later in the day, for quiet time, sometimes we'd watch movies. Disney movies were their favourites. They liked to watch the same movie over and over again until they had the words and songs memorized. Movies were interactive, and they liked to dance and sing with their favourite characters. Watching movies was a relaxing time for us all. I could fold laundry, tidy up, or get dinner started while they were occupied, often mesmerized by the movie. Sometimes I needed to just sit and relax, cuddle, and enjoy the fantasy with them.

I love to read! I discovered many new authors of children's books that were funny and refreshing, and many of them taught important lessons. When I seemed too exhausted to take another step, I could be revived by relaxing and reading a good story. Reading stories gave us quiet times at the end of usually hectic, activity-filled days. At bedtime, if Mike was home, I'd read to the children one at a time so I could give each child individual time, attention, and cuddles. Most times I read to them all together. As they got older, I began to read chapter books, so I would read a chapter a night as we followed the stories and adventures that took us to far-off, wonderful places. Reading captivated them and developed their imaginations.

I told them stories about things that had happened in my childhood living on our family farm. I recounted tales of my brothers and sisters and my own antics as a child. I told them about us swimming, skating, building snow forts, tobogganing, and playing in the hay barn. I told them family stories about my grandparents, family gatherings, and playing with my cousins. I loved growing up on the farm and had many tales to tell. We lived in a small city, so tales of farm life were intriguing to my children.

We had many farm buildings on our property, including an array of buildings used for particular functions, such as a car garage and a milk house, where we kept the large stainless steel milk cooler in which we stored our cow's milk. Attached to the milk house was the cow barn for the cattle and milking equipment. There was a loft for storage of hay, and a granary that stored the grain used for cow feed. There was a chicken coop and the pump house, which housed the water pump above the well. We also used the pump house as a cold storage building. Inside the pump house, shelves lined the walls of the 10-foot square building top to bottom. They were filled with canning jars, assorted pickles, jams, tomatoes, fruits, and sauerkraut. Drying herbs, garlic, and spices hung everywhere. We had a cement block silo for grain storage that stood beside the cow barn for the convenience of feeding grain to the cows, as well as the hay barn, which was the largest of our outbuildings. The big barn was massive and became the best playground possible.

One half of the big barn was for storage of farm equipment, such as tractors, a baler, a combine, discs, and a plough. Most of the necessary tools and equipment for our farming operation were stored in the big barn. It had a huge set of sliding front doors centred in the middle, where machinery could drive inside to unload or get work done, like grease and oil changes or machinery repairs. The back of the barn had another set of doors to drive through and out the other side. All the buildings were practical and had particular functions. All were used to the maximum, with little wasted space.

The other half of the hay barn stored the bales of hay and straw for bedding and feeding the livestock. To me as a child, the hay barn was gargantuan. It was a veritable fortress of fun and adventure. I was an outdoorsy girl, so throughout my childhood, I practically lived in the barns, trees, and fields, working and playing. I'm guessing the barn was 120 feet long, 50 feet wide, and approximately 45 to 50 feet high at the tallest point in the middle upper peak of the roof. Above the floor, about 20 feet up, were the main wooden structural beams, which were square and about 10 inches by 10 inches in size, by the length and width of the entire barn. At that level, 20 feet up, there was no floor, only support beams and open spaces. Attached to these beams were the triangular support beams that rose up to support the roof. Running down the full 120 foot length of the highest centre peak of the roof was a pulley system with a series of ropes attached to the highest centre beam. These ropes and pulleys were used to lift and move bales of hay or other heavy items to different parts of the barn.

Well, for us children, you can imagine that the big barn was a playground made in heaven. The rope system made an ideal Tarzan swing. My two brothers, my cousins, and I could maneuver the ropes over to the person standing on a beam on the side wall of the barn. That person would grab the rope and swing across the width of the barn, kick the other side, and swing back. What a hoot that was. Sometimes we would swing, let go, and leap onto a pile of hay or just hang on tight and swing back and forth. We had awesome fun in the "BIG" barn for hours on end!

Another favourite game we played in the barn was tag, but this game of tag was a bit more risky than the schoolyard version. We played this tag on the 10 inch beams, 20 feet up in the barn. Hey, we were children, and we had little fear of falling. And if we did, so what? We'd get scraped up a bit and continue to play. We raced and ran along those beams like we were flying to escape some terrible monster. I think the trick was to not look down but to look where you were walking/running and to the destination—the next triangular support beam going up that you could grab onto briefly for stability and then continue to run. At the same time, you had to watch out for whoever was "it" to keep away from them. When you tagged someone, you yelled, "You're it," so that everyone knew who to watch out for next. It was a great game. Amazingly, none of us fell or hurt ourselves badly. We were lucky!

As children growing up on our farm we had space and freedom. Our house was small, 30 feet by 30 feet on the main level with two bedrooms on the second level. One result of our small living quarters was that we spent the majority of our time outdoors. We played baseball, built a tree house, played games in the barns, and climbed trees. My grandmother got angry with us for climbing one of the apple trees, because we sometimes broke branches, and those fruit trees were one of our food sources. Now I can see her point, but at the time we felt she was being crotchety.

We had apple, pear, walnut, and plum trees, which I enjoyed climbing very much. The top of a tree full of leaves provided a quiet, peaceful space where no one could see me, but I could see everything and everyone. One particular apple tree I liked to climb had the best vantage point. It was situated along the driveway that separated our home from Grandma's, and the tree was close enough to the road to see the comings and goings. I was hidden by the leaves, which nurtured my imagination. I felt like a bird or a spy, and I felt powerful. I would sit high up in the tree and relax on a comfortable large branch, watching the leaves and the sky and enjoying myself. When I heard the noise of someone approaching, or a vehicle in the drive, I'd observe the activities of the farm from my hidden lookout tower, where no one could see me. Up in that tree was a special, safe, and peaceful place for me. I loved it!

My children loved it when I told them stories of my brothers and I getting into trouble in one of our many mischievous schemes, like when we tried to ride the cows or catch the chickens, or ate the tar paper, or smoked cigarettes in the barn. We didn't escape all these activities unharmed. My brother Frank and I were injured many times. I got stitches five times, and Frank got stitches in odd places, like on his tongue when he fell and landed on a tin tuna can and cut it open. Frank had a habit of holding out his tongue when he was concentrating. He got stitches and it healed quickly. Playing hockey once, Frank landed on his own skate, and the blade cut open his butt cheek. Imagine the embarrassment of that one! Seeing a doctor and having them sew up his bum. Ha ha! But he didn't think it was very funny. My brother also broke things, like his arm and leg. These consequences of our actions did not deter us one bit. They were more like battle scars we were proud of.

One time, Frank suggested I drink the contents of a glass Coke bottle that had black liquid in it on a shelf in the garage. I was about two years old and he was three. Neither of us knew any better. He said it was Coke, so I drank it. It was some kind of poisonous fluid, paint thinner or something. My mother had to rush me to the hospital and get my stomach pumped. Mom said it was awful. She said I looked like a rubbery rag afterward. It must have been horrible for my mother, but I don't have any memory of the event. I survived with no permanent damage that I am aware of! I had many funny stories about life on the farm, and a few scary and strange ones as well. Which story I told depended on our mood, and sometimes strange or scary was appropriate. We had our own "Kotow Reality Show," which may not have been too unusual then, but now it would sell TV time.

Besides these real-life stories, I made up stories as well. I created what we termed "space stories." This began with a story I made up about me and my kids travelling in space and having an adventure. Soon the story grew into a series of events, and then it expanded to include us as characters. I included their ideas as we went along. Nothing was too crazy or outrageous to belong in these space stories; in fact, the more dreadful and disgusting the ideas, the more interesting the story became, and the more my kids liked it. The imagination is an awesome thing; it doesn't have to be grounded in reality. Anything was possible. My imagination soared, as did theirs, as we created our adventures in space. We improvised and included the day's events or our anticipated plans in the plot as it thickened.

In the space stories there was a scientist, a pet, a driver or spaceship pilot, and a baby. Sometimes we included extra characters, like their grandparents, cousins, or friends, if someone was visiting. We would figure out where we would go that night, which planet, moon, or some made-up place. The story would always start with us waiting until the parents were asleep and then going to our hidden space lab. We'd get into our spaceship at our laboratory and get ready for another adventure in outer space.

We met aliens of all sorts in various states of dangerous dilemmas. Somehow we would fix their problem with creative resolutions or help them find their own solutions to save their worlds. We got into some precarious situations and always narrowly escaped. My kids would input their ideas as we went along, and it became a community plot line. Like a master mind, we brainstormed ideas, and one thought built on the other. It was a "create your own adventure" each time. Sometimes the story would be an extrapolation of our last trip, so it became a series, and other times the plot was new and altogether different. We always had to start our adventure late at night, after dark, and it was critical to get home before the first light at dawn. Our travel was classified and confidential. No one was to know what we were doing or where we were travelling.

To begin, we'd make our way to the space laboratory and start planning our journey. Then we'd each give suggestions or say which character we wanted to be that night. They absolutely loved it! Some were very funny stories, like volcanoes spewing green alien poop, and some were serious, like one of our members having a close brush with death. Some were outrageous, like the cat genius who solved an alien crisis. Those stories certainly kept our imaginations working at full tilt. I should have written the stories down at the time, but I didn't. We had dozens of space stories, and we retold our favourite ones again and again. We enjoyed them for many years. The interactive nature of the stories was delightfully entertaining for us all.

Swimming was another activity we thought was an essential life skill. All four of my children took swimming lessons from when they were about six months old through their teens. When they were babies, I needed to go in the pool with them and basically play around to help them get used to the water. Our plan was to have them all be capable swimmers and not afraid of water. My mother had almost drowned as a child and was still very afraid of pools, lakes, and water in general. We felt swimming was an activity that could be done by all of us anywhere for family fun and exercise. It could also lead to many other interesting sports, like boating, diving, snorkeling, sailing, and scuba diving. Two of the kids swam competitively as teenagers.

Another activity my children expressed interest in was dancing. I played music and we danced around our living room. Lisa wanted to take ballet lessons; she did dance for a few years when she was four to six years old. She loved to wear dresses and had many beautiful ones with frills and lace, and velvet and satin, items given to her by her older cousins, Clare and Giselle. She liked to wear a fancy dress every day. She delighted in wearing those pretty clothes and twirling herself around. Ballet lessons came from this desire to dress up and her joy of dancing.

John took tap dancing for a year when he was five years old. He was the only boy in the class. He had rhythm and loved to dance. He picked up the dance steps and moved readily and was actually quite a ham who loved to be in the limelight. He was a cowboy/gunslinger in their year-end show. I made him a blue metallic vest and pants to wear for it, and he gave quite a good performance.

John grooving, dancing on a log at his cousin's wedding in Petaluma, California

Mike was an avid hockey player and fan. He wanted all of our children to play hockey, male and female alike. Hey, we lived in Canada, and hockey seemed a natural part of our lives. At five years old, all my kids started to ice skate in the CanSkate learn to skate program. They would slide along the ice pushing orange pylons and getting their ice legs under them. It was comical to watch them stumbling around the ice, slipping and sliding and trying to get to the puck to the other end of the rink, which was a major accomplishment.

Lisa, John, and David played hockey throughout their childhoods and into adulthood. They still enjoy the odd game of hockey today. Rachel chose not to play hockey after her first year. She tried figure skating for a year, but moved on to other sports that were warmer. She didn't do well with the cold. She shivered and shook and didn't enjoy the activities on ice. It was fun to watch the others as their hockey skills developed.

Our great Canadian sport; Dave, Lisa, and John in full hockey gear

Rachel ready to play

I was adamant not to place gender roles on them or their activities. I wanted the boys to learn to do housework, engage in creative arts, enjoy dancing, and play with dolls, which are traditionally female activities. I wanted the girls to experience hockey, soccer, and activities that traditionally were geared to boys. I promoted equal availability to all four to choose what

195

they wanted to try. After they had tried it for a while, it was their choice to continue or not.

Each of my children had a favourite doll, stuffed toy, or blankie that they used for comfort. They soothed themselves with and showed affection toward these items. Affection and caring are natural human emotions and not gender specific.

I was held back from playing organized hockey and taking automobile repair and mechanical and woodworking shop in school when I was growing up because I was female. I would have liked to learn and would have enjoyed those classes. I was interested in how machinery and engines worked and wanted to build stuff. Back then there was no accommodation for girls in male sports or auto mechanics, welding, or other shop activities. I played hockey in outdoor rinks and on the frozen pond in the winter with my brothers. When I got old enough for organized sports, I had to take figure skating instead of hockey because of my gender. I enjoyed the figure skating but missed the competition of hockey and playing the sport with my brothers.

I've always loved sewing and doing crafts. I learned to sew from my mother, sister, and grandmother. When I was growing up, sewing was a functional and practical activity. We repaired and mended clothes to extend their lives because we didn't have the money to go out and buy new things. It was a practical skill that I took to naturally. I learned further how to create clothing items by experimenting with making my own clothes. Basically, I learned by visualizing what I wanted to make and then building it. I also learned how to alter clothing to fit perfectly by adjusting the garment to my body. I was guided by family members but fine-tuned the skills with practice.

I taught all four of my children basic sewing skills. It couldn't hurt them to know how to repair a seam or sew on a button. A basic understanding of how clothes are assembled, repaired, or altered is a useful life skill. Maybe they would pursue more advanced seamstress work, as I had done, or maybe not. My sewing skills had turned out to be practical and useful throughout my life.

Looking back now, I realize that the variety of play and the many traditional and alternative activities I offered my children were responsible for me surviving having four children in five years. The creative energy and enthusiasm I sustained during my years of motherhood made our lives interesting.

I felt satisfied with my work as a mother. The reward of seeing my children active and happy made me feel secure that I was a good mom. There were no measuring sticks or grade levels to tell me I was succeeding, but there were glimpses and flashes of proof in my children's laughter or when they cooperated with each other or helped another human unselfishly.

Motherhood is a difficult profession as far as knowing if what you're doing is right. I made the conscious effort to be with my children each moment and make the best of every day. While I certainly influenced their personalities and attitudes, each of my children had to make their own decisions in life. As they got older, I hoped I had equipped them with enough tools to live an enjoyable life that contributed to our family and the community. Only time would tell. I did the best I could at the time. I tried my hardest and used my intelligence and my creative and physical energy to create a fun and loving environment.

# CHAPTER 15

## *Creative Cooking, Sharing Food, and Family Meals*

Cooking was another essential skill I wanted to teach my children. A big plus about cooking was spending the time together doing it, and the results were usually edible. We had so much pleasure making meals together. Planning the menu, shopping for the ingredients, and creating the dishes became a fun event, and the resulting food was a delightful bonus. When my kids were young, they had to stand on a chair to reach the bowls to stir and add the ingredients. They really wanted to participate. Simply pouring the ingredients into a bowl or pot was not at all simple or boring for them—it was an adventure. We were creating together, and they were so proud of becoming little chefs. I encouraged and praised every effort of their help and participation.

All my children learned how to put meals together. I would say, "The kids and I made spaghetti for dinner," because they did help and were proud of themselves. We experimented with spices and tastes and tried new flavours. For example, when making chili, we would taste it and I'd say "Hmm, do you think it needs more chili powder, or salt, or pepper, or cayenne?" We'd add a bit, simmer, and taste again. I encouraged them to expand their palettes. We tried different food together as well as a variety of recipes we gathered from family members, friends, and various cookbooks.

When my children were between six and twelve months old, while I was still nursing, I began introducing foods, starting with rice pabulum. Then one by one I introduced mashed-up foods, beginning with fruits and vegetables. I started with mashed banana, carrots, squash, and potatoes.

As I started introducing more solid food, they would nurse less because they were getting more of their needed nutrition from their diet. The kicker was that I got pregnant again each time I slowed down on the amount of nursing. When I was pregnant, I had to wean them off the breast milk. I was so tired. I was continually hungry when I was pregnant and didn't seem to have the energy to nurse and be nourishing the new baby at the same time.

When my children were six to twelve months, I also gave them finger foods, like cheerios, digestive cookies, and small chunks of banana or cooked vegetables. This was before they learned to use a spoon. Their fingers worked okay, but they needed practice getting things to their mouth. Soon they graduated to using a spoon. What a mess my kitchen was then. As you know, it takes a while to figure out the spoon to mouth action. They felt so good and independent when they could feed themselves.

When we travelled, I bought jars of baby food for convenience. I looked for the ones without salt, sugar, or other additives. They loved the apple sauce, sweet potato, and squash. When they were between one and two years old, I introduced meats, mainly chicken and beef, as well as other vegetables like tomatoes, cucumbers, broccoli, and beans (green and pinto). Then I added carbohydrates like pastas and rice. I prepared large pots of soup, like beef vegetable, vegetable, and chicken stew. I made them from scratch with fresh meat and vegetables.

When I was first married, my cooking skills were poor. I really hadn't cooked much in my first twenty-five years of life. I'd been more interested in farming, sports, and outdoor activities, so I never spent a lot of time learning to cook and clean. I just wasn't interested. Now I had kids of my own to feed and had a reason to learn. I was motivated. I wanted my children to have a nutritionally healthy, balanced diet and grow up strong and well-nourished.

My mom is a great cook and an awesome baker, so I was constantly calling her for instructions and recipes. When I needed a particular recipe or ingredient that I'd forgotten about, my mom was available to help. I was twenty-six years old when I cooked my first turkey dinner. I was asking Mom on the phone, "Do I cover it? How much water do I put in? What spices should I use?" It worked! I made a lovely, delicious turkey dinner!

As I learned to cook and bake and became good at making tasty meals, I began to enjoy the process. I found cooking and baking to be a great creative outlet. I began by gathering a few good basic cookbooks, and I wrote down recipes of dishes I liked from relatives and friends to start my own collection of favourites. My first two favourite cookbooks were a hardcover *Chatelaine's*

*Adventures in Cooking*[17] and a wire-bound *More with Less*[18] cookbook written by a Mennonite group. The Chatelaine cookbook had lots of basics in it, like shopping lists, meal plans, temperatures, and conversion tables. It had basic step-by-step, detailed instructions, which I needed in those early days.

I used these two cookbooks as references and experimented with different recipe ideas in them. The *More With Less* cookbook suggested alternatives, like using whole wheat flour, less sugar, fat and salt, and substituting brown sugar, apple sauce, or honey for healthier choices. It also provided many vegetarian dishes that were nutritious and tasty. Plus, it had ideas about cooking for large groups, which I sometimes needed. I often used its recipe for pancake mix, making the dry mixture in a gallon jar. It was simple to add the wet ingredients to create a quick meal anytime.

Those were my two starter cookbooks, and I learned much from them. I also got an excellent hardcover *Traditional Ukrainian Cookery*[19] from my sister as a gift, and I added *The Joy of Cooking*[20] as well. The Ukrainian cookbook had a plethora of information about traditions, customs, and cultural background that added depth and meaning to our holiday meal celebrations. It included our favourite recipes for perogies, Christmas and Easter breads, cabbage rolls, etc. The *Joy of Cooking* was also a great book for the Caesar salad dressing recipe, which we love, and for general cooking knowledge.

My kids and I used the pancake mix to make creative pancakes of all sorts. We added food colouring to make "space pancakes," like Pluto, Saturn, Earth, moons, and so on. We divided the batter into four bowls with red, yellow, blue, and green food colouring mixed in. The batter was our pallet, and the pan our canvas. We created edible art forms that were a shame to destroy by eating them. But we ate them, and they were oh so tasty and loads of fun. When the boys were into Ninja Turtles, we made the four Ninja Turtle characters' faces and heads with their coloured masks and ties. Each turtle cake was an individual creation that looked awesome. My kids loved to eat them. I began to bake as well, once or twice a week. Our favourites were banana muffins or bread, oatmeal chocolate chip cookies, and carrot muffins.

Another breakfast favourite treat was what we called "dinosaur eyes." My mom made these for us when I was a kid, but we didn't call them anything in particular. I called them dinosaur eyes because my children were fascinated with dinosaurs. They wanted to learn everything they could about them.

They had plastic dinosaur figurines, puzzles, and games. It seemed fun and logical at the time to name these breakfast treats as dinosaur eyes.

I'd take a slice of whole wheat bread and cut a hole in the middle with a glass cup about 3 inches in diameter. In the frying pan, I put butter on medium heat. I placed the bread in the pan, put an egg into the hole, and cooked to about over-easy doneness. I then turned the bread and egg over together to cook the top. I grilled the bread that had been cut out on both sides in the same buttered pan until crispy. I served the toast and egg combination on a plate and placed the toasted circle over the egg yolk in the centre hole, like an eyelid to cover the "eye" so the dinosaur could blink at the children. They could dip the toasted circle into the yolk of the egg and enjoy eating it. Simple, healthy, and fun!

I consistently made an effort to provide nutritious meals and snacks for my children. Creating meals together became our family norm. My children enjoyed an occasional treat, as did I. For some strange reason, they loved hot dogs and Kraft Dinner. This was not my favourite, nor did I think it was nutritionally sound, but once in a while it was okay. KD and hot dogs was a quick comfort meal. They also liked pizza and ice cream. What kid doesn't like ice cream? We even had a toy ice cream maker that was a cool contraption. David thought it was the cat's meow. He made us some yummy ice cream that he had to mix by hand with much effort. This method took forever, but so what? We had time. We made our own whole wheat pita pizzas, and each child got to pick the ingredients to create their own personal pizza. I learned to combine nutrition with enjoyment and good taste. I believe my children learned to appreciate preparation and enjoyed good meals.

Breakfast was usually cereal and bananas. I only bought the cereal without sugar coatings, and we never added sugar. Cheerios, bananas, and oatmeal were our staple breakfast foods. We all loved yogurt. I would use seasonal fruit and mix it into a large bowl with plain yogurt. Fresh berries and yogurt makes a delightful dessert or snack.

When we had visitors, we often invited them to come early and join in the fun of the prep work. Done alone, cleaning up or washing dishes are just chores, but in groups they become social events in themselves. In our home, cooking was as much a communication time as the actual meal. Sometimes it was more intimate. While peeling piles of potatoes to make perogies, we could share stories about our days and lives. Questions arose and were debated, history was told, politics and current events were discussed, stories were told, and feelings were expressed. We cried and laughed until we cried. This time became a great opportunity for me to connect with and listen to my children. Often the chance arose for teachable moments, a little story or information I would give to help them through a thought process, or a discovery that guided them toward a decision. Bottom line, I listen to my children often. Preparing meals together provided another opportunity for us to communicate.

Lisa and Beth perogy-making for Christmas dinner

The meal itself became a family ritual, from planning menus, making the list, buying the necessary groceries and specialty items—like candles, flower arrangements, coloured napkins, and seasonal decorations—to creating the meal together. We all were expected to participate. If one of the kids was busy and couldn't cook, they were on cleanup duty. Each child had their favourite jobs while cooking, and if Aunt Bethy was there, she joined in, usually by peeling potatoes, chopping onions, cutting vegetables, or making bread or biscuits. If Mom and Dad were visiting, they took over the preparations while I took a break. Cooking and eating was an inclusive event.

An example of this family cooking on a larger scale would take place at Christmas, Easter, and Thanksgiving every year. The day before the holiday was spent cooking together with whoever was visiting, friends who wanted to learn and help, and family who were in town. Of course, Mary Beth, myself, and my four kids all helped.

First thing in the morning we would start with perogy preparation. Beth and John and Mom usually peeled 10 pounds of potatoes and chopped four or five yellow onions. When the potatoes were cooked, we mashed them with Cheez Whiz and shredded cheddar cheese, salt, and garlic. This was the filling we used in the perogies. Then we set the potato filling aside to cool while we did other prep work.

I wasn't good at making bread or pastry dough, so I asked my mom to teach my kids these skills directly. Mary Beth was the bread maker when Mom wasn't visiting. She would organize the kids to help her prepare the dough. While the dough was rising, I'd start making the perogy dough, and we'd spend the afternoon filling and squeezing the potato dumplings together. In the times between the rising, punching, and braiding of the bread, we'd work on other parts of the meal. We placed the layers of perogies on cookie sheets with flour and wax paper between the layers so they didn't stick. If we weren't eating them right away, they went into the freezer.

My mom's theory was that it was bad luck to count how many perogies we were making, so we guesstimated the numbers. Usually we made fourteen to sixteen batches of dough, and each ball, rolled out and cut, made twelve to fourteen perogies. We kept on filling and making until most of the potatoes were used. We'd make somewhere between two hundred and two hundred and fifty perogies. It would take six to ten of us all day to finish.

At the same time as I was orchestrating the perogy making, Beth was patiently timing and kneading the bread dough. When the dough was punched down sufficiently, Beth and the kids took the paska or kolach, the Christmas or Easter bread, and made it into designs. They would braid long strips of dough and create beautiful decorative loaves, long braids, three-ball buns, and one large decorative, braided round loaf with a hole in the middle for a candle as the table centerpiece. We loved making and eating the home-made bread and perogies. Fresh, hot from the oven, a slice of bread lathered in butter! Delicious. That's why we made such a huge amount. We ate them for dinner and gave plates to friends. We especially loved the perogies fried to a crispy brown in butter and onions and lathered with sour cream for breakfast.

Spending the whole day making bread and perogies was a big commitment of time and work, but it was a family tradition that was well worth the effort and mess. The time we spent preparing these meals was time we talked, laughed, and told stories, jokes, and tales about each other. We got ourselves and the kitchen covered with flour. Every time when we neared the end of the day, we were all getting tired of making them, and we started to get giddy and silly. Much brainless chatter began; nonsensical laughing fits ensued with our cooking weariness. Our words made little sense and our topics became cruder. The laughter helped us to plough through to finish the task. I loved those days of cooking and still do.

Mealtime was family time. My rule was no TV, radio, or talking on the phone while we ate. There were to be no distractions. Dinner was time we focused on us as a family and any guests we had at our table. We sang "Johnny Appleseed" as grace. I'd learned that song/prayer as a Girl Guide years before. Funny how those nursery rhymes and songs were etched into my mind and sprung out years later at appropriate times. Singing grace is a ritual we continue to observe, and it signifies the beginning of our special time together sharing food and life.

Another tradition, or courtesy, at mealtime was that no one started to eat until I sat down and was ready to eat myself. I learned this from my family growing up. Mom worked so hard to prepare the meal, and out of respect for her, Dad made us wait until she sat down before we could begin to eat. We said grace and started to pass the dishes around. I was grateful for this courtesy, because we did work hard, and I would have felt resentful being left out of the fun. I hated to miss out on any of the conversation during dinner. Plus, I'm a slow eater and usually the last to finish, so if they didn't wait for me, I could have been sitting by myself long after they were all finished their meals. Our courtesy extended to waiting for whoever was cooking, just to show respect and thanks for their efforts. Because everyone waited for me, I could be fully involved and engaged in the lively, joyful, and telling conversations as they flowed during our meals. We were blessed with much laughter and sometimes tears and serious discussions about life. Many wonderful memories were made in our kitchen and around our table at mealtime.

Sometimes we all got bored of the regular everyday meals and would change it up. When John was about four or five years old, he'd often ask for pizza and ice cream for breakfast. Old tradition says no to that concept, and I said no to him many times also. Then one day I reconsidered the idea and said why not. So what if we have breakfast food for dinner, and dinner food for breakfast? It all goes to the same place, just at different times of the day. That thought grew and expanded into ideas that germinated into "Backwards Day."

On Backwards Day we did just that—everything backwards. Yes meant no, clothes were worn inside out, pajamas were kept on all day, and we ate pizza and ice cream for breakfast. At dinner we had breakfast food, like cereal or bacon and eggs. The best part for the kids was having pizza first thing in the morning and then ice cream. Oh heaven! It was great for me as well, because I love ice cream too.

We made delicious pizzas from scratch with fresh ingredients. One of the kids had the idea to eat under the table, since it was backwards day, so we did. We put a cloth under our kitchen table and all went under to enjoy our pizza and ice cream picnic-style. It felt like we were camping or on holidays. That change from our routine was refreshing and energizing. We enjoyed Backwards Day whenever we needed a break from the norm.

Another alternative to our traditional cooking and meal plan was picnics. I had a history of enjoying picnics with my family, and especially good memories of picnics on Saturdays with my grandmother. My grandmother, dad, and I often had informal, impromptu picnics after we went to the farmers' market in Windsor. We'd buy homemade Ukrainian ham and garlic kielbasa, pickles, cheese, and fresh bread and then stop somewhere on the way home and have a picnic. I have fond memories of those special times with my grandmother and my dad.

Besides those pizza picnics under our kitchen table, we had picnics pretty much everywhere and in any weather. In the winter we spread my African cloth on the carpet in front of our fireplace and ate our lunch picnic-style. I'd light a fire and we'd enjoy the warm glow, the scent, and the comfort of the wood fire. We would eat, talk, and snuggle as we shared our food and our dreams.

John picnicking at the beach. Life is good!

Picnic in the mountains; Cathy, Rachel, and Dave

Indoor picnic: Airdrie home

Lisa picnicking with John and Dave, wearing their race car jumping suits

Lisa and John, in their jumping suits, rock climbing with cousin Francis

Picnics on our deck were common in the summer months. We had the two picnic tables I'd made, an adult one and a kid-sized one, and the deck over top of our double garage was large, so we had lots of room for play. I put a small kids' swimming pool on the deck for the kids to cool off and play in. Many hours in the summer were spent in the solitude and privacy of our deck. Beth would come and we would visit and enjoy a picnic with her. The menu varied, but was usually kielbasa, bread, cheese, pickles and maybe olives, or specialty cheese or ham or lunch meat to make bunwiches with mustard. It was easy to have picnics there, because we didn't have to pack up everything to go somewhere else. We just moved the food from the kitchen to the deck and were ready to share the food and the company. We would laze outside on the deck and bask in the sunshine, enjoying the balmy summer days.

Family picnic at a lake park in southern Ontario

We also liked having picnics in the park. I'd plan ahead and purchase some special treats like granola bars, chips, and sparkly drinks. Then we'd head to Nose Creek Park, Big Hill Springs Park, or the playground and park down the street from our home. The kids could play on the equipment, check out the creek, and play in the water. Sometimes we hiked through Big Hill Springs Provincial Park, made a fire, and cooked hot dogs on sticks in the large outdoor stone fireplaces.

One time when we were picnicking at Big Hill Spring Park we tried hiking on a different hill that was beyond a fence in a farmer's field. I stayed below with Dave and Rachel, and Lisa and John began to climb the cliff. The hill wasn't too high, and I was sure they could safely climb it. I climbed up a ways so I could keep an eye on all four of them. Lisa and John were climbing beside each other. John yelled at Lisa to stop and stay still. She looked at him, questioning why. He told her that there was a snake just above her. She thought he was simply trying to scare her with another practical joke, but then she looked up and saw it, not 2 feet from her, rearing its head and rattling its tongue. Fear struck, and Lisa froze. Move or not move? In those few seconds the snake stopped, turned, and slithered away. Lisa and John were spooked. They scurried down the hill at record speed. We were all relieved to have avoided the imminent danger.

There are many ways to have a picnic; the sky is the limit. It simply takes some imagination and willingness to do it. Many of our picnics turned into adventures, like the time Nana Eileen and Harry were visiting from Ontario and we went out to Banff for a tour and to go swimming and soaking in the hot springs. It was winter, and the temperature was around -30 degrees Fahrenheit. It was frigid. For lunch we found a lovely park with tables and a playground. We managed to get the food on the picnic table while the kids played for five minutes. We threw together our sandwiches while we shivered from the blisteringly raw wind. We laughed at ourselves for our optimism in thinking a picnic might be fun on such a wintery day. Well, it was fun but short and memorable. We certainly needed the hot springs following that picnic.

Occasionally we went out to a restaurant to eat, but not often, as bringing four young children to a restaurant and trying to keep them seated and quiet was stressful. Sometimes I broke down and took them to McDonald's. The one in Airdrie had a playground where the kids were reasonably safe and could play and let out some of their energy while I relaxed and enjoyed a coffee. If I felt I needed a break, that's where we went for me to regroup.

Having limited financial recourses was also a reason we ate at home most of the time. If we couldn't go out to a restaurant to eat, then why not make our own restaurant at home? That's exactly what I did. My kids wanted to go to McDonald's, and I didn't have the money or energy, so I created our own McDockman restaurant at home. I designed a menu with pictures and wrote the food and drink choices with a calligraphy marker. I added the foods one could get when out at a restaurant, like eggs, ham, English muffins, bacon, and orange and apple juice. The children sat at the kitchen table and looked at the menu. I played the server/waitress and took their orders. They could sneak into the kitchen and help me prepare the food, or they could sit and colour while they waited. The pretending worked. It satisfied their desire to eat at a restaurant.

We created an elaborate French restaurant scene in our home once when Nana and Uncle Harry were visiting us. My children were young, and I didn't want to bring them all to a fancy, elegant restaurant, so we created our own French cuisine and atmosphere in our living room. The fireplace was the perfect spot to set up the table and create a beautiful ambiance. The kids and I planned a special meal menu. I designed lovely menu cards in calligraphy that explained the various courses.

The menu included white or red wine, vodka and tonic, fresh Caesar salad with homemade dressing, hot, toasted, garlic-buttered bread, French onion soup in brown crockery with crusty French bread and two cheeses, barbequed steak with baked potatoes and all the trimmings, and broccoli with cheese sauce. We finished the feast with brandy or Bailey's Irish cream, homemade cheesecake, and tea. I was the head chef, and the kids were my assistant chefs and served as waiters and waitresses. We all played our parts in making Nana and Harry comfortable, keeping their drinks full, and taking away their empty plates. Eileen said she couldn't imagine ever eating in such an elegant restaurant, and they both raved about the quality and taste of the food. The evening was a smashing success. I felt proud of myself and of how my children worked together and played their parts. It was an excellent evening.

During those early years of marriage when my children were young, I learned to cook healthy, delicious meals from scratch. I could do some basic desserts, but I never mastered the art of bread and pastry making. My mother was a master at making pastry, particularly pie crust. She made a strawberry rhubarb pie that was so scrumptious it was to die for. I don't like most pies because they have too much crust and not enough fruit in them. Mom's strawberry rhubarb pie has a light, flaky crust with lots of fruit, so the crust doesn't overpower the filling. It's truly a fruit pie, and I love the flavour combination. The unique mixture of sweet and tart. . . mmm, yummy!

I decided that, since I don't have the talent or knack for making pie crust, I'd get my mom to teach my kids this skill herself. One summer we were visiting family in Ontario. I was in Windsor with my four kids, and my sister Cris organized events for my siblings and my nieces and nephews to go on outings together. One of those outings we called a blueberry fest. That summer my kids were in the age range of five to ten years old. John and Cris and their two, Sandy and her two, Bern and her three, me and my four, and Mom all participated. We piled into two vans, six adults and eleven kids, and headed out to the U-pick berry farm in Leamington.

It was a typical hot, humid southern Ontario summer day with hints of carefree timelessness. We talked and picked, ate blueberries, and picked and laughed and picked. Someone suggested the idea of a contest. Who could put the most blueberries into their mouth and swallow them all? Okay, the competition began. John and Andrew managed to stuff fifty-five or sixty at once and swallow them. Andrew almost upchucked, barely managing not to vomit. Clare and Theresa tried and did a bit better, as did Crystal, Vicki, Francis, Dave, Rach, and Lisa. The clear winner was Joey, who managed to stuff ninety blueberries into his mouth and swallow them. It was hilarious to watch and quite an amazing feat. We had great fun picking and gathering the five-gallon pails of blueberries for our fest. After about an hour of eating, picking, and silly antics, we paid for the buckets of berries and headed to Cris's home to cook with them.

Mom, Betty with Cris, who finds happiness creating in the kitchen

Sisters cooking together: Cris and Cathy

Blueberry fest: buckets of berries to process. Dave and Cathy

And so the marathon began. Mom was instructing interested kids on pie crust making. At the same time, we had groups making blueberry muffins and freezer jam. We made crepes with berries and whipped cream for dinner. Of course, Mom organized the pies. About a dozen pies were made, two for each family. We froze the last of the blueberries plain. It was an all-day adventure in cooking, fun, and family time. We were exhausted by the end of the day, but we were happy. It was good fun, and we were pleased with the amount and variety of scrumptious foods we'd made and put away for our later enjoyment. We have fond memories of that lovely family bake-off on very special summer day.

Mom, Betty creating her delicious pies at our blueberry fest day.
Mom makes amazing, flaky pie crust!

On another occasion during a Windsor summer visit, we had a banana split party. My sister Cris had participated in a trough party and decided we absolutely needed to have one. Now, what the hell is a trough party? I will explain. Cris asked our brother Joe to build an 8-foot feeding trough with legs for support as a stand. Joe was handy with building things and creating unique inventions with wood and other materials. He bought an 8-foot plastic eaves trough from the hardware store for the top feeding part, and he built two sawhorses on each end for the trough to sit on at about waist height. Food could be put into the trough while everyone stood around it and ate. Interesting concept!

My siblings, our spouses, and children were all at Cris's house for the dinner and the trough party. Still, we were unsure what this trough party actually was going to be. After dinner, Joe set up the trough in the backyard on the grass. He secured the sawhorses into the dirt to make the trough sturdy.

Cris orchestrated all of us to assemble an 8-foot-long banana split in the trough. We had gallons of vanilla ice cream, about a dozen bananas halved lengthwise, cut up fresh strawberries, caramel and chocolate sauce, and whipped cream. We built the largest banana split I'd ever seen. It was incredible!

Trough party with our 8-foot banana split

Trough party antics

Our family also likes to play practical jokes on one another and tease each other. We decided the joke would be on Cris this time. Dad had been in a nursing home for years, so he wasn't able to participate. For some reason, Mom had kept Dad's extra set of false teeth in a jar high up in a cupboard in her bathroom. Someone dreamed up the crazy idea of putting the teeth in Cris's part of the banana split. That wasn't all. Clare, Cris and John's daughter, had a new boyfriend, Jason, and he was coming that day to meet the extended family. We decided it was a good time to initiate him into our wild family.

We put a gold foil-wrapped condom at Clare's spot in the banana split. We were giddy and giggling with anticipation and sneakily trying to insert these two items without being seen. Mom was in on all the dastardly deeds, and Cris and I worked on secretly inserting the condom into the ice cream. John was shaking his head and smiling at our unbelievable antics.

Once the 8-foot banana split was built with its hidden treasures in the trough, all twenty-one of us gathered in position around and on each side, with spoons held and ready. Photographs were taken, and Cris started a countdown: three, two, one, go! Everyone began to eat the banana split in front of them. There was much laughter and watching each other as we enjoyed the extravagant treat. We had one eye on Cris and one on Clare, watching for the discovery of their special prizes.

Clare found the condom first. We cracked up laughing! When she realized what it was, she began to laugh and couldn't believe we'd done it. Jason is a candy lover, and he thought it was a gold foil-wrapped chocolate coin. This misunderstanding made us crack up more. Clare was trying to explain to Jason through laughing tears what it really was. He was a real trooper and went along with the gag. He fit right in and enjoyed the humour.

Then the "pièce de résistance." Cris found the teeth! She was poking with her spoon on something hard and thought it was frozen fruit or hard ice cream. We all watched waiting and trying to hold our composure intact, with great difficulty. Then she said, "There's something in here!" She pulled out the false teeth, coated and dripping with melted ice cream. She screamed and howled and then doubled over with hysterics. When she got control of her laugher, she stood up with the teeth in her mouth, ice cream dripping down her chin like creamy-white vampire blood. We lost it, almost falling down laughing.

Surprise! Cris says, "There's something hard in my ice cream?"
Poking it with her spoon, she finds the false teeth and buckles over laughing

John and Jason watching Cris put the false teeth in her mouth. Ice cream fangs!

Cris losing it, hysterical laughter

Cris putting the teeth in her mouth took us all to another level of hysterics. We could not believe our eyes. We never thought she'd actually wear the teeth. Tears rolled and stomachs ached from roaring with laughter. Then all hell broke loose. It was chaos, and the shiet hit the fan. Cris began to chase the kids, death walker style, like a zombie. That was it—ice cream fight! Gobs of sticky, melted ice cream were spewed in all directions. No one was safe. The kids went wild, as did many of the adults. We all got lathered with the sticky, white, sugary guck. It was everywhere—on our clothes, in our hair, and all over our bodies. What a mess—a ridiculous, unthinkable, and hilarious mess!

Ice cream fight after the trough party was sticky business with flinging gooey masses. We garden-hosed everyone off. Wild fun!

When the ice cream war died down, happy, gooey bodies were hosed down with water from the garden hose. The afternoon trough party took on a mind and energy all its own. The teeth in mouth and ice cream fight took us to a whole other level of untamed fun. Totally unplanned, the trough party ending in the ice cream war was perfect.

Sharing food through whatever means we did it—be it in the traditional way, eating at the dinner table, going picnic-style, enjoying a fondue or

Backwards Day—was quite simply a family affair that often turned into an adventure. More than any other activity, cooking meals and sharing food together became our family motto, our go-to for any time of celebration. We continue this tradition to this day for birthdays and holidays. Family meals have the power of consistency and longevity in our family.

We have to eat. I believe life is full of choices. One of them is whether to eat in a boring way or memorably. I chose memorable. Sure, lots of days were just normal eating at the dinner table with traditional North American foods, but regularly we enjoyed different, creative, and memorable family meals.

# CHAPTER 16

## *The Trek West*

I lived in Ontario for the first thirty years of my life. During that time, most of my family lived in southern Ontario, with a few exceptions. I loved my family and spending time with them, and I had longings to travel and experience more of the world. I have an adventurous spirit and a passion for learning. Living somewhere else, anywhere else, was a desire of mine. So the concept of moving west and living near the Rocky Mountains was a thrill for me and fed my exploratory nature.

I was sad to be leaving my family, and I vowed to visit every summer and at Christmastime. At the same time, I was excited about our new adventure. We were starting a new life in another part of the country. The Rocky Mountains were only one hour away from our new home. In fact, on a clear day we could see the mountains from our backyard. I was thrilled to be able to visit and explore places like Banff and Lake Louise.

I had seen the magnificence of the Rocky Mountains when I was seventeen years old and took a touring trip with a girlfriend to Calgary for a month in the summer. When I saw the first mountains of my life, I was astounded by their size and magnificence. I remember being dumbfounded by their beauty. The mountains seemed so near to Calgary, like I could just reach out and touch them. I fell in love with the Canadian Rocky Mountains as a teenager.

We drove and drove. It seemed like an eternity. Suddenly, we were surrounded by vast, awesome, and powerful rocks. Like many people when they see these miracles of nature, I took unnatural amounts of pictures. I was so awestruck. I took film upon film of these massive monsters.

During my trip as a teenager, we'd camped in Banff, near a lake. That night, sitting around a campfire, the moon's radiance permeated the air and hung protectively above the ragged peaks. It was a perfect picture! Even better was the complete reflection of the mountains, trees, and hovering full moon on the lake, duplicating its visual potency. I was hypnotized by the power and peace. I sat by the glowing fire and stared at the magical grandeur before me. Those awesome feelings and wondrous images left a lasting impression on me that became a very special memory. Here I was fourteen years later returning to live near their rocky majesty. I was delighted to be returning to the mountains and eager to repeat those wonderful experiences!

Although I didn't always speak my mind, I definitely had my own thoughts and drew my own conclusions about situations and life. I was a thinker, a questioner, a seeker of knowledge. I had made decisions about how I wanted to live and how I would parent my children. I knew the kind of mother I desired to be, and I wanted to become the best of what I saw as a combination of what my parents did, the experiences I had with my friends' parents, and my own thoughts and conclusions that came from my extensive reading. Being away from my family allowed me more freedom to raise my children the way I wanted to. I treated my children with respect and trust and had a very creative and alternativistic philosophy. Now came my true life test. My husband, my four children, and I were journeying toward this unknown territory. I was scared as hell, but the overriding emotions were hope and enthusiasm for a better life and new growth potential. I would have the freedom to become the kind of mother to my children I envisioned.

The timing was right for the sale of our house in Cambridge. It was 1988, and the housing market was very good in the southern Ontario area. We'd bought the house for $52,000 three years earlier. In the time we'd lived in it, we'd completed lots of upgrading. We rebuilt and fixed the wire fence and repainted the wooden fences. We had the exterior brick sandblasted to remove the old paint and residue and painted the brick a cool blue-grey colour. We painted all the exterior doors and trim black. The consistency and flow of the colours brought a calm and stately look back to the turn-of-the- century home. I was proud of the changes we'd made and loved the spruced-up look of our home.

On the inside of the house we refinished the original hardwood flooring. We removed the wallpaper and repainted the walls in classic neutral colours, and modernized the upstairs kitchen. Grandpa Dockman installed a new door frame to rejoin the upstairs and the main floor. We sold the house in

Cambridge for $137,000! The combination of the increase in value from the work we'd done and the rising cost of the housing market both worked to our benefit. It was wonderful. We had money to make a nice down payment on a home in Calgary, with extra money saved for emergencies.

We now needed a place to live in Alberta. It was the beginning of August, and the Olympics were in Calgary. Mike flew to Calgary during that week of the Olympics on a work-related trip and to find us a home. I wasn't able to take the trip, but I gave him a wish list of what I wanted in our new home. We had friends who lived in Airdrie, which was half an hour north of Calgary, so Mike contacted Linda and solicited her help and advice about where to buy a home. Linda said she loved living in Airdrie, as it was a smaller, friendly town of about 10,000 people, and it was great for raising children. She had a blended family with five children.

Mike found a realtor and looked at several houses in Airdrie. Driving back to the airport, he noticed a sign for a house for sale off the side of the highway in Balzac. Balzac is a very small farming community halfway between Airdrie and Calgary. He pulled in to investigate and followed the signs. The lady who owned the house was there and showed him around the home and the property. It was a beautiful, 2,100 square foot bungalow on 20 acres of land. The house had everything on my list and more! We could afford it with the salary from Mike's new job and the money we got from the sale of our home in Cambridge. The property also had potential for subdivision into several lots that we could sell to pay off our mortgage and still have our home on 4 to 5 acres. We were thrilled with the price of $250,000. It had space, a beautiful kitchen, a two-sided stone fireplace, a large garage, and a full basement with a hot tub. The home had everything we wanted, and it was out in the country with lots of space for the kids to run and play and grow. It was perfect, so we bought it!

We filled up a massive U-Haul moving truck with all of our worldly possessions in September of 1988. We were supposed to be moved out of the house by noon on closing day. Well, we were some of those horrible people who were still moving stuff out of the house when the new owners showed up to move into it. How embarrassing! I still had much of the housecleaning to do. Having four children underfoot and trying to keep them safe and happy while we were packing was no simple task. So here we were with a massive moving truck in our front driveway and a pile of the leftover stuff from the house on the front lawn waiting to be squeezed into the truck. Impossible, you laugh! Yes, okay, I see your point. I guess in hindsight the situation was really quite hilarious. Totally unrealistic, really!

We had masses of stuff that we'd accumulated. It was extremely silly of us to bring all of that paraphernalia clear across the country with us, but we did. We should have saved the time and energy and sold it or given most of it away. Hindsight can be so clear!

Mike was calculating his storage spacing figures so that everything would fit into the truck without an inch of it left unused. I was herding our four small children while a few people helped to load the truck. I don't know how I survived! I agreed to the trip, the move, the whole banana stand, and I did it wholeheartedly. I must have been out of my mind, or thought I was superhuman or some such warped thinking. OMG! But hey, I agreed fully with the decision to move, so I wasn't complaining. I was making things happen and organizing the move forward. I was simply wondering what I had got myself into.

Rachel was only three months old, David had just turned two, Johnathan was three years and eight months, and Annalisa was the ripe old age of five years and one month. Whatever possessed me to move with these four young children was big enough to motivate me to overcome all odds and succeed at this new adventure. When the new owners arrived, they assessed the situation and dug right in and cheerfully began to help with the cleaning process, the angels that they were! Surely they were as excited to get into their new home as we were to move and get into ours.

There were half a dozen items that didn't fit into the moving truck—a child's swing set, a small kids' swimming pool, and a few other assorted pieces of miscellaneous junk that I'm sure we could have purchased in Alberta! But oh no, we had to move it all clear across the country. Give my head a shake. Oh well, certainly hindsight is 20/20! We were moving west for adventure and opportunity and to travel more. We got all these things in spades from the beginning.

There are always two sides to every coin, or alternative ways to look at things. The tail side of the coin had my life thrashing wildly about with seeming randomness, yet the other side of the coin could be construed as courage. Courage brought to me a willingness to venture beyond what was comfortable and be willing to try new things. I had sufficient desire to explore and learn, which overrode the fear of change. I believed I was quite sane, and I viewed the move with an optimism that bred solutions.

Mary Beth was our designated driver of the moving truck as we journeyed across the country, brave soul that she is! Thanks, Beth. Mike and I travelled in our turtle top van with our four children while Mary Beth drove the massive moving truck that shivered and throbbed at maximum capacity, threatening to explode and spew our precious possessions to litter the Trans-Canada highway. Our goods were held tight in the confines of the truck, thank God! The trip ran smoothly and without a hitch.

I don't know if you've ever seen a turtle top van, but it was the coolest thing. The top of the van had a pop-up hard roof with an accordion-type canvas circling the roof. It had metal supports that extended the height of the interior of the van in that back by about 1.5 feet and held the pop-up roof, thus earning its name. This allowed for standing room in the "kitchen area," which included a small refrigerator, stove top burners, a table and benches, and cupboards for storage.

The back of the van possessed a "turtle tail." I don't remember if we came up with that name or if the person who sold the van to us had used the term when they explained the set-up. In essence, it was a tent that extended out the back of the van 6 feet into a double, wood base-framed bed that sat on stilts of steel. This bed easily fitted together. The frame was surrounded by a tent of canvas that snapped onto the edges of the open back doors of the van. Two adults could easily sleep in the turtle tail. It was a mini-transformer van! The turtle van was unique, functional, and awesome.

The van worked for travelling with four children and for camping, which saved the cost and hassle of finding a motel room or restaurants. It also had a chemical toilet, sort of a mini porta-potty, which was very useful. We could travel easily with four children in reasonable comfort. . . well, as easily as possible with four small children.

By the way, did you know that some motels have a limit of five people per room? We have six people in our family! What do we do with the sixth person? Smuggle them in, or have one of us sleep in the car? I guess most families have the typical 1.7 children. Maybe this limit of five people per room works for most families, but definitely not for us. The turtle van was a great solution to this problem.

The turtle van ran on propane gas. There was a price war going on in 1988 during our trip across the country, because we paid $0.03 to $0.04 per litre of propane. Yes, that is three to four cents! We were filling up the two propane tanks for $3 to $4 total each time. Incredible! That was great savings. There were two tanks, so we could switch from one tank to the other when one propane tank got low in fuel. We never ran out. . . well, once we came very close to running out of fuel. We were going through the United States, and some states didn't sell propane at all! Hey, we asked for adventure! Running out of propane in the middle of nowhere added adventure, but also stress and drama. But we made it to the next state, where we found a gas station that sold propane. We learned not to let the fuel tanks get so low to avoid this problem repeating itself. It would have been horrible to be stranded on the side of the road with our four small children, but we somehow got through by the skin of our teeth.

We drove in tandem with Mary Beth across Canada from Cambridge, Ontario, to Calgary, Alberta, on the Trans-Canada highway. It was approximately 3,300 kilometres, or 2,050 miles, which was approximately thirty hours when driving straight through if you travel across Canada, or twenty-four hours of direct driving when travelling through the United States. I felt like an old-time settler travelling west to a new frontier. I was simply bursting with excitement and anticipation!

When we travelled with our four children, there was constant buzz of activity and usually high levels of noise. We met their ongoing needs as we ventured across the country. Many things took my time and energy, like nursing the baby, changing diapers, making snacks and meals, and doing activities to occupy their little minds. We made regular stops for breaks and running time, getting the children out of the van and playing in a park to expel some energy and have some fun while getting some fresh air. We also travelled late into the night. I loved to drive at night, because all four children were asleep and it was quiet. I could relax, listen to some music, and enjoy some rare peace and solitude.

I was a well-organized mom. I had anticipated challenges when driving across the country with four small children and prepared what I called a "lap box" for each child. This box was a plastic container 12 inches long by 8 inches wide by 3 inches deep with a flat, secure lid. The box could fit on their lap and double as a drawing or play surface, like a lap desk. Inside the container I had prepared and wrapped ten numbered items with name labels on them. I included healthy snacks like granola bars, dried fruit, and fruit gummies, as well as small kits of activities, such as a small Lego set, a drawing pad and markers, and play dough.

When the kids got a little rambunctious, I'd instruct them to open their lap box and pick a certain number to open. They could eat the snack or play with the toy or game. They soon caught on to the lap box system and looked forward with excitement to the next surprise package. They had fun playing with the activities, and it curbed the boredom and restlessness that comes from such a long journey. I planned the opening of these items to last the three-day journey. The result was amazing! My plan worked well, and we had loads of fun with the lap boxes and their contents.

At the end of our journey, we drove past the Calgary city limits and the population sign as the sun was rising. The sky burst open with brilliant colours of pinks, yellows, and oranges that took over the darkness and welcomed us to our new province and home. It seemed like a good omen that confirmed we had made the right choice to relocate our family west.

Excitement and joy filled us as we anticipated arriving at our new home in Balzac, a home only Mike had seen. They say Texans do things oversized. Well, my first impression of our new home was "Are we in Texas?" Everything seemed to be oversized, including the big rocks, the Rocky Mountain range, and those gargantuan rocks that we could see from our own backyard. We had a wonderful plush-grassed lawn that extended from the house to the road along the driveway for about a quarter of a mile, and a vegetable garden that could feed an army, which I would need to use and fill with food to feed those four young'uns as they grew older! The view of the mountains from our back deck was magnificent. I fell in love with the place immediately. Space. . . we had lots of space for the children to play and grow and be safe. I was thrilled!

We utilized much of the enormous space. I planted a vegetable garden. I'll correct that—it was a small field rather than a garden. We had raspberry bushes galore, which expanded rampantly. We enjoyed the space and the privacy.

One part of the basement was developed and housed a six-person hot tub. Oh the luxury! We promptly installed a lock on the door so the kids couldn't enter without one of us adults. We spent an abundance of enjoyable hours in this heated mini pool with the kids.

Mike worked near the Calgary airport, which was in the northeast section of Calgary. It was only a twenty-minute commute with little traffic compared to Toronto. This saved Mike time so he had more time at home with us, hypothetically speaking. He worked long hours and still spent small amounts of time at home. He was trying to achieve and succeed at his new job.

I found it interesting how some things changed while others stayed the same in life. I noticed many changes in the way things were done in Alberta, which I took for granted while I lived in Ontario. Because I did something a certain way my whole life, I concluded that everyone in the world did things that same way. I couldn't have been more wrong, but I learned quickly. Some aspects of living in Alberta felt like I was living on another planet! It sure opened my eyes. I grew up a bit more and matured because of this experience. I was able to see life from other perspectives.

Living in Alberta was a mind-expanding experience that helped me understand varied points of view. I learned that people had different ways of thinking about and approaching life, and I became more open to alternate ways of life. I became a more rounded and understanding individual. We were still in Canada, not even another country, but many things were done differently. For example, I thought Bell telephone ruled the world in phone services, but apparently not. The phone company in Alberta was Telus. Who would have thought? The hydro company was different; in fact, Albertans called it power or electricity, not hydro. The gas and water service providers were also different. I adjusted to the many new ideas and ways of doing things in western Canada. Farms and farmers in Ontario were called ranches and ranchers in Alberta. Cows were called cattle. Traffic lights, which were hung vertically in Ontario, were horizontal in Alberta. This could be an insignificant difference to most people, but not to my brother Joe.

Joe travelled to Alberta and lived in Edmonton to work for a couple years as a young man. When he first arrived in Calgary driving his car, he came to a traffic light. *Okay, it's sideways,* he thought to himself. *Oh sh\*\*!!??* He's colour blind, so he didn't know which side was green and which was red. In

Ontario, he knew that the top was stop and the bottom go. He made a quick decision to observe the intersection. He paused and watched the traffic stop and go and figured out his dilemma. Confusing, yes, but it made him change his way of thinking and seeing. Many things in life were done differently, and we made adjustments accordingly to fit into our new life in Alberta.

We began the research and completed the necessary paperwork to develop our 20 acres of land into three to four building lots. The plan was to sub-divide, sell the lots, and pay off our mortgage with the revenue from the sale of the lots. Real estate was inexpensive compared to the Toronto area, so we got much more house and property for our money. About a year later, we decided to buy another 20 acre parcel of land near our home as an invest-ment and to sub-divide that property as well. Life was good. We were well on our way to settling and succeeding with our new home and ventures.

My mom and dad were visiting us from Ontario in February of 1989. Mike was in England for a business trip. When he arrived home from the trip, he informed me that he'd been let go from his job. I was shocked. OMG! Apparently, the company didn't stand by their promises, and Mike was vocal about this infraction. They decided he wasn't doing his job to their requirements and fired him. Justified or not, we were left with no income and an abundance of property and expenses. The second property hadn't closed yet, so we were able to cancel the deal. This left us with our home, which was approximately worth $250,000 with a hefty mortgage. Immediately the pressure was on to make a decision about selling the house.

I was a stay-at-home mom and had no income to contribute, but my contributions were significant—the nurturing and caring for my children's needs. It was a tragic and horrible day. Thank God Mom and Dad were visit-ing, because I needed my parents' support to get through the emotions and deal with this sudden problem and difficult time. Mike decided to take a break from work and become a stay-at-home dad for about a year. I pur-chased and operated a small sewing, alterations, and dressmaking shop in the mall in the nearby town of Airdrie. The shop was called Lili's Needle, after the name of the previous owner. I began sewing hems and doing clothing repairs. My work and business brought in some income, but it was far below what Mike's income had been at his job.

The reality was we had to sell the acreage and wonderful spacious home in Balzac and downsize to a more reasonably-priced home that we could afford. I had to let go of the dream home for now and accept the fact that we had to move for financial reasons. We bought a cute, small but functional home in the town of Airdrie about a block and a half from my business and close to shopping and schools.

Mike needed time to recuperate and regroup with his work plans, and he wanted to spend more time with the children. He felt he'd already missed a lot of their lives due to his work commitments. I ran my shop while he stayed home. The problem was that when I came home, I needed to prepare meals, clean up the disasters, and try to spend time with my children. Mike was spending time with the children but not doing much else with cooking, dishes, shopping, laundry, or other chores that needed to be done in our home. It was a very difficult time for me with too much to do. When I spoke up about the inequality of the situation with Mike, we argued or my words fell on deaf ears. Nothing changed. He couldn't cope with all the demands of the home, and I was exhausted trying to take care of the business, the children's needs, and our home.

I did enjoy being back in the business world. It was challenging, and I found working with my hands and fixing and creating garments rewarding, and dealing with adults refreshing. I missed being with my children full-time, though. I realized that I loved being a full-time, at-home mom and cherished my time with my children much more.

Somehow, we survived. Mike got his needed rest. My kids survived. . . they were alive. I got refreshed by working for a year and appreciated being able to be a mother at home with my adorable munchkins. For financial reasons, we withdrew Lisa and John from the Montessori school in Calgary and enrolled Lisa in kindergarten at the French immersion program at a school in our local town. I was so pleased and grateful to find such a great establishment in French and in our own community. After a year of Mike being at home and me working full-time, he began to work and I hired some staff so I could be at home again.

Mary Beth came back to Alberta, transferred to a job in Calgary, and lived with us for six months. It was so nice to have her, a family member, for companionship and support. Mike and I would have date nights once a week to try to get some alone time and fun together, and Mary Beth would watch the kids for us while we went out. Mary Beth and I shared our struggles and successes and became close friends.

Through all the ups and downs of our move, we were happy to be in Alberta and striving to build a life for ourselves and our children. When Mike's job ended, we chose to stay in Alberta as opposed to moving back to Ontario. Alberta became my home and home for my children. The growth and learning I experienced because of the move changed me. I became more mature and confident in my resilience and ability to make decisions for my family and execute them successfully. I loved the time I spent being a full-time mother at home with my kids, regardless of the outside circumstances. I was happy taking care of and nurturing my children. I grew into motherhood smoothly.

# CHAPTER 17

## Sex, Drugs, and Rock 'N' Roll

When I was growing up, we didn't talk much about sex, drugs, and the horrid new rock 'n' roll music. These topics were feared and avoided like the plague. They were considered taboo and looked down upon scathingly, particularly sex and drugs. It was like maybe if we didn't discuss these deeds, they didn't exist. Denial!

I was raised in a Catholic family, and it was believed that a good girl waited until she got married before she lost her virginity. Drugs were a fairly new phenomenon in the 1960s, especially for my parents, and little information was available or shared with us, either by the schools or at home. We only heard many scary warnings to stay away from and say no to drugs. As for rock 'n' roll, this was a whole new kind of crazy, loud and verbally graphic music. During the 1960s and 70s, freedom of speech was paramount, especially for teenagers, who ran rampantly out of control and engaged in all of the above "pleasures," often in the name of freedom of speech and action. In fact, you weren't "cool" if you didn't have sex, try illegal substances, and listen to rock music. Those temptations were available and enticing to all of my generation.

My parents' generation didn't discuss sexuality at all with their parents. There was a general tone of hush-hush about menstruation, sex, and how babies were made. When I started my period, I was very naive about what was happening to me. I didn't know why I was bleeding. I have to give my mother credit—she tried to talk to me about my menstrual cycle, and I acted like I already knew everything from my friends. I was just as queasy talking about the "facts of life" with my mother as she was with me. I'd only heard bits and pieces that didn't really make any sense to me, and most of the information I got was wrong, like getting pregnant from the saliva when a boy kisses you. My older sister, Cris, gave me the necessary pads and a few basics tidbits of information about my period. I was still left mostly in the dark about my body and the changes that were happening.

I was totally unaware of contraceptives or details about sexual activities. I knew you did "that" to get pregnant, but I was in the dark as to what exactly "that" entailed. Other teenagers I knew talked about "going all the way," which I deduced meant having sex with a guy. What "that" was exactly I had little clue. Having sex was something a woman did to please her husband and have children. That was the Catholic concept I learned from the nuns at school and from my parents. In hindsight, I expect I got that attitude from society in general. Pleasure and enjoyment had little to nothing to do with sex for females. Sex was simply seen as a means to procreate and keep our species alive.

I learned that making love was a marital obligation. Any sexual feelings I had were bad and should be subdued and not acted upon until later in life when I got married. Being a virgin for females was a virtue society held in high esteem. But there was a double standard, because for boys it was okay to lose their virginity. In fact, it was joked about boys "sowing their wild oats." This was just another way females were discriminated against, and no one spoke out about this dichotomy.

But times were changing, and speaking out about injustice and inequality became a part of the times during the 1960s. As we know, it took decades before those old thoughts in society changed and women became more respected and treated on equal terms as far as having their voices heard and making equal pay for equal work. Certainly we still have a long way to go, but much progress was made in creating awareness in the 1960s and 70s.

The 60s was a decade of revolution. Young people were challenging their parents' values. At that time, sexual freedom was encouraged, but such freedom without knowledge was dangerous. Many young girls had unwanted pregnancies. Abortion became an option, but a scary and dangerous one, as it wasn't legal or safe. Questionable and unhygienic abortions were performed, leaving girls damaged, sterile, or dead. I'm not saying challenging old, out-dated values was wrong. It was necessary for change. What I observed was the negative fallout that happened because of a revolt against old ideas, and the system not changing quickly enough to support the new ideas. Ideas, actions, and views were evolving that would change rules and laws over time, but slowly.

My parents believed there was safety in numbers when it came to us going out as teenagers from thirteen to sixteen years old. I was allowed to go out with my brother, his friends, and my friends if we went as a group. This was true for the most part; we hung out as a group and went to movies, dinners, and parties. In the group we coupled up and were still able to engage in some sexual experimentation, but the group safety factor was definitely there. We felt responsible for each other, so we looked out for each other and had each other's backs.

We would get alcohol and have bush parties or drink wherever. We drank while we drove our parents' cars and trucks. Wearing seat belts was not the law then, so we never wore them. We practiced many unsafe activities in the name of fun and freedom and were damn lucky to have survived unharmed. My brother Frank and I had a group of eight friends, four of each gender. We were a tight group of peers and looked after each other and spent most of our free time together.

My father had a green Fargo pickup truck. At times when we gathered as a group of friends to do something, we would have four of us in the front cab of the truck and five or six more in the back open box. It was a travelling party machine, and we were having the time of our lives. We were footloose and fancy free. The possible negative consequences of our actions never occurred to any of us. We were extremely fortunate, super lucky in fact, that we weren't hurt in any accidents, and didn't cause anyone else harm. We engaged in very dangerous and scary activities on a regular basis. I feel very lucky to have survived those years.

We had bonfires in the bush while we consumed cheap alcohol that had explicit warnings right on the bottle that said, "Dangerous. Do not consume straight or in large amounts. May cause death!" We drank it straight anyway. We were young and felt indestructible. How we survived those antics, I'll never know. Thinking back, I'm surprised we survived unscathed. Alcohol was easy to get and not expensive. I recall going into liquor stores with fake identification, (ID) and buying alcohol on our lunch breaks at high school.

My cousin Ron was not so lucky. We called him "Whitey" because he had white- blond hair. He was my mother's sister's son. Aunt Bern had five boys.

We were close with her and Uncle Harry and our five cousins, and we spent lots of time visiting at each other's homes. They lived in the town of Essex and had an above-ground pool in their backyard, so we went over often to swim. They all came to our place to visit, play, and do farm stuff. Whitey and I were the same age.

On this occasion, Whitey and his friends were drinking and driving, thinking they were having a wild and wonderful time. They were travelling on a winding gravel road and were in a horrible accident and flipped the vehicle. My sixteen-year-old cousin was killed! It was horrible! We all thought that we were invincible and nothing like this could ever happen to us. Then it did. We attended Ron's funeral, and it was very sad. His death made us aware of the possible dangers, but it was a hard and costly lesson to learn. We drank at home more often, as our parents suggested, and didn't drink and drive so much. But we didn't stop.

During my teenage years in the late 1960s and early 1970s, many drugs were readily available to us. Teenage use of drugs for pleasure was very common. Most parents, including mine, knew very little about these new mind-altering substances. My parents' generation was afraid of drugs, as they should have been. They gave us dire warnings about the dangers of using any drugs. I remember my brother and me smoking cigarettes under the combine in our hay barn. Both my parents smoked tobacco at the time. They'd buy two cartons of Export cigarettes a week—that's twenty packages of twenty cigarettes per week.

There was usually a package lying open on the kitchen table, so Frank and I would take one or two cigarettes and hide under the old John Deere and smoke them. We were about eleven and ten years old. We thought we were very grown up, and the act of smoking was exciting for us. Stupidly, we left the butts in a pile on the dirt under the combine, and one day my father discovered them. Naturally, he was extremely upset. He had a right to be angry, because we were smoking very close to the large storage of hay in the big barn. We could have burnt the barn down. Farming was my family's livelihood, so this possibility rocked my dad's world. We were young and naive. My dad took his belt off and chased us. I'm sure he intended to give us both a good "lickin". He had never hit me with the belt but he only needed to threaten. This time we deserved punishment, and he fully intended to give us a lash with his belt, but we ran faster and got away and hid.

Later that day, when we were probably safe from being strapped, we came to face the consequences. Dad made us smoke and inhale a full cigarette each. He was trying to make us sick so we wouldn't want to smoke. I couldn't do it. I wasn't inhaling the smoke. When I tried, I felt sick. He said if we were going to smoke, we had to smoke in front of him. I was too embarrassed and shy to do that, but my brother did occasionally. Dad also said to us later in our mid-teens that if we were going to drink alcohol, we were to do it at home, where we were safer under his supervision and not driving.

A few years later, my mother caught my brother Joe and me smoking in one of the upstairs bedrooms. Mom never came up the stairs, so we smoked up there thinking we were safe and blew the smoke out the window. She must have seen the smoke coming out the window or suspected something was going on. We heard her voice and her steps coming up. Afraid, we frantically put out the cigarettes and hid the butts. When she accused us of smoking "dope," we admitted to smoking cigarettes and showed her the butts. I don't know if she believed us or not. She was so afraid of drugs, I'm sure she thought we were smoking marijuana.

My brother Frank, whom I looked up to as my hero, gave me a scary and serious warning. It was a threat, really! He said to me, "If you ever try any kind of drug, I'll kill you." I knew he wouldn't ever hurt me, but I heeded his warning and stayed away from drugs. Years later, I discovered that Frank had been using a variety of drugs himself and was trying to protect me. Well, it worked! "Lucky" for me I listened to my brother, because I didn't get into trouble from using drugs.

My father had a problem with alcohol, as did his mother. In my grand-mother's and previous generations, little was known about alcohol abuse. My grandmother had extreme mood swings and sometimes got violent. She kept small bottles of whiskey—mickeys, we called them—hidden in the house, kitchen, and barn. Looking back and talking with my parents, we see now that she displayed many clear signs of alcoholism through her attitude and behaviours. Drinking alcohol was her coping mechanism for dealing with the loss of her husband and son and the subsequent responsibilities of raising her family and running the farm alone. My father was raised in that environment and had the genetic predisposition for alcoholism.

I was nineteen years old and studying at the University of Waterloo when I found out about my father's alcohol abuse. My mother had had enough! There had been an episode in which Frank had a twenty-dollar bill on top of the fridge. The money went missing, and Frank thought Dad had taken it to buy a case of twenty-four beers. In his anger, Frank found the case of beer out by the cow barn. It had been smashed, the glass bottles beaten into deadly chards with a baseball bat. Dad's drinking had progressed to unbearable levels, and his behaviour had sadly deteriorated. In her frustration, Mom told Dad that he would have to leave if he didn't quit drinking and got help. Frank and Mary Beth were also there. Dad angrily slammed the door after Mom gave him this ultimatum. The money, the smashed bottles, and the angry violence were the last straws. Change needed to happen, and Mom took a stand. Frank went to try to talk with Dad. Fortunately, Mom had foreseen this event happening and was prepared.

A neighbour and friend of the family had quit drinking, gone to an alcohol recovery centre, and had joined Alcoholics Anonymous, (AA). Mom asked Norm beforehand if he would help by talking to Dad and taking him to the recovery centre when Dad was ready. Maybe that day Dad was ready, so Mom called Norm. He came and talked to Dad. Dad agreed that he needed help, and Norm immediately took him to the recovery centre for detoxification and time in the recovery setting.

He lived there for three months and partook in intensive daily education and treatment. He couldn't drink and had to attend group meetings and adhere to a strict schedule. He began to see that he had the disease of alcoholism. Drinking was a form of escape for him, and he started to learn better ways of dealing with his emotions and stresses in life. My father worked hard in that program with the help of a serious "hard ass" priest, the program director, and counselors. My mother supported him and began to go to groups to help her understand the disease and her part in it. My father was a gentle, kind, and loving man when he wasn't drinking. When he drank, he became unpredictable and angry. That program saved Dad's life. Many things changed in Dad and our family after he started in his recovery from alcoholism.

My father had a steady, consistent, and friendly disposition. He farmed and then kept his job until retirement after thirty years of working at Chrysler. Prior to going into recovery, he drank, but only on the weekends. I had difficulty believing that my father was an alcoholic, and I denied it for a long time. I thought that alcoholics were drunks who lived on the street. They were bums. I had old, stigmatized ideas about alcohol addiction. I needed to open my mind and learn new information. Over time, I became informed and understood that alcoholism was a disease—an addictive, compulsive, progressive disease.

Since I wasn't living at home, I wasn't exposed to the final stages of the alcoholic chaos happening in my family since I'd left. Then I didn't see the recovery stages that followed. Three years after Dad quit drinking and started his new life, my sister Cris sent Mary Beth and me a book called *Adult Children of Alcoholics* (1983).[21] Mary Beth and I decided to search out our own recovery and discovery about alcoholism and how growing up in an alcoholic household had affected us. We started to attend an Adult Children of Alcoholics recovery group.

A new chapter of growth began in our family with the awareness of alcohol addiction, and our perceptions and behaviours changed from the old patterns we'd learned while trying to cope with Dad's drinking and mood swings. We learned healthier ways to deal with our emotions and relate to one another. My dad didn't simply quit drinking, which was a huge and difficult undertaking, but he also got help from counselors and other recovering addicts that supported him in changing his belief system. Dad learned how to recognize and express his feelings, and a new way of communicating evolved within our family relationships. Anger and resentments were talked about, and healing grew and spread. That was the beginning of the change from the destructive cycle in our family to recreating more positive, healthy relationships.

The result of my parents developing this awareness and changing their behaviours reflected on us, their children. Frank experienced numerous instances of out of control behaviours after consuming excessive alcohol throughout his teen age years. At the time we thought it was normal teenage behaviour to drink in excess and do silly, destructive, or random things. But Frank's behaviour was anything but normal. He had several altercations with the police and a few violent drunken outbursts over that period of time.

Frank was a very large young man, 6 feet and 250 lbs. Many people were afraid of him because of his sheer size. I swear he looks like Hulk Hogan. Often when he drank to excess, he would pass out cold and blackout, later not remembering his behaviours.

I thought this was normal, but it wasn't. One time at a family wedding, Frank drank too much and passed out under the table. It was very embarrassing for my parents and relatives, but no big deal to me. A couple of my uncles got him up, and I tried to help them get Frank out to the car. My uncles told me to stay back, that he might hurt me. I was shocked. He would never hurt me in a million years, even in his drunken state. I continued to talk with him and try to calm him down. Someone had said something that pissed him off. He got mad and put his fist through a window beside the doors in the community hall. There he was a hulk of a man/boy out of control, bleeding, and me and my uncles shuffling him out to the car to sleep it off.

The fact that he could be dangerous when he drank did occur to me briefly when I witnessed his rage and destructive behaviours, but I had no fear of him. I was very naive. In Frank there was the mixture of unresolved anger and inherited alcoholic tendencies that created a very volatile situation when he drank. He had the illness, the disease of alcoholism.

Another alcohol-induced incident landed Frank in jail overnight. One year after my father went to the recovery centre; Dad talked to Frank and brought him to alcohol detoxification (detox) and the three-month residential treatment and recovery program. Frank was twenty-one years old. His decision to quit drinking and enter recovery changed his life forever, as it did for my father. This was another of the many ripple effects my Dad started. The wave effects of Dad's and Frank's recoveries affected our family for the better, as well as our children and future generations to come. The cycle had been recognized and broken, for which I am grateful.

One very healthy result of this recovery process was that our family had more open and honest communication with ourselves and each other. Over the years, I slowly adjusted my thinking and became receptive to information about alcoholism and the possible heredity link to the disease in my children. When my four children were in their teens, I took them to open birthday meetings with Dad and Frank. They attended Alcoholics Anonymous (AA) meetings to help maintain their sobriety over the years. An open AA birthday meeting welcomes friends and family to celebrate another year clean and sober. At the birthday meeting the recipient shares their story. I wanted my children to be aware of their genetic history and educate them about my family's addictions and the recovery process. The potential for these same problems was in them. In fact, the addictions have surfaced in our family in a few places since then.

Along with the free expression of sexual desires and the experimentation with altered states of consciousness with drugs and substances came another form of wild and free expression of personal freedoms—new music. It seemed that the social views of the time spoke out in the lyrics of songs that reflected the larger political and social movements. The youth of the 1960s became vocal about "Peace, not War," demonstrating against the war in Vietnam and expressing these views at political rallies, in the streets, and at massive concerts like Woodstock. Free expression of love for our fellow human beings became part and parcel to the long-haired "hippie, flower power" era. It was an exciting time, frightening for many, enlightening for some, and a catalyst to changes in our society. I think rock 'n' roll played a major role in this transformation of thoughts and ideas.

My parents loved their music and dancing. In fact, they met at a community dance. They loved country music, big band music, and dancing to waltzes and polkas. My father played the harmonica and the accordion. He used to play tunes in the kitchen and as children we would learn the steps, dance, and have wonderful times. Dad taught us to do the waltz, polkas, and the Russian Kazoks. We had loads of fun. Dancing was great exercise with lots of laughter. I remember watching my parents dance together with awe. They adored each other and danced so smoothly together. They were completely in sync with each other as they floated across the dance floor. Dad would lead, and his right arm never moved from its distance to the floor. It was a beautiful and touching experience. I was mesmerized by their movements and the oneness they portrayed. I was proud of how they danced together.

Then rock 'n' roll stormed in, literally crashing and burning its way into a music scene that previously had been controlled, systematic, and pure. This new music was deafening with crude realism and wild costuming. Freedom of speech and action permeated the music scene, making this new music drastically different from its predecessors of my parents' generation. When

241

you compared it to big band music, or Lawrence Welk kind of tunes, it was radically different.

This mind-boggling change was difficult for my parents to accept or comprehend. They simply didn't like this new rock 'n' roll music one bit. They called it noise, not real music. We totally loved the new music and listened to it loudly and often. We used to tease Dad about his old country tunes and would wolf howl at them. Dad would reply by saying that our music wasn't real music, just a bunch of loud, aggravating noise. I have to say, I have thoroughly enjoyed the big band sound and particularly loved watching couples dance to the music of Mom and Dad's era. The polkas and waltzes were lots of fun to dance to, but rock 'n' roll music was more spontaneous, modern, wild, and sexy, and much of it was radical and spoke of freedom, drugs, sex, and many previously taboo subjects. This new music was an expression of who I was as a teenager and the freedom I desired in life.

Needless to say, the music of the 1960s was very controversial. It was overtly sexual and emotionally expressive. It was quite a scary time for my parents—a time of hippies, flower power, drugs, and thunderous music. Looking back, I can certainly understand their fear and uncertainty about how these strange new times would affect their children. The music of the Beatles, Elvis, Jimi Hendrix, and Janice Joplin, for example, was unacceptable to my parents. They had reason to be afraid. "Freedom" was the word of the day to do whatever one liked to do, including freedom of mind through hallucinatory drugs that were "far out" and "too cool" and "funky." There truly was danger lurking within the rock 'n' roll scene. The stability and tradition of our culture was threatened, and our future altered.

With the era of the 1960s and freedom of speech came a heightened level of the women's rights movement and a surge of feminism. Women banded together to voice their outrage at inequality in all forms. Issues from equal pay for equal work to sexual equality between genders were at the forefront of debates. Women burned their bras to show solidarity and express their sexual freedom. Men grew their hair long to rebel against tradition and expectations. The 60s were a time of massive rebellion against standard beliefs and values. Major changes had begun. One of those changes saw a major shift in the style of parenting.

As the pendulum swings through time, it often goes from one extreme to the other, and change becomes inevitable. The 1960s were a turning point from a period of strict Victorian parental control to the quest for total freedom of the hippie parents, who gave their children power. Children were meant to be free, not suppressed. It was a time of no boundaries and little supervision. Children were encouraged to speak their minds against their parents and society as a whole.

With the 60s came two-income families, mothers going to work and finding fulfillment through jobs. Kids were put in daycare, left with family members, or even left at home by themselves, garnering the name "latchkey kids," as they'd let themselves into their homes after school because Mom and Dad were both at work. All changes in the name of progress—or was the cause of this double income also consumerism? Part of the "work hard to succeed" idea was to buy the stuff like big beautiful homes, fancy cars, toys, and travel, and to give kids better opportunities. But at what cost to human and family relations? What happened to the family unit? What balance do we need to find between total control and total freedom in our parenting?

So we learned by practice, research, and trial and error. As I said at the beginning of this book, no one taught me in school how to be a mother or raise my children successfully. There is no consensus on "the" best way to raise children. It's really a personal choice based on our own childhood environment, social status, education, and philosophy of life. In our world of instant gratification, parenting doesn't fit the mould, as the results of successful or unsuccessful parenting will take decades to show.

Studies may help to prove what has worked and what hasn't worked for the next generation of parents, but by the time the research results are tallied, our kids' generation will have their own philosophy, which will include the relevant issues of their day. The world has changed, and parenting views will change with it. So what's the answer? It's not a universal one, because there's a plethora of conflicting information and advice out there on being a parent and a mother. I guess I realized this when I began my own personal journey of motherhood. I believe it's important to read, research, ask questions, have a role model, and form your own opinion from your life values and morals. Then the bottom line is to trust yourself, trust your instincts, and go with what you believe to be right and best for your children in your situation. As a favourite teacher of mine in college, Pat, said when I would often ask specific questions, "It all depends." And she would go on to explain a variety of situations that required different approaches. There are many answers to the same question. The answer will depend on you, your child, family circumstances, and the specific situation.

The social and political environment in the 1960s changed society's view of parenting. I formulated my own views from the information I gathered and my own experiences with the topics of sex, drugs, and rock 'n' roll. I was not as radical as the times, but I wanted to help my children develop independence, find their voices to speak up, and respect themselves and others. That is precisely why motherhood is such an ongoing challenge. There are no all-encompassing answers, no mould that will work across the board. Each family is different and must make choices that reflect their values and beliefs and relate to the personalities of their own children and themselves.

# CHAPTER 18

## *Love and Affection: Showing Emotions!*

When we consider our environment and the social climate in which we live, we must include the changes in emotional awareness and emotional intelligence. During the 1960s, emotional outcries were common, which was a change from the Victorian standards of behaviour, the attitude that said you kept a stiff upper lip, that you didn't show your feelings because it was a sign of weakness. I was of the opinion that showing and speaking about emotions was important. I felt demonstrating love was crucial.

What about love and motherhood? Would showing affection toward children be beneficial to their development into secure, confident, and independent human beings? Of course it would. This is a logical assumption, but human behaviours aren't always logical. Unhealthy behaviours can be passed on through generations without thought or explanation, meaning that the behaviours will be repeated automatically from one generation to the next. Emotional decisions are made in stressful situations, and environmental circumstances can place undue pressure on a person to behave according to societal norms and expectations. For these reasons, there are times and circumstances in our human history when motherhood had little to do with love, and love little to do with motherhood.

As mothers, we can often feel that we're not in control of our own lives, let alone the lives of our children. This is a sad state of being, as we're usually the main person in charge of raising the children. If we as mothers feel powerless to make decisions in our parenting, our results may be sabotaged and we may feel that our efforts are insignificant and unrecognized. As a result, we can feel that our job of being a mother is of less importance than an external job that brings home financial support. How do we as mothers bring back our power and work together with our families and society to raise our children

245

in the best possible environment? We must feel that we are doing important work ensuring the safety, nurturing, and education of our offspring.

Let's examine how emotions fit into our work as mothers. If only emotions rule our decisions, where are we? Females have long been considered the emotional gender, but we also use logic to inform our decisions. We think and feel, so the combination of logical evidence and emotional clues are both important in making the best choices for ourselves and our families. I conclude that love and emotions are an integral part of motherhood, but—and that's a gigantic BUT—how do we show love?

We live in an increasingly materialistic culture, where love can be equated with stuff that money can buy, like toys, electronics, houses, and cars. Objects are given to show love rather than showing love by spending time and sharing companionship with people.

It's a dilemma many parents in two-income families face. There's not enough time to get everything done, and so much time is spent rushing around to get errands done and drive kids to sports and extracurricular activities. Dual-income families often go for quality time with their children as opposed to quantity time. That may be a necessary compromise due to the higher cost of living for some, or it could be a cop-out because we're too busy making a living to acquire all the stuff we think we need. Our consumerism has become a normal way of life, which can be costing us quantity of experiences with our children.

It's your choice how you operate your family, because we live in a free, democratic society. But I suggest taking time to express your love to your children. They will remember the times you played cards with them, or built snow people, or went on a picnic, more than they will remember the toy they received but played with without you. I am reminded of a quote I love from the great *Maya Angelou*: "People may not remember what you did or what you said, but they always remember how you made them feel."[22] Children learn from how they are treated, and if emotions are commonly expressed, their emotional intelligence will grow and be nurtured. They will feel loved and secure. Children need to feel important, that they are wanted, accepted, and cared for.

I read an interview with Dr. Maya Angelou in *Oprah* magazine. At eighty-five years old, Maya had gained incredible wisdom. Here is an excerpt from that interview:

"The love of the family, the love of one person can heal. It heals the scars left by a larger society," Dr. Angelou said in the May 2013 issue of *O, the Oprah Winfrey magazine.*[23]

From my early life observations, I formulated that my goal as a mother would be to provide an environment where freedom of emotional speech was as welcome as freedom of verbal speech. I wanted my children to feel free to speak their mind as well as express their feelings. In my family of origin, and my early Catholic schooling, I learned that emotions were rarely expressed, especially negative ones. Crying was considered to only be done by the weak. "Negative" emotions like anger, pain, sadness, frustration, and hate were discouraged from being shown. "Negative emotions" were considered "bad" and were to be avoided, stuffed down, and ignored.

As children, we were encouraged to suppress such "negative" feelings, hide them, and pretend they weren't there. We were expected to only show the positive, good feelings and emotions, like happiness, joy, contentment, and satisfaction. We were to put a smile on our faces no matter how we felt or what was happening in our life at the time. I quickly learned to hide behind this mask of a smile to cover up my true feelings. Therefore, a part of me was suppressed and put aside. As an adult, I've spent much time in study, reflection, and therapy to uncover and retrain myself to reintegrate my complete range of emotions. My aim has been to develop and grow my emotional intelligence.

I was in my mid-twenties when I became aware that something was missing inside of me. There was a void that I'd always felt, but I didn't know where it came from or how to fill it. I tried to fill it with other people in relationships, or with substances like alcohol. Neither worked. I tried to work excessively, study excessively, to keep so busy that I was unable to recognize the pain of the missing parts. My healing process started a few years after my father began his recovery journey through alcoholism. My father began to value all emotions and express his feelings with us and our mother.

I recall one particular conversation Dad and I had about love. We had gone for a walk around the farm, and he was asking me about my relationship at the time with a boyfriend. He wondered if I still loved this boy. My feelings were jumbled, and I was unclear, but speaking freely about my feelings helped me to gain clarity. Dad taunted me about another problem, deliberately provoking me to prove his point. He persisted until I got angry and showed my anger by yelling at him. Following my outburst, Dad laughed. It had been a set up! I was startled and simply stared at him. Then I too began to laugh. We laughed for many minutes at the absurdity of the situation. Dad said he knew he'd taught us to suppress our anger, and he was feeling 100% better since he'd learned to show whatever emotions he felt. He wanted the same freedom for me and the rest of his family, perhaps to repair what he saw as one of his mistakes of the past. It was awesome! I learned much that day, and thus began my wonderful journey toward wholeness.

I began to understand where this behaviour of suppressing my emotions came from. It was a form of coping with extremely difficult times. My parents and grandparents spent decades in survival mode, which meant toughing life out, doing without, and dealing with the hardships of wars, the depression, and disastrous financial times. Both sides of my family had been farmers for many generations, so they were accustomed to working long hours, often sixteen to eighteen hours per day, seven days a week, and doing physically hard, intensive labour to put food on the table. A person who was a hard worker was valued and held in highest esteem in their generation. There wasn't time or tolerance for figuring out or talking about their emotions.

As I've said previously, thoughts and behaviours are passed on from one generation to the next. If nothing changes, the behaviours remain the same. For example, my grandparents on my dad's side came from Russia and the Ukraine. They survived horrible times of pain and atrocities in their home country, almost to the point of genocide in the Ukraine. My grandparents, like many others, left their home countries in Eastern Europe with very little money or material goods. Life had become too dangerous to remain. There was little hope of their survival, let alone creating a better future for their families.

I can only imagine the courage and strength it took for them to pack up and leave their countries of origin, their homes, and some of their family members behind in questionable circumstances. Often they could bring very little with them on this journey, because they were escaping and it had to look like they were only on a holiday. They could bring only what they could carry inconspicuously while walking, riding the train, and finally on the boat.

They would have felt much uncertainty about where they were heading and what their new lives would be like as they travelled across the ocean to a foreign and strange new world. I image they were driven by two main things: the need to escape the horror and devastation of their home countries, and the hope of building a new, safe, and better future for their families. My grandparents took a huge risk leaving their country and travelling thousands of miles across Europe, over the Atlantic Ocean, and across the huge expanse of most of Canada. It was a long and treacherous journey in search of peace and safety.

I had been aware of a shift in the way of life in North America from the survival mode of the first half of the century to a life of affluence after the Second World War. Through the 1960s and 70s, most Canadians lived peaceful and secure lives. They weren't drafted into the military, as our military services are voluntary. War was and is basically a foreign concept and event in my world. I had no direct link to war; even my father was too young to serve in the Second World War. My life and world was very different from that of my ancestors and the previous generation of Canadians, who experienced wars and flight from them.

As a child, we didn't have much money, but we always had an abundance of good food, dry and warm shelter, and free education. We weren't lacking in opportunity. When our needs are met in this comfortable environment, the seed of reflection and change can be sown. My environment created fertile ground for the consideration of new concepts and a higher scale of mind exploration, as seen in Maslow's hierarchy of needs. The basic needs were being met, so we were able to pursue more complex desires.

I was an excellent observer of my surroundings. I learned to read people. I watched their expressions, body movements, inferences in their speech, and their behaviours and made predictions and conclusions of my own. I carefully observed and made mental notes of how my friends' parents treated them. Most of them were strict with rules and curfew, not allowing their children any freedom to make decisions or try something new or different. I saw some strongly controlling parenting in action. I related these kids' behaviour to how they were parented and realized that strict control didn't work. Most often those highly controlled kids were the ones who were outwardly defiant or secretly mischievous about breaking those strict rules.

Many of them learned how to look good in front of their parents, but when they were with us, they went wild and tended to do just the things they were restricted from doing. I recall two of these girlfriends having makeup and skimpier clothing hidden in their lockers at school, two things that weren't allowed by their parents. They'd put on colourful, usually excessive, makeup at school, change their clothing, and then remove it on the bus going home. I didn't agree with this method of parenting. Even as a child, I understood that parenting methods that used control looked deceivingly effective, but in reality weren't effective at all. To demonstrate, try telling a child, "Don't do that!" Whatever "that" is. Usually this statement makes the child curious to try just the thing they're told not to do. I've experimented and read about this concept and was amazed at how the mind works. The mind says to itself, *Hmmm why can't I touch it? I wonder what will happen.*

The other behaviour that comes out of control may be defiance, an "I'll show you" attitude to prove they can do it. As my youngest daughter used to say to me and to her siblings, "You're not the boss of me!" Sometimes I tried to use control and be the boss, which of course I wasn't.

Some of my friends' parents operated at the other extreme and let them do everything they wanted. They also were wealthy and bought these children any material items they desired. Basically, these kids ruled the house. They learned to manipulate their parents through deceit, emotional outbursts, and guilt. It was an ugly game they played. In these cases, the child became spoiled and self-centred. They never learned how to deal with someone saying no to them. They learned to deal with disappointment by having a tantrum and being extremely rude until they got what they wanted. As a result, they became selfish and were unable to engage in healthy interactions with their parents or others. I disagreed with both methods of parenting. From my observation as a child and a teenager, I felt there must be a better way to parent that balanced these two extreme philosophies and gained better results.

My own parents' philosophy was less extreme, but still much of they did was random and unconscious behaviours they learned from their own upbringing. My parents gave us much freedom, perhaps because they were extremely busy on the farm. We did have some rules that were inflexible, like no drugs. I found that this way of parenting encouraged trust and the ability to make some of our own decisions. We learned to make choices and deal with the consequences of those choices. I liked that freedom and responsibility.

I learned an incredible amount about motherhood from my observations as a child. Some methods worked and others didn't, while some methods made matters worse and created havoc. I logged that information away in my mind for future reference.

Another example came from the teaching methods used at the Catholic school I attended. We were taught for the most part by nuns, with a few male laypeople as teachers. The rules were ridiculously strict, and if broken the punishment was being hit on the hand with a strap. This was called "getting the strap," and we were warned about and threatened by this punishment into behaving uniformly. This form of enforcement scared the hell out of me and left an indelible mark in my mind. I was a shy, quiet child. I went about my work and did not like any form of attention. I was given the strap in the principal's office once. My crime had been leaving a few bread crumbs on my desk after eating lunch! Even as a seven- or eight-year-old child, I was aware that the punishment did not equal the crime. It was humiliating, but I learned a valuable lesson. The incident stuck in my mind as unfair and inef-fective. I disagreed with using violence to elicit desired behaviours.

A few of my classmates got the strap regularly. They were those students who acted out to get attention, or who mocked the nuns by laughing and making fun of them behind their backs. Okay, I agree that they deserved some form of corrective response to their behaviours, but hitting them didn't seem like a useful answer. I could easily see that this form of discipline was not effective. Behaviours weren't changed; they were simply hidden and became manipulative. The acts went underground or became drastically worse. This form of discipline uses fear as the motivation, and I didn't like that feeling. Fear didn't motivate me in a positive way. I didn't like fear tactics being used on me then nor do I now.

I recently re-read the book *Think and Grow Rich* by Napoleon Hill (1960).[24] Hill's book presents a wonderful life-understanding concept and is a self-awareness classic. I read this book the first time when I was in my early twenties and was looking for financial success, management strategies, and personal development. I read it again because of my interest in life awareness and creating a more balanced life. It contains great successful life messages throughout its pages, not simply money-making ideas.

I've always believed in the power of the mind, so I agree with Hill that "thoughts are things" and the energy of our thoughts is transferred into our actions. Hill makes a profound statement about fear in his chapter about the six ghosts of fear. He says, "Criticism will plant fear or resentment in the human heart but it will not build love or affection." This makes total sense to me. I didn't feel love or affection for my critics or the ones who used fear tactics to try to control me. These harsh forms of attempted behaviour modification weren't conducive to building healthy relationships. They felt demeaning and manipulative and made me want to crawl into a hole and hide, or to strike out and fight. I felt that criticism tore down relationships and niggled away at a person's self-esteem.

I remember well one of my teachers, a male, and he wasn't a nun! He was my favourite teacher, Mr. Harvieux. I remember him because of the way he treated his students and me in particular. He demonstrated a different approach toward teaching and relationships that didn't use control or manipulation. He showed us respect. He never belittled or criticized me but encouraged and engaged me into doing interesting work, and we held intriguing conversations. He noticed and made comments about my strength of character and my intelligence and abilities. I recognized his alternative approach and loved it. This experience changed me. I identified his approach as a significant alternative that I fully embraced.

Mr. Harvieux offered me a new view of myself and how to relate to others because he saw and expressed the potential he saw in people. I began to feel that I had talent and strengths and could succeed and do something with my life! Being taught by Mr. Harvieux made me feel smart and special. Previously, I was a good student, but under his supervision I became an excellent student, the best! He encouraged me to want to become better. I found my stride. With his guidance and inspiration, I realized I loved to learn. This was an extremely significant realization in my life! I happily discovered that I had a mind that was smarter and more capable than I had ever imagined. This awareness has served me well throughout my life in whatever circumstances came along. I knew I could learn what was necessary to overcome any obstacles and succeed at what I pursued. When I expended my energy usefully, I became a powerhouse. I thrived under his instruction and gained much self-confidence.

I am forever grateful for the experience of having a teacher and mentor who invested himself in me. What a great life lesson! I knew how his method of encouragement worked for me, and I wanted to become like him, so I emulated him. I'd use positive reinforcement, point out people's strengths, and show them their potential. I decided to use his approach of respect and encouragement when I had my own children.

From my personal experiences, I learned which styles of parenting I agreed or disagreed with. The basis of my philosophy of motherhood began with those childhood observations and conclusions. Further study, reading, and research clarified my stance and gave me theories that backed up my ideas or challenged my concepts. Putting my philosophy into action while I was learning to be a mother was my life's greatest challenge. In the midst of my busyness and insecurities, I needed to be present to the moment and consciously aware of my thoughts and behaviours so I could change the automatic responses into my desired way of mothering. I knew positive encouragement and expressing my feelings verbally and with my actions would give my children the feelings of love and security they would need to feel secure in themselves. That goal was never far from my mind when I was mothering my children. I gave them my time, attention, and love in abundance.

# CHAPTER 19

## Education: Primary School Years, Kindergarten to Grade Four

I stayed at home with the children and unpacked and made our house comfortable. I also began researching the local school systems. Lisa was three years old, so she still had two years before she started school. I investigated some alternate forms of education, preschools, French language schools, and others. The public school system was overloaded with students and under-financed because of budget cuts in Alberta. There were between thirty-two and forty students in each classroom with one teacher. I felt those numbers weren't conducive to meeting students' needs. It was unfortunate, because any child who had difficulty learning could easily fall through the cracks and miss the basics of reading and math that were required for life. I considered different options.

Mike wanted me to home-school, but I was not a teacher. I wasn't confident that I could provide my children with the best education or fulfill their needs academically. I also was concerned about the social aspects that may not be addressed adequately with home-schooling. Seriously, my main concern was that I didn't think I had the patience or the stamina to do the twenty-four seven regular everyday care plus add schooling to my already full agenda. The thought of looking after all of my children in all ways, plus overseeing their education, was overwhelming. It would have been too much for me to handle. I vowed to Mike and myself that I would find a viable alternative and thus preserve my sanity.

In my research, I discovered the Montessori schools and began reading about their philosophy. I read Maria Montessori's book *The Discovery of the Child* (1967),[25] in which she wrote about her views on educating children with the purpose of preparing them for life rather than teaching them to recount facts. The Montessori program used hands-on, experiential approaches that utilized a child's natural curiosity and search for understanding of their world. She deduced that learning made more sense to children if they used all their senses. I liked what I read and decided that this holistic approach would enhance learning. I felt that one to two years of Montessori schooling would greatly benefit my children before they attended the regular public school system. I found a Montessori school in Calgary and enrolled Lisa and John. Lisa attended for two years, John for one, and David for a short time. Here was one alternative solution for supplementing their educational experience.

For the next step in their education, I checked out the French immersion programs in Alberta. I was surprised and extremely pleased to learn that in my small town of Airdrie, French immersion education was alive and well. My mother's family was French-Canadian, but I never learned French growing up, except for a bit of high school French. My parents spoke English at home, even though Mom was fluent in French and Dad spoke some Ukrainian and Russian. These languages were lost in my generation. Canada is bilingual, and I felt strongly about my children picking up the French language that had been lost in my generation.

I believed that if my children were bilingual, they could reap future benefits from having this skill. If they spoke two languages, more opportunities would be available to them. My research told me that children learn and retain languages rapidly compared to adults, and if they know two languages, the brain is somehow programmed to learn the next language more easily. The ratio of teacher to student was much better in the public French school, with approximately eighteen to twenty-five students in each classroom with one teacher. My children would have a better opportunity to get the help and guidance they needed in a class with fewer students. French immersion seemed like an excellent choice.

I had my own ideas about child rearing. I felt that hands-on, experiential learning was most effective. I wanted my children to enjoy childhood without having undue pressure to succeed or grow up prematurely. I was their mother, not their teacher in the academic sense. My role included teaching values and morals, but not math and reading. I wanted to instill a desire to learn as part of the enjoyment of childhood for my children. I knew if they had the desire and the motivation, the learning would follow throughout their lives.

I have a passion for reading, and I read and told stories to them daily. As their vocabulary grew, they began telling the tales each in turn. I did this for fun, not particularly for teaching them how to read, although that was a side benefit. They learned to appreciate and love the wonderful places words and stories could take us. We shared laughter, tears, joy, and adventures through the stories we made up and the books we read. I watched their imaginations grow and work as their minds wove tales of battles and wit and good conquering evil. I held imagination as precious and wished to nurture it in my children. To quote Albert Einstein in the 1929 *Saturday Evening Post*, "Imagination is more important than knowledge. For knowledge is limited, whereas imagination embraces the entire world, stimulating progress, giving birth to evolution."[26]

As for math, I was always good with numbers and enjoyed working with them. Mike loved math also and was excellent with figuring numbers in his head. He played number games with the children constantly. The kids and Mike were always counting, sorting, and figuring sums, particularly when we were travelling in the van. They also played the alphabet game, where you start at A and find the letters of the alphabet in order on car license plates. The aim is to go through the entire alphabet in order. It was a fun game that passed the time in a constructive way. My children spent their time prior to kindergarten enjoying being kids, having fun, and learning basic life skills.

Lisa's first day of school was worrisome for her and for me. Mike and I had chosen the French immersion program. I was emotional because she was growing up and leaving the nest, so to speak, to fly off to school. She was afraid. She was in tears and clinging to my legs. Clearly she didn't want to go to school or leave me. I was her security. Somehow she didn't have the same reaction at the Montessori school she attended previously, maybe because she had John with her there. She was definitely worried about kindergarten. I dropped her off every day for a half day, and she cried and clung to me for dear life. The teacher would guide her into the class with a gesture for to me to go. It was dreadful for both of us. I would sulk away feeling guilty about leaving her. Eventually the crying and clinging decreased and Lisa adjusted to being in the classroom. She made a friend, and as she became more comfortable with her new environment, both our fears subsided. Thank God! She began to enjoy some of the activities, and when her attention was focused, she became absorbed in them. It was a difficult transition, but we both managed to survive it.

During that first year in the smaller home in the town of Airdrie, we sponsored a foreign exchange student from Sweden to come live with us. Her name was Charlotte, and she was in her late teens. She came to Canada to work as a nanny in exchange for accommodation and the opportunity to travel. Charlotte was a charming girl who was very helpful to me and my family. She eagerly assisted me with the children, and I was grateful to have her living with us. We are a bit unusual in our thinking, and our household was pretty crazy sometimes with four children who were all under five, but Charlotte was a great sport. She was curious, willing, and had a wonderful laugh and sense of humour that helped us survive in many situations. We took her to the Rocky Mountains, Banff, and Lake Louise, where we did some touring of local attractions and she skied. Her mother and sister came to visit her from Sweden. They were a lovely family. Charlotte fit right in and became an important part of our family.

Family New Year's celebration with Charlotte

We had some money put aside from the sale of our home in Ontario, which we used to live on while Mike was off work and to renovate our first home in Airdrie. We managed in that first home for about a year, but the space was small, especially with Charlotte living with us. Therefore, we decided to purchase a larger home. We sold this first home and bought another one that had more space, had more bedrooms, and was within a block of and easy walking distance to the tri-school area. The three schools covered kindergarten to Grade 12, English and French immersion. The location was ideal. The house was also close to grocery stores and the main amenities. It needed upgrading, and it had an unfinished basement, so we got an excellent deal that was well below market value. I could walk the kids to school and be available for them to come home for lunches. This was a good move for all of us.

John's birthday was January 8, and the school system had an age deadline of five years old by December 31 to start kindergarten the following September. This meant John had to wait another year before he could go to school, putting him two grades below Lisa. David went to school the year after John. I was okay with this arrangement, because even though John was physically advanced, I knew he needed to mature emotionally before he would be prepared to attend school and succeed with peer interactions. Lisa being in school also gave John and David time together to bond, and it gave me more time to spend with the three younger children individually without being uninterrupted by Lisa's needs. This enabled me to give some catch up attention to the younger three. I could spend some quality time with Lisa in the evenings doing crafts, cooking, playing, or reading. The individual alone time was needed and special for both of us.

I found the teachers and their programs at the French immersion school to be exceptional. The teachers were dedicated and hard-working, and the class sizes were smaller because fewer students were enrolled in the program. Smaller classed allowed for extra individual teacher attention to be given to each student to assist them in grasping concepts and encourage them to overcome their difficulties.

Lisa's teacher recommended that she be moved to the English program at the end of Lisa's kindergarten year. Lisa was experiencing difficulty grasping French language arts, therefore she was behind in her reading levels compared to the other students and the curriculum standards. She wrote some words and letters backwards like a mirror image, and we thought she may be dyslexic. I did some research and discovered that many children write letters backward in the early stages of learning to write. Most children grow out of this habit through time, practice, and maturity.

Lisa showed signs of intelligence because she had a grasp of numbers, she was able to figure out math problems, and her verbal speech and vocabulary were above average for her age, with the exception of enunciating the letter "L." She said her name as "isa." I remember her Nana working with her, showing her how to place her mouth and tongue to say the sound of L, "leh, leh, leh" over and over, again and again. This took a few more years of toiling work, patience, and practice before Lisa was able to speak "L" words clearly and correctly. Because of her understanding of numbers and mathematical concepts, and her grasp of oral vocabulary, we decided to keep her in the French program and do the extra work necessary to help her catch up and learn the language arts skills at home.

In Grade 1, Lisa took an Intelligence Quotient, (IQ) test and was tested for dyslexia. The results showed an excellent overall knowledge level, above average vocabulary, clear understanding of math concepts, but an inability to read written words. She wasn't dyslexic. There seemed to be some connection to reading in her brain that did not happen in the "normal" fashion. We felt this was good news. We could work with this information and help her learn through alternate methods. The trick was to find out how she learned. We struggled with this for three more years.

Lisa learned languages differently than most kids. Her brain saw letters altered somehow. It seemed she saw pictures, whole words, phrases, or images instead of the individual fragments, the letters. I was determined to work with her as much as I could to help her overcome this challenge. She had the same teacher, Madame Pothier, for Grades 2, 3, and 4 because of split classes and by our design. This teacher took a special interest in Lisa and spent much time doing extra work and created alternate programs that involved phonetics, pictures, and experiential worksheets that she designed just higher than Lisa's level of reading. She saw Lisa's strengths, believed in her, and was determined to help her overcome this language difficulty.

Through parent-teacher meetings during Lisa's first four years at school, we all agreed Lisa would do better if she remained in Madame Pothier's class, because each year a new teacher would have to learn how to work with Lisa and begin the learning process and relationship at point zero. A continuum of teaching methods was used, and Lisa was comfortable and trusting of Madame Pothier. She progressed slowly but steadily. I spent time with her in the evenings doing word flash cards, letter games, and practicing the activities her teacher sent home for us. The school, her teachers, and I cooperated together in a concentrated effort. We all contributed to her progress and eventual success.

We were unsure of what workings went on in Lisa's brain, but we were trying everything we could to reroute the pathways to discover a way for Lisa to learn to read. Lisa was focused and determined and worked very hard. She never whined or complained or even seemed discouraged. She was eager to learn and motivated by her desire to learn to read.

By the end of Grade 4, Lisa had overcome her struggle and began to read fluently. We didn't understand why, and to this day we don't really know what exactly happened. No one event in particular seemed to precede her "getting it." It was one of those things that I just had to accept and be grateful for. I think it was an accumulation of the many things we tried, time, maturity, and persistence. Lisa explains that one day she looked at the word "the" and spoke it out loud. The word, meaning, and letters somehow came together and suddenly made sense to her. She appeared to see words as pictures rather than individual letters. Finally these pictures made sense and connection in her brain. Something turned the light bulb on in her head! It was a great breakthrough for her. We were all delighted and relieved.

From that day on she began understanding and putting the letter puzzles and pictures together smoothly. She was able to compensate for her alternate learning style by creating alternative pathways in her brain. With time and persistence and using alternative methods, Lisa retrained her brain. One result of this reading challenge was that she developed excellent study habits at an early age. She learned how to work hard in her schooling and saw the rewards for those efforts. I found she struggled with self-worth some of this time, but she was consistently reminded of the fact that she was smart because of her ability and results in other subjects in school. For the most part, her self-worth and confidence were left intact. I worked hard to help her keep a positive self-image through this process by encouraging her and never belittling or criticizing her reading. She was smart. I knew this and we told her often. I believed in her and that together we could overcome this difficulty with reading, which she did. In hindsight, all our efforts were well worth the time, energy, frustration, and worry. The important thing was that she could read. Poor reading would not be a barrier to her learning and advancement in whatever she chose to pursue academically.

When the boys began school, they adjusted more quickly. Maybe I was more relaxed and a little more experienced as a parent, or maybe the boys were different people. Also, we all learned from Lisa's experience. They saw Lisa come and go to school unscathed, and going to school became a normal activity. Whatever the reason, I was happy that the boys' transition to school was much smoother and less traumatic.

John struggled as well with reading and language arts, possibly for different reasons. He too was great with numbers and could figure out how things worked if he could see and feel them. He was a hands-on learner. If he was seriously interested in something, he was able to fully concentrate on it. I learned how to funnel his energy into organized physical activities and sports that kept him happy and used up some of his bountiful, endless energy. I learned that focusing his energies kept him mostly out of trouble.

The most challenging time for me handling John's excessive energy was from the ages of one to five. This was a time when I was learning about how he ticked, his personality, and what motivated him. They were the years before he got involved heavily in organized sports. When he was three years old, we travelled through the United States on a holiday. We had Grandpa Dockman with us. We were somewhere in the hills of the mid-western states and had stopped at a lookout sight to have a picnic and enjoy the view of a deep and beautiful valley. There was a set of wooden stairs heading down to a river. Of course, John wanted to check it out. Remember, he was only three years old. So Grandpa and John began the journey down the stairs, which was an adventure for both of them, since Grandpa was elderly, deaf, and mostly blind from macular degeneration. From the top of the stairs we couldn't see the full extent of the pathway or the length of the stair setup. They were gone for some time, and when they appeared in our sights again, they were counting the stairs from the bottom up. John was still walking on his own two little legs, and Grandpa had counted over three hundred on the way up. John was persistent, determined, and had incredible endurance, even at that young age.

If I was busy cooking dinner or trying to help Lisa with her homework and John was getting antsy, he'd need to do something physical, so I'd send him off on a mission. I learned that if I challenged John physically, he would react positively and do what I suggested with gusto. So I would suggest things like he run around the outside of our house five times, and I would time him to see how fast he was and how long it would take him compared to last time. If I sent him to the basement to fetch something out of the deep freeze for me I'd time him to see how long this task took him. He needed some time and attention from me, and that acknowledgement combined with some running did the trick. The physical activity and focus on a task kept him happy. I'd give him a little attention and encouragement and continue my task. The timing part kept him motivated, excited to be fast, and usually out of mischief.

John, Dave, and Lisa were in a week-long hockey school in Canmore, Alberta, one summer when they were around eight to ten years old. I recall going to the hockey rink at 5 p.m. to pick them up after a day of skating, hockey, and physical training, which had started at 6 a.m. John was not exhausted by the full day of exercise but was hyper and energized by the physical exertions. He wanted to show me some off the ice activities, so he proceeded to run up and down the cement stairs of the arena, I'd say around fourteen to sixteen stairs. John ran up and down, did ten pushups at the bottom, and then ran up and down again and repeated this half a dozen times. He was like the energizer bunny! He just kept on going and going and going! Unbelievable! I was getting tired simply watching him. He had amazing stamina and energy. I discovered that when John played sports, his hyperactivity was focused. He was happy; he used his energies to learn the skills of the various sports and totally enjoyed himself. His energy was focused and used creatively instead of destructively.

By the time John began school, he was able to focus and do well in his learning as long as he had ample physical activities dispersed throughout his days. John played hockey in the winter and soccer in the summer, as well as participating in gym activities at school. Dave was a totally different personality than Lisa or John, a fact that often startled and shocked me. I somehow thought that two boys with the same parents and from the same family would be more similar. Not true. Their innate personalities were actually very different yet complementary.

When Dave started school, he made friends easily and did well in his learning. He didn't have the same difficulty with learning to read as his siblings had. If he did, he overcame those difficulties with Lisa and John's help. Being a third child, he had a calm and reflective personality and enjoyed the social aspects of school immensely. The peacekeeping qualities he showed for his siblings were equally demonstrated for his peers. Dave was loyal and protective, even showing signs of conflict resolution during his school years. He was of solid stature with large, muscular shoulders he could have used for intimidation but did not. He used words and logic.

Dave was involved in sports, such as hockey and soccer, and creative activities like cooking, art, and building things. He had a keen interest in math and science. In kindergarten, David made a friend for life, Eddy. They are best friends to this day. I was relieved to not have to worry about Dave academically or socially.

Then there was Rachel! Her position as fourth and youngest child was somewhat of a challenge for her from day one, partly because of her personality. She was strong, demanding, tenacious, and naive, which made for an interesting and challenging mixture. She had a need to understand situations, and fairness was of optimal importance to her. If Lisa could do something, why couldn't she? The age difference of almost five years was irrelevant to Rachel. I would often take the time during her toddler years to explain the "whys" for Rachel to help her understand the reasoning behind what was happening. She was very literal and took words as they were said, often missing inferences or humour in statements.

When I was busy and didn't have time to explain situations to her, like in the grocery store, she'd often have a temper tantrum. You know the type of crazy theatrics you see in the movies. She'd jump up and down, yell, scream, fall to the floor, and kick her feet and flail her arms. She was totally out of control and completely unmanageable in that state. I realized that when she got herself into such a tizzy, there was no point in trying any type of discussion or discipline. Logic fell short in the face of such intense emotions. She was emotionally distraught and unable to see or understand consequences. I'd walk ten feet or so away and watch with interest, commenting on what an unruly child she was and saying that some mother should so something about her. I was able to distance myself from her antics most times and keep calm and let her express and release her frustrations. Then I'd walk up to her if she was done and finish shopping. If she wasn't stopping, I'd pick her up without a word and carry her to the car, put her in, and take her home. There was no reasoning with her until after she calmed down.

Rachel's tantrums had become rarer by the time she went to school, but occasionally she became indignant when she felt unequally treated. Several times in her kindergarten year, Rachel took offence to the words or actions of her sibling and sat down on the sidewalk on the way to school and refused to move. I believe that for Rachel, her learning was challenging not because of intellect or ability, but because of her emotions and her deep need to understand her surroundings and how things worked before she could move on.

There was seriousness about her, an air of wisdom beyond her age. Some would say she was an old soul. I think she is. She approaches her life here as a quest, a journey to understand human emotions and interactions. She was a big-picture seeker from a very young age. She is loyal and dedicated to family to the maximum and loves her family members deeply and fiercely. I was challenged regularly with her questions and behaviour, and I would ask myself, *how important is this in the large scheme of things? Will this problem matter five years from now?* If the answer was no, then I'd drop it and let the situation go. In other words, I carefully chose my battles with Rachel, because even at three years old she was a formidable opponent, and I didn't want to get into a war with her if I could avoid it.

I wanted to become her ally and support, which I did by not confronting her. I used gentle persuasion and tons and tons of patience with her queries. As her Nana used to say, "Rachel will need to be lead, not driven." I discovered that leading her, engaging her in understanding and conversation was the best form of communication for her personality type. She always knew I was on her side and loved her dearly for the unique individual she was. My goal was for her to feel that she belonged in our family and was important and played a vital role, as each one of us did.

I made every effort to do this with all four of my children. They were all unique human beings with different qualities and attributes, which made none of them better or worse than the others, simply individuals. I wanted to celebrate these differences and help them see that there is value in being different, and we can learn from each other's individuality yet still be a closely knit, loving family unit.

Lisa's school picture—80s crimped hair!

John's school picture

Dave's school picture wearing his saxophone and music two-piece suit mom made

Rachel's school picture

I cried the first day Lisa went to school. My first child, all grown up! I cried on Rachel's first day of school, as my last child flew the coop. Each of those occasions was another transition in my life and theirs. The transition from being at home with Mom full-time to being at school five days a week brought significant physical and emotional changes to learn to cope with, understand, and grow from. My intention had been to be a stay-at- home mom until all four of my children were in school full-time—then and only then would I consider employment outside of the home. Well, life some-times throws us unexpected curve balls that alter our direction and change our plans. Oh, the best laid plans of mice and men can get scattered and blown away.

When Rachel was in kindergarten, I realized my marriage was in distress and would not last. My husband and I had what I saw as multiple irresolvable problems that we had discussed and tried to fix together, but were unable to agreeably solve. It came down to some value differences that I was unwilling to compromise on. I had suspected the eventual demise of our marriage just after Rachel was born, but I was unwilling to accept that our marriage was over, because I was in a vulnerable position as a stay-at-home mom with four children under five years old. I made the final decision to postpone the end the marriage and make every effort to resolve our relationship problems before all four of my children were in school full-time. I pushed those fears aside and focused on raising my children and trying as best I could to con-tinue to make a stable home environment for them. I spent much of my time supporting early childhood learning at home and working with the school programs. At the same time, I was trying to mend cracks in our marriage.

Over the next three to four years, it became clear to me that I would soon be a single parent and would need to work full-time to support myself and my children financially. I felt I had given my four children a stable first five years of life, and I was deathly afraid of failing as a single parent. The decision to separate from my husband was the most difficult decision of my life.

# CHAPTER 20

## *Separation and Divorce*

I chose to have my children, and when I did I made a serious commitment. I brought these four little human beings into this world; therefore, I felt responsible for them. If I was responsible for my children's arrival on this planet, then it was my duty to take care of them to the best of my ability. Because of the magnitude of this commitment, I didn't take my parental responsibilities lightly. I was determined to do my very best for them, no matter what circumstances life threw at me. I would provide a supportive and happy family environment for my children to ensure that they thrived.

When I got married, I believed that marriage was going to be "till death do us part" and "for better or for worse" and that we would stay together forever. That was it! No negotiating or faltering, the decision was final and set in stone. There could be no ifs, ands, or buts in the matter. Marriage was a permanent and done deal as far as I was concerned. Since I had taken my marriage vows so literally, it took me a very long time to admit that we had some major problems in our marriage and wouldn't be together forever. Our life together wasn't working, and we would be better if we were not together. I learned some valuable life lessons about never saying never, and about not thinking in absolutes or making hard-line decisions that can invariably be challenged.

The whole concept of separation and possibly ending our marriage went against my core beliefs and values. I was in an extremely difficult predicament and was living a life diametrically opposite to my belief system. It was an unhealthy situation emotionally and mentally, and because of this disconnect, I protected myself by being in denial about the breakdown of my marriage for a long time. In hindsight, I guess denial was my way of coping. How could this be happening to me? It couldn't really be real. Other people get divorced. . . I don't.

Making the decision to separate and admitting that I had failed in our marriage was emotionally devastating. No matter what Mike and I tried, we couldn't seem to fix our relationship. Our marriage became a poor example for our children, and I was in a constant state of unsettledness and sadness. I knew in my heart and my gut that separation was the right decision, but that didn't make the process any easier. I was simply more determined to figure out a way to ensure that the separation had as little negative effect on my children as humanly possible.

Mike and I made a deal that we would put the children's needs first and foremost in our discussions and not blame or bash each other in front of them. We would not be critical of the other parent or let the kids use one of us against the other to get what they wanted. We would share custody so that the children would continue to have us both in their lives regularly. Mike and I would live in the same city so that the children had easy access to both parents. Their schooling and friendships would not have to be disrupted. We opted for minimal change to the children's lives to reduce the trauma created by their parents getting a separation.

I borrowed enough money to purchase the same sewing business I'd bought and sold a few years prior. By operating a local business, I felt I could work hard to make enough money to support myself and the children and have the flexibility in hours to be available for school events, sports, and other activities. I could be home on school days for lunches with my kids.

Mike demanded to move to the basement of our home and said he would not move out into his own place until he and I had a signed a separation agreement. Hammering out the agreement took us about six months. It was awkward being in the same house after making the decision to separate, but it seemed necessary to have the time and each other available for meeting and making concrete plans. After approximately six months, we had come to a formal written agreement of how our lives would be organized and who would be responsible for which tasks. After those unusual six months, Mike moved to a townhouse three houses down from me. I stayed in the original family home.

I was concerned about us living so close to each other after the separation, as we would see each other come and go, and it would be difficult to have any privacy. If either of us chose to date, the close proximity of our living spaces could cause problems. But living so close to each other actually worked very well. Mike and I had to make appointments and schedule times to meet and talk if we had something to work out, as we were both very busy people. The set-up for the kids was very convenient, as they didn't have far to go from their dad's place to mine or vice versa. We had no driving time, and the kids had an easy few-minute walk between the two homes.

I had the kids from Sunday evening to Thursday afternoon, and Mike had them from Thursday evening to Sunday evening. This arrangement used both our strengths. My strength was in helping the children with school stuff, homework, projects, making lunches, and cooking meals. Mike's strength was in supporting their sports activities and taking them to weekend activities. This arrangement supported the children and their needs best.

For the first six months, the children came to my house often when they were on their dad's time to get clothes, have food, or just talk. This happened because the majority of their possessions and their comforts were at my house. And, of course, I was their mother! I was the main chef and baker in the household, so I always had an abundance of food. My refrigerator was consistently well-stocked with healthy foods, and I prepared homemade meals every day.

Mike and I tried to make it clear to the children that the separation was not their fault, and that they had done nothing wrong. We reiterated that the cause of our separation was an adult problem. We expressed this to them often. Still, it was hard for them to understand and not take on some blame for the separation. David seemed particularly concerned about what had happened to cause the end of our relationship. He was keenly aware of his environment and asked me on many occasions why we had split up. I told him that the problems were between his dad and me, and that he or the other children were not the cause. I explained that when he was older and I thought he could understand, we would tell him more details. I felt at Dave's young age it wasn't necessary to give him any details.

I had every weekend without my children. It was weird, really awful, at first, being a mom part-time after years of being with them twenty-four seven. It was horrid. I felt like I'd lost an arm, like a large part of me was missing. In fact, a part of me was missing—my children. There was a huge, empty hole left when my kids were gone for three and a half days each week. I knew I had to find something constructive to do with my time so that I wouldn't be so sad, lonely, or worried about them.

On the weekends when they were with their dad, I worked Fridays, Saturdays, and most Sundays during the daytime hours at my sewing shop, Catwork's Sewing Centre. I took that opportunity to catch up on sewing projects and work that needed to be completed, and to connect with my staff and customers. I enjoyed my work greatly. In the evenings, I'd rest, relax, or go dancing and drinking with girlfriends. I have to admit, I went a little wild at first, being single again. I was like a crazy teenager who was suddenly free to do whatever she liked. So when the kids were at Mike's, I had some fun, intense times of drinking, partying, and rock 'n' roll dancing extravaganzas. It was a strange thing to feel alone but responsible at the same time, but only half of the time. It took six to twelve months to adjust to being separated and parenting my children only half the time, and being single and alone the other half of the time. It felt like I had a split personality by consciously switching roles each week. I learned much about myself, including that I was flexible and resilient.

After a year of separation and settling somewhat into our new routines, I figured it was time for me to buy my own house—something smaller, more efficient, and with a finished basement for more flexibility. I bought a duplex halfway between my business and the tri-schools. It was in a central location within easy walking distance of all our needs. I was very fortunate to find a great place at a reasonable price. The house had five bedrooms on two levels, a one-and-a-half-car detached garage (funny, how do you fit half a car in it?), a wooden front deck, and small front yard with an enclosed backyard. I could afford the mortgage payments and had enough space for everyone. It was perfect!

The house had a suite in the basement with its own kitchen and bathroom. Mary Beth moved into the basement suite, the girls' and my bedrooms were upstairs, and the boys' bedrooms were downstairs. The arrangement worked amazingly well. Beth had her space to cook and eat downstairs and have her privacy, and we could all get together upstairs for family meals some evenings and on Sundays. Beth and I were always close by to support each other. I loved the navy-blue kitchen cupboards, the island for cooking, and the open-concept living, dining, and kitchen area. When I was preparing meals in the kitchen, I didn't have to be separated from the activities going on in the living room and dining room. Great for family meal preparation, eating together, and sharing close family times!

The kids were between the ages of five and ten, so they were all out of diapers and into schoolwork and sports activities. It was a very busy time. All four kids participated in hockey and some combination of swimming lessons and/or soccer, gymnastics, ballet, or tap dancing. I had full days of sewing, customer care, and business work to do at my shop. When I came home, I had kids to care for, homework, and housework—and I tried to have some fun time with them. We created healthy meals from scratch and tried to eat together most nights. I drove them to their sports and got homework started in between. If there were sewing jobs for the next day that were unfinished, I'd go back to work for a couple of hours late in the evening after the kids went to bed, or take the work home and complete the next day's jobs. I had Mary Beth at home to keep an eye on the children when I needed to go to the shop to work late at night.

We plodded on in this fashion for almost two years, with the kids coming to my place Sunday to Thursday and then going to Mike's from Thursday evening to Sunday dinner. I was nicely into a routine of this schedule when Mike expressed his dislike of our separation agreement and child-sharing arrangement, particularly because he had no weekends off. He felt it was unfair that I had all the weekends to myself. That was hilarious! I worked like a maniac on weekends to make up for the work that was neglected the first half of the week. Sure, I went out some weekend evenings, occasionally, if I wasn't too exhausted. Sometimes I simply went home after work on weekends and fell into bed and slept for twelve to fourteen hours to try to catch up on rest and recuperate from my nonstop life. I was able to have a small bit of a social life—I will emphasize the *bit* because I was struggling to make financial ends meet and still be available for my children's needs and extracurricular activities, homework. . . you know the drill.

When you have children, there never seems to be enough time for all that is needed to be done. Down time for, say, reading a book for pleasure? Well, that just didn't happen. I remember spending whole weekends cleaning, doing dishes, trying to catch up on laundry, and then collapsing into a dead sleep. Of course, there were times I needed to take sewing work home so that I could hang out with the kids and stitch some hems or draft a pattern. Killing two birds with one stone, as they say! What a terrible thought! Or the times in the evenings after the kids went to bed that I went back to my shop in the mall and sewed until the wee hours of the morning.

So because of Mike's need to have some weekends off, and our inability to come to a compromise, I gave in and we switched our deal to having the children on alternating weeks. That way, Mike had every second weekend off, and I took them to weekend sports, which I loved to do, but it cut into my business and busiest work time—the weekends. He had to take care of weekday school stuff and make meals and some lunches. I still kept my Tuesday and Friday hot lunches at home every week, so all four kids and usually their friends came home for hot, homemade lunches two days a week. I decided to continue this so that I could see my kids and check in with them when they were on their dad's time. This also ensured they got some healthy food when they were away from my home.

The only constant is change, and my life was changing constantly. At times the changes exhausted me. As the children grew and came into new developmental stages, I tried to keep abreast of the newest research in psychology and child and adolescent growth. I kept my mind open to their changing needs, new awareness, and questions. I also researched how I could support their growth in healthy ways.

It was a huge challenge to keep the broader picture in mind when the activities kept us moving and busy 99% of the time. I had to focus on the now and try not to worry about what wasn't being done. Sunday dinners were our weekly connect time. Conversations, attitudes, and body language at family dinners were how I kept a finger on the pulse of each child's successes and challenges, attitudes and behaviours. I would watch and listen to the tone, words, and body language and either open the discussion for all to give their input or, if the situation was delicate, I would approach them individually after dinner. I knew problems needed to be dealt with immediately to prevent a snowballing effect that could create a larger problem or even a disaster later. I didn't like to dwell on the negative or problems in life, but I believed in addressing them as they arose. I looked for any advancements and/or positive growth in each child and gave them positive recognition generously for any steps forward. We all like to be praised and acknowledged for our efforts and growth. I wanted my children to know I appreciated them and was proud of who they were.

Through the separation years of my marriage, I somehow found the strength and courage to be a single parent of four children. I drew on my many family resources for support financially, emotionally, spiritually, and physically. There were times I couldn't have made it through a situation without help. I had to ask for help to get kids to their sports or to a doctor's appointment. Other times, like when my furnace went on the blink and I needed a new one, my family gave me money to pay for it. Mary Beth helped me immensely by being there and being willing to look after the kids if I needed to go to work, get groceries alone, or go to a medical appointment. Being a single parent was a major challenge that I could not have succeeded at without much help and encouragement. I was and am extremely grateful for my family's support and encouragement, which got me through challenging times. Of course, there were many great times as well, which we celebrated together, but I could not have survived and overcome the difficult time to the extend I did without my family's constant help and encouragement.

Decorating Aunt Beth for New Year's! She's such a good sport

Dave giving hugs to the Christmas reindeer

# CHAPTER 21

## *Middle School and Early Adolescence*

The school system in Airdrie, Alberta, was divided into three segments: kindergarten to Grade 4, Grades 5 to 8, and Grades 9 to 12. As my children began moving into middle school, which happened from the ages of ten to thirteen, the pre-teen and beginning puberty years, their minds and bodies grew. My challenge as a mother was to grow with them and try to understand and support the changes going on in their lives. Keeping a finger on the pulse of the multitude of emotions and physical changes was overwhelming at times. Often I noticed particular changes in each child and responded appropriately; at other times, a friend or a family member would bring the change to my attention, and sometimes I missed it altogether until after the fact. I did my best to be present in their lives and aware of their growing and changing bodies, minds, and emotions.

The physical work of being a mother of young children was demanding. I was constantly moving to care for, feed, and manage the activities of my four children. At those young ages, physical safety was paramount. I had to watch out for them at all times and often predict problems before they arose in order to prepare for and prevent accidents. Although teaching emotional intelligence was important in those early development years, I believe the physical often became my first priority because of my children's inability to keep themselves safe. At that point, they were too young to know the dangers around them; I had to be their protector.

As they grew, I taught them the rules of our world and how to observe and be aware of their environment so that they could protect themselves and avoid dangerous situations. A transition happened from focusing on my children's physical needs and demands to spending more of my time on their emotional needs. As my children became more aware and learned further about their environment and relationships, my support shifted. Therefore, the demand on my time during middle childhood changed from non-stop physical needs to understanding, teaching about, and supporting their emotional needs.

At the same time as this was happening, they became more involved in school projects, reading, and learning about the world and its workings. Their intellectual needs grew alongside their emotional ones. It was fascinating to me how much they learned and the intensity of their curiosity. They were seekers of understanding of how their lives and the world worked. Child development is a complex mixture of physical, emotional, and intellectual growth. Sometimes the physical would outgrow the emotional or intellectual, or vice versa. The challenge was to try to balance them all and encourage the growth in all areas simultaneously.

Their physical growth at this same time, call it middle childhood, changed from basic muscular coordination to developing particular large muscular skills, like riding a bicycle, swimming strokes, running, and kicking a soccer ball. At the same time, they were continuing to develop fine motor skills like using a pencil and a paintbrush, and typing on a computer keyboard. Video games became a part of their leisure time, which developed excellent hand-eye coordination. As their bodies learned and absorbed all these skills in middle childhood from the practice of repetition, they became more functional in daily living skills and more knowledgeable about their world. They also developed the beginnings of a foundation of emotional intelligence.

My children's middle childhood was an interesting time of learning for me as I evolved my mothering skills in parallel with my four children's growth and development. There was a constant barrage of questions about anything and everything, questions ranging from every topic one can imagine. Many subjects I had never imagined and some I had no clue as to possible answers, such as: Why is someone mean to me? What is gay? Where do babies come from? Why does war happen? Will we blow up the world? Can we save the environment? How long do I have to go to school? Is there a God? Do other beings live in the universe? How long will I live? How long will you live, Mom? And on and on and on. The curiosity of children is endless. I did my best to give factual, correct, objective answers, and if I didn't know the answer, we would research and/or ask the questions of others who had the required knowledge. Many times one question led to others, and informative discussions ensued. Other times a simple, few-word answer would suffice. Depending on the age of the child asking, their maturity level, and how much I felt they needed to know appropriate to their age, it was a judgment call. I had to decide how much to disclose, but usually I was frank and to the point.

For example, when John was twelve or thirteen, he was curious about sex and how it worked. Lisa was embarrassed by some of his questions and told him he shouldn't be asking such things! I preferred to give him informative books and/or discuss the questions directly. One time he asked me, "How many times, Mom, have you had sex in your life?" What the hell? How do I answer that question? Should I even consider answering it? Obviously, I stalled. I replied that I would have to think about it and give him an answer the next day.

The next day John said that he'd been thinking about the question and had changed it to, "Have you had sex more or less than ten times in your life?"

I breathed a sigh of relief and said, "More than ten times." John was satisfied and went off on his way to whatever he was doing. The delay saved my ass and gave him an adequate answer, as well as giving him a chance to clarify his thoughts to specify what he wanted to learn.

Another situation and inquiry came from a conversation with Rachel about her vocabulary. Rachel's position as youngest child often gave her information that was beyond her years as far as understanding and emotional or mental maturity, but if siblings were talking about something, she took it all in. Well, one day when she was about five or six years old, I overheard her call someone a "blow job." I stopped in my tracks and listened. It was obvious she had no clue what this meant. When I talked with her alone and asked her about it, she confessed that she didn't know. I thought about what I should say. Knowing Rachel, I explained it in simpler terms because of her age. She looked at me with shock and indignation! I could see her little mind trying to understand and digest the information. After a moment, she looked at me with such wisdom and asked, "Why would you tell me this?"

Amazing, who would have thought. I looked at her knowingly. Of course that would be her reaction. She knew this information was beyond her age. I explained, "If I didn't tell you the truth, you might have continued to use the words in public." She nodded her agreement. She never used the term again.

I learned a great deal about myself during those years of my children's inquisitions, when they were trying to figure out how the world worked. Their questions were challenging, and I needed to take a good look at my beliefs and examine their origins. I did not wish to pass on my biases or mis-information to them. I was trying to be responsible and conscious about the answers I gave. I also asked them about their interpretations and what they believed the answer was for each particular question, and we'd explore the alternatives together. I was hopefully instilling in them the value of flexibility in thinking, that there are often no clear black and white, right and wrong answers. We all have our own perceptions based on our experiences in life. I felt open-mindedness was important, and I attempted to mentor them in it and practice the art of lateral thinking, not simply linear thought with one-answer solutions. I felt it was important for them to learn that differences of opinions were valid and that we could learn from other people's differing ideas and thoughts without having to agree with them.

Thankfully, Lisa progressed well enough in her reading and language arts by Grade 4 that she was able to handle the change from one school environ-ment and teacher to another—middle school. Her reading difficulties had been resolved and as she progressed into middle school, she had gained an academic confidence and strong work habits that allowed her to excel in her studies.

There's a saying that goes, "What doesn't kill you makes you stronger." Well, Lisa ploughed through her struggles with reading and broadened her learning style and scope. Basically, she taught herself how she learned and then fine-tuned her specific learning style. This is a major skill to possess. At the tender age of nine, she had already learned that she was persistent, consistent, and resilient in her pursuit of learning. As a result of experienc-ing the difficulty, struggling through it, and consequently overcoming it, she developed compassion and empathy for others. She felt for them and knew what they were experiencing. What a gift for Lisa.

When her siblings were struggling to learn a concept, Lisa was able to mentor them in creative and supportive ways. This was particularly impor-tant, because all four of my children were in the French immersion program. They had surpassed me in French language capabilities, so Lisa's French lan-guage skills became a useful resource for her siblings as they came up through their school years. Throughout my children's school years, including university, Lisa aided her siblings and friends with concept or process challenges to help them in understanding and practical use of learning theories. I am happy to say she uses this skill to this day in her adult job at the university and in her relationships.

I chose to have four children at a time in history when the average family was having 1.6 kids. I grew up with four siblings and was well aware of the challenges of sibling relationships, but I also know well the incredible support and strength I have gained from those relationships. My goal, my quest, my desire was to instill in my children that passion for family. I wanted them to have close and secure relationships with their three siblings that would carry them through all of life's ups and downs. I expressed my feelings about my family, and my children observed how my parents and siblings helped us and how we kept in contact with each other. Also, my children were aware of the times I helped my siblings and parents. It was a give and take relationship built on trust and willingness to help each other.

Children fight with each other, that is a fact. They fight about physical stuff like toys, or emotional and mental stuff like "I'm right and you're wrong." My kids competed for my attention and for their place to fit into our family. At times, my own siblings fought, and at times my kids yelled at each other, threw things, bit, scratched, or hit each other. This behaviour drove me absolutely batty. I couldn't stand it and would not allow physical abuse. Dealing with conflict was a huge challenge for me, because I abhor conflict. What was I to do? I couldn't ignore it when they were fighting verbally, and I wouldn't allow them to fight physically. I was in a conundrum. I had to face my fears of conflict, talk, read, and learn how to address and diffuse it. I then had to teach skills to express and deal with anger issues. That was a massive learning challenge for me.

The disagreements and fights were often between Lisa and John. They fought over what seemed to be silly things. I think the bottom line was that they each sought power and control in the family. Lisa, being the eldest girl, strove for intellectual supremacy. John, the eldest male, strove for physical superiority. Really? I know, those relationships were intense. I often became a referee between them. I observed the before and after when I could and knew that neither was to blame, so I didn't take sides. They were trying to learn and grow as best they could. I took a neutral ground and mediated their disagreement. I stopped any physical confrontation and discussed with each person separately and then together after the emotions had calmed down.

I was frustrated with the fighting between them and afraid they would hurt each other. I remember one particularly loud and intense fight. I stood between them, arms stretched out, with my palms flat out and facing each of them, attempting to stop the altercation. I was frustrated! I told them that if they couldn't resolve their differences, how could we resolve the problems of the world? Their fight could start World War III! They stopped and stared at me with dropped jaws, like I'd lost my mind. What the hell was I talking about? World War III? They were simply having a brotherly/sisterly squabble. What did that have to do with World War III? The yelling threats they were issuing to each other were anything but brotherly or sisterly behaviour.

We sat down and I proceeded to explain my thoughts. I said that individual people start fights and they can resolve fights. If we don't learn to discuss our differences without letting them escalate into emotional shots and threats of actual physical attacks, how can we expect to become leaders and contribute to the world as responsible people who can discuss differences and diffuse aggravated situations? They looked at me, tipping their heads to the side, not really understanding what I was trying to tell them, but obviously in thought about my comparison.

Many more discussions ensued about how one person could or couldn't change anything, let alone the world. Can one person make a difference? Do we need to learn to express ourselves effectively without trying to overpower people? We had a discussion about using fear and force tactics versus eliciting discussion and inducing cooperation. Pretty serious topics for young people, for anyone, but I felt they could handle the topic, and these discussions helped them to think about what they felt and about their values. They learned how to be more rationally effective, to debate, and use compassion in family relationships over time. This set the communication foundation for their future relations with friends, teachers, and co-workers, and it helped to develop their morals and values.

My children's middle school years became a time of discovery about themselves and clarification of their beliefs. They developed friendships and learned how to be a friend. They were active in school and sports activities as well as family gatherings, outings, travel, and meals. An extremely busy time for me as a mother, but a rewarding one because they were developing relational tools and we had conversations regularly about life: What would happen if? What do I do if? I learned from my kids to be more open- minded that there was more than one way to tackle a problem or view a situation. They wanted to explore alternative solutions, and we did.

I learned there was wisdom in their youth and enthusiasm. Sometimes their ideas didn't work, but we would learn from trying and then try a different tactic. But sometimes their alternate ideas worked better than mine, and I had to sit back and say, "Wow, that's a great idea! Good for you." It wasn't easy; we all had different and often strong opinions about strategy and how to approach things. Consensus was strived for and sometimes achieved, but other times compromise and fairness had to prevail. I wanted them to respect each other's differences and even admire their different qualities as something worth striving for in themselves. I complemented strengths and gently helped them to become aware of their weaknesses and how to accept and improve them.

It was lovely to see their relationships develop and their love and care for each other grow. As a mother, at times I felt like I was spinning my wheels, and my hard work and advice was falling on infertile ground—discouraging times when I questioned my strength and ability to guide them successfully. Mostly times when I was dog-tired, worn out from working so hard at work, mothering, and running a household. I remember praying for a full night's restful sleep. Ah, that would have been heaven! Then I'd remember my mother's advice: "I'll sleep when I'm dead, now I'm going to live!" (Hey, look at that, me listening to my mother's teachings. Whoop, maybe some of what I taught my kids would stick in their minds for them to use later. There was hope!) ***108 Mother needs a nap! Single parenting.

So I pulled up my bootstraps and attacked the next project or activity with my fullest attention and enthusiasm. Big or small activity, it didn't matter, I treated it as if it was the most important thing in the world, as it was in that moment. If it was making Kraft Dinner and hot dogs for lunch, then it would be the best KD and HD we ever had. I gathered my energy and strength and used my creativity to make everyday tasks fun and memorable. I had to let go of my ideas of being the perfect mother, which I was not, and that I had to have the cleanest, tidiest, perfect home, which I didn't have. I admitted when I was wrong and asked for help.

My kids were reaching the teenage years. I'd heard so much about the rebellion and disrespect of teenagers, how different they would be to deal with, and how they would lose respect for me. I saw the teenage years like the terrific twos, a time of experimentation and discovery of who they were as humans. A time to question laws, rules, boundaries, and authority. I remembered my teenage years clearly. I'd pushed the limits of thoughts and actions with my parents and teachers in order to express myself, discover my separateness, and develop my independence. I figured it would be a challenging time as a mother, and I had prepared myself for the worst. My aim was to support and encourage my children through those possibly impossible and unpredictable teenage years.

Teen siblings relaxing in Nana's hot tub

Christmas with the sibs

Oh joy! Group hug with Cathy and her four teenagers

Lisa and John during Christmas stocking openings,
showing their love and affection for each other

Cozying up to a winter fire at Nana's with Auntie Christine

# CHAPTER 22

## *Motherhood and My Social Life*

What social life? Ha, very funny, you've got to be kidding! I embraced motherhood with a passion that left little room for parallel pursuits. Although I worked at my business with commitment and intensity, it was a means to an end, and the end was earning the funds to support my family. I enjoyed being a businesswoman and I loved to sew, but this was a vehicle that allowed me to become the kind of mother I felt my kids deserved and I desired to become. I threw myself into motherhood with a passion that pushed me to be all I could each day, and to be with my children and experience each moment to the maximum. Living that way was highly fulfilling but also extremely exhausting. The majority of my social life was related to my children's activities. I had acquaintances who were parents of my kids' friends, and girlfriends that had kids with whom we could do activities together as families. My social life involved my kids and family almost exclusively. I rarely took the time for other pursuits.

Back in Ontario, our neighbourhood was an older, established one with few small children. Most of our neighbours were retired. I knew only one lady who was a stay-at- home mom like me, so we visited each other and did some park outings together. I was very busy with the care of my three small children, so my social life was almost nil. My adult interactions were mainly with family at holidays, birthdays, and the odd visit in between.

Between raising my four children and operating and managing a small business, my days were full. When I was married and when I was a single parent, I found little time for romance, relationships, or fun unless it had to do with my children's activities. I belonged to a babysitting service and had some camaraderie with those mothers, but again it was child-related. I realized that this was not the way to live a balanced life, but that's how I chose to live through my motherhood years.

My personal life as far as dating when I became a single parent was sparse. There were a few men along the way, but I refused to date on the week I had my children living with me full-time. I only went to social activities when Mike had the children.

An incident that happened when I was transitioning from being married to being separated stands out clearly in my mind. Mike was living in the basement of our house, and I was working at my shop and had gone in early to catch up on some sewing projects. It was about 8 a.m. The mall was empty except for a few staff members in other businesses. I was working away with my glass sliding door partially opened, standing at my glass counter and marking and measuring some garments for alterations. A man came up to the counter and asked me a question. I was concentrating on my work and gave him little attention and replied with a simple, courteous answer.

When I looked up at him, I felt a physical shock to my system. Our eyes locked, my green to his blue, and time was temporarily suspended as we stared into each other's eyes. Everything stopped except for my pounding heart. A knowing familiarity touched and consumed my being. It's hard to explain, my knowing a stranger's soul. At a glance I had the memory and feeling of a pull from a long and connected history. It seemed fate had brought us together again. Incredible how I sensed all that in a few seconds of eye contact and presence. I instinctively knew him. The feelings and experience caught me unawares. It had been a long, many years since I had seriously looked at another man.

I felt a wave of heat flash through my body, a flush of my cheeks, and a vibration in my core that rocked me. The sensations were so foreign to me that I quite simply ignored them and proceeded to speak calmly and in a professional manner. When he left, I had to sit down to relieve myself from wobbly legs and shaky knees. What the hell just happened? I tried logically to comprehend the sensations spinning throughout my body like an aftershock. There was a tremendous attraction between us, but that alone minimized the experience. The connection was so much more. I had never seen or met him before, yet I felt I had known him always. I was blasted with his familiarity. I sat there hidden on the bench in my fitting room, confused, overtaken by emotions and sensation. I felt like a bumbling idiot who stumbled over her words and blushed like a young schoolgirl. The worst part was that in that moment I met him, I was completely out of touch with the sensations happening in my body, or perhaps afraid of them, and I ignored the messages they were trying to send to me.

When the cloud lifted in my brain a little, I felt I had missed an incredible opportunity. I jumped up and ran outside and tried to find him. I looked outside the entranceway of the mall, and inside the mall itself. He was nowhere to be found. Was he real? Had I imagined this? Wow, it took me most of the morning to calm down and try to make sense of that early morning's happenings. At first I panicked because I couldn't find him. Then calmness came over me, a knowing. I had the sense that I would see him again, and when I did, I would act on my feelings and talk further about meeting again.

A few days went by with no further sign of him. I was constantly aware and looking for him to appear, like he was ethereal. On the following Friday evening, I went out to the Old Hotel in downtown Airdrie after work at 9 p.m. It was a huge old country bar that had wooden beam structures and floors. It was decorated in a western, rustic, cowboy style with pool tables and a dance floor. Bands of all sorts played on the weekends to jam-packed crowds that ranged in age from eighteen to sixty. It was a rockin' place back then, such fun.

I love to dance and went to the Old Hotel when live rock or country bands were performing. I walked in this particular Friday evening, glanced around the bar, and saw him sitting at the bar. Instantly I got excited and nervous. What if he didn't feel the same connection? I wasn't going to miss the opportunity, so I assertively walked over to him. When he saw me, his face broke into an enthusiastic smile, showing he felt it too.

The feelings I began having as we talked and made plans had long been buried. I felt alive, feminine, attractive, and desirable. I had forgotten the elation of that feeling and how energized it made me feel. The rush of feelings made me re-evaluate my life and my relationship with Mike. What was I doing? The next day I contacted Mike and said he needed to move out so we could both get on with our lives. I didn't feel right having another relationship while my ex-husband was still living in my house, even though he was living in the basement. For me to move on I needed the freedom of Mike being in his own place and me having my space. The relationship with that blond angel was intense and full of emotion and energy. I called him my angel because he was the catalyst that pushed me to make the decision to express and assert my needs to Mike.

I soon found out that the hunky angel was not long-term relationship material, which I was absolutely fine with accepting. We had great fun dancing, taking country drives, and having many meaningful conversations. We went to Banff in his red convertible on a beautiful summer's day. We had the radio blaring, our hair blowing in the wind, and not a care in the world. I remember the song "Life is a Highway, I want to ride it all night long" by Rascal Flatts, and us both singing at the top of our lungs and grooving to the tunes. He made me feel young and free. He was exactly what I needed at that point in my life. He was around for three glorious months, and then he simply disappeared. We both got what we needed and moved on. I still smile when I think of that blond-haired, blue-eyed, hunky angel who came and gave me such a gift with his presence.

As a result of that brief fling, I got the confirmation I needed that I was doing the right thing by separating from my husband. Our relationship no longer gave me any of those wonderful feelings I had during those three months with Mr. Blondie Angel. I felt validated in my decision. The example Mike and I were setting for our children was that of an unhealthy relationship, not a caring, compassionate, and loving couple, and I felt responsible for teaching them the wrong values and behaviours. That's why I'm grateful for my blond angel who came into my life and helped me to open my eyes to what was actually happening, and what could be again.

Moreover, I did something about it. I looked at our relationship in a new light, with fresh eyes, and I acted to resolve the ambiguities. I felt so much better about myself and my life when I was being authentic in my feelings and they matched the way I was living. When my thoughts and actions were congruent, I felt peace and balance in my life. My angel brought me to that point of understanding, and then he was gone. I was grateful for the important lesson he taught me about being in touch with my sensuality and being true to myself.

As my body went through the changes of being pregnant and nursing, my focus became maternal almost exclusively. As my body changed and the baby inside me grew, my health and the health of my baby dominated my being. I didn't feel sexy or interested in having intercourse. Loving intimacy and closeness would have been helpful, but somehow intercourse seemed to be an invasion of the oracle that held this precious being. Maybe subconsciously I was trying to protect the baby inside me. With the subsequent pregnancies, I felt the same way—not sensual.

After my first pregnancy, when I got pregnant so easily, having sex brought with it the worry of getting pregnant again so soon when I felt I wasn't ready physically, emotionally, or mentally. It's hard to enjoy sex when you're so fearful of the life-changing consequences. Nursing a baby apparently lowered the chances of getting pregnant, but I had no menstrual cycles while I was nursing, so I had no idea when I was ovulating. Each time I slowed down my nursing schedule, I got pregnant again. So after my third child was born, and even more so after the fourth, I was terrified to have sex at all for fear of getting pregnant again.

I didn't date for some time after that eye-opening experience with my angel. I didn't feel the need. Approximately six months later, I took a part time job at a fabric store where I met a new girlfriend. She was in a similar situation as a single parent—a bit lost and trying to find her power again. We became fast friends and spent the next six months partying hard on the days we didn't have our children. We regularly frequented the Old Hotel, whether it was day or night, whenever we were both off work. It was a wild kind of revisiting of my teenage hood in my forties.

We were fearless together and challenged each other to take risks and meet and date men. We danced all night and drank too much alcohol. She had an unreal ability to handle her alcohol. We were bold and crass and had tons of laughs together. We partied with businessmen, cowboys, bikers, and young dudes. She had a great sense of humour, and we lived on the edge. One time we drank and partied all night, and then we went to work intoxicated. Not something I'm proud of. . . we just did it. We were intense about our partying and men. It was a crazy, acting out time. I barely got my work done and was living those two separate lives again—one week being the mom and doing kids' stuff, and the next partying and being cougars. Fortunately, she decided to move to Vancouver, and our wild lifestyle came to an end. Again, there was a reason for our behaviour. We both needed the freedom to explore our sexuality and build our confidence in our ability to attract men. We needed to feel and exert our sexual and womanly power. We enjoyed this wild lifestyle every second week for about six months, and then it was done.

When she moved, I drove her U-haul truck for her to the west coast. She had the truck full of her belongings, and her children had already been sent ahead. She wasn't comfortable driving the massive truck, so we made a deal. I'd drive the U-Haul truck out, and she'd fly me back to Calgary. I thought it was an awesome plan. We sat in the cab of the truck and were excited about a road trip as our final hoopla together. Just outside of Banff, the engine started to smell like smoke, so we pulled off the side of the road to check it. The truck stalled and wouldn't start. We let it cool down for half an hour, it started, and we decided to drive into Banff to get the engine checked. The engine died when we came to a full stop at a service station. Bottom line, it would take two to four days to get parts and repair the engine and get back on the road again.

Awwh, tough luck, eh? Two women stranded in Banff for a long weekend. My girlfriend ranted and raved and got the company to put us up in a hotel for the weekend—not just any hotel, but the Banff Springs. Ooh la la! We were getting a holiday weekend on them. We relaxed, went to the spa, and enjoyed the hot tubs and sauna. We drank all the baby bottles of refreshments in our bar fridge in our room. We lived the high life for a couple days and felt like queens. We had a wonderful little interlude of quality and class. The truck got repaired, and three days later we proceeded on our trek to drive to Vancouver. That ended another phase of my life. After she left town, I resumed my normal lull of life with kids and business activities. Looking back, I see that phase as a frantic time of seeking, but the seeking turned out to be internal. Who was I and who did I want to become? The party girl was not it. I calmed down to a healthier lifestyle.

When Mike and I separated, I hadn't dated in fifteen years. I was a teenager when I met Mike. I was now unfamiliar with the current dating protocol. Also, a high percentage of men my age at the time, around forty years old, were married. I learned the hard way about finding out a man's marital status. I needed to ask several questions before dating someone, and that was no guarantee that they'd told me the truth. One question I asked regularly of a new potential man I was thinking of dating was, "Are you married?"

I asked this of one fellow and he said no, so we proceeded to date and see each other for several months. Several red flags began to appear, like we never went to his place, and he was secretive about where he spent much of his time. We ended up at his home for lunch one day, and I discovered he lived with a woman. Upon questioning him, I learned that he had been with his woman for many years, but he said they no longer had an intimate relationship. Maybe you've heard that line before. His admission stopped me in my tracks. I felt deceived. He didn't lie directly, but he did through his actions and omission of information. I was torn, because I'd become attached to this man and enjoyed his company. For all intents and purposes, he was married, common law. Although I should have stopped seeing him altogether, I did see him occasionally. On the day I found out, I decided to end the relationship. I had been the wife who was cheated on, so I didn't want to be the "other" woman having an affair with a married man. It went totally against my values.

I don't know if I was a magnet for married men. Maybe they were safer, because I didn't have to get so emotionally involved, but I seemed to attract them. Another fellow I met was very attractive. He was tall with dark hair, a lanky build, and was serious with a dark side. He was the typical type I was attracted to. We met at the local dance club and had lots of fun dancing. He didn't hide the fact that he was married, but of course he was unhappy in his marriage and felt obliged to stay because of his children. I thought it was such an unhappy state of society when marriage vows were taken so lightly. He felt guilty, but we did have a casual relationship that lasted about a year.

Sometime later, I met a fellow while sitting at the bar. After my friend moved to Vancouver, I occasionally went to the Old Hotel to sit and think, visit with friends, and have a drink. This man and I talked about life and relationships and shared our philosophies. He was smart, had an interesting life, and made me laugh. We hooked up a couple times. I found him very attractive physically and as a person. He had that wild side, a desire for adventure and perhaps chaos that I seemed to be comfortable with and attracted to.

In fact, within the first week of dating, we were at the Old Hotel one afternoon playing pool. The bar was empty except for three other young men playing pool at a table beside us. An altercation ensured, typical when macho-men and alcohol are involved. My guy friend and these three men got into a bar fight! I stood back in shock. Does this really happen? Is this happening now? I was not impressed. The three other guys had my friend on top of the pool table and were hitting him with their fists. Appalling! The bartender broke up the fight and kicked the other three men out of the bar. My friend and I sat and tried to calm down from the incident. It was like a movie happening in slow motion in front of me. Wow, an eye-opening experience for sure.

After a few weeks of seeing each other regularly, the subject of age came up. I assumed he was in his mid-thirties, and he thought I was also. Turned out he was twenty-three years old! I was forty-four at the time. We simply gaped at each other open-mouthed. We were both shocked with disbelief. There was such a connection between us, such a familiarity, and of course he looked older and I looked younger, but the reality of the situation was that I was twenty-one years older than him. We both found the age difference amusing and complimentary, and we mutually decided to be friends and not to date further. We were at very different places in our lives. He wanted children, and I was done with that. Another life lesson and experience that actually makes me smile upon recollection.

I have tried to analyze my behaviour based on my childhood relationships. What I have concluded is that basically I was looking for someone like my father on a subconscious level. I wasn't aware of my comparisons between men I dated and my father's character and behaviours and looks. Dad was an attractive man; when he was younger, he was movie-star striking, with dark hair, strong facial features, a nice smile, and that shy yet mysterious and mischievous look. I idolized him. My mother was beautiful as well with a similar look to Judy Garland in her youth.

My dad had a gentle personality, unassuming and compassionate. He was caring and giving to others and was a gentleman and a romantic. It was difficult to compare any man to him, because he was such a nice human being.

When I was looking for a partner in life and seeking a male relationship, my habits brought me to men similar to my father. I was attracted to men who were kind but who also had addiction and self-image problems, relationships that were familiar. I know from later learning and education that what is learned can be unlearned, but at that time in my life, I was unaware. My father going into treatment and admitting he had a problem started my journey of self discovery. For a long time, I denied the fact that my upbringing in an alcoholic household had affected me negatively. I saw so much of the good things my parents did to help me be strong and independent that I thought those issues I had with self-worth were unrelated, but they were directly related to how I learned to be as a child. After several years of Dad participating in addiction recovery and finding peace in his life, I began to accept that he was an alcoholic and that I could benefit from education and healing therapy.

My eldest sister, Cris, sent my younger sister, Mary Beth, the book *Adult Children of Alcoholics.*[27] Beth was in denial about the effects on her as well. So as the co-dependent people we were, Beth went to a group therapy session to help me, and I went to the session to help her. Kind of humorous in hindsight. In any case, we mutually supported each other in discovering how our upbringing had affected us and how we could change our thinking and our behaviours. The awareness I gained from those meetings was amazing. I saw the origins of my beliefs and was able to question some of them. Many were coping mechanisms for my childhood but were no longer useful in my life. I needed to learn some new ways of thinking and healthier ways of behaving. Maturity in my emotional life was my goal.

In hindsight, I needed to spread my wings and feel the freedom of dating again, even though it was for a short time. I got the wild bug out of me. I regressed for a time into some pretty wild, teenage-type behaviours. I believe my partying and dating craziness can be attributed to my search for my new identity at that moment in my life. After that short rebellious stage of somewhat careless behaviours, I felt revived and empowered to proceed with courage and self-confidence. I was able to be content with being a single parent and a business owner again.

When the men I dated expressed their opinions about my parenting style, or tried to alter my parenting, I became defensive about their interference. I was strong in my views about treating my children with respect and dignity and did not appreciate what I saw as negative input. I refused to be involved with someone who tried to change my focus, as my children came first in all my decisions. So having a man in my life became very low on my priority list.

I put thoughts of having a relationship in the back of my mind until well into my future, when supporting my children may not be my main task in life.

I have no regrets about the decision I made to remain single throughout my motherhood years. I guess I thought finding a new partner in life would not be as difficult as it was. I assumed I'd be married within a few years of my divorce. Not so. In fact, I've been mostly single, with the exception of a couple of live-in boyfriends that did not last long. I became quite comfortable and happy with being single and able to make my own choices and decisions about my life without conferring with a partner. I was free to travel, read, and spend as much time as I wished with my children. Times of loneliness and alone time were few because of how busy my life was as a mother. I think my life worked out as it should, because I am very proud and love who my children became as a result of my choices.

# CHAPTER 23

## *High School Years and Career Aspirations*

I remember hearing it said of teenagers that their brains are taken from them at the age of twelve and not returned until they reach eighteen years old. I thought, *How ridiculous!* Dealing with teenagers couldn't be as bad as people said it was. I thought they were obviously exaggerating. I managed successfully through the "terrible twos," which I preferred to call the "terrific twos." Sure, it was challenging, and my children tried to push the limits of their abilities and the rules in many ways, but I saw this as a natural learning progression, not an intentional behaviour trying cause trouble or to break the rules or a deliberate attempt to make me crazy.

Two-year-olds and teenagers are in a time of life filled with self-discovery and experimentation. In fact, I believe much of childhood is just that, discovering who we are and how we fit in our world. I believe if we simply do what society says without questioning or thinking carefully about our beliefs and actions, we fail to discover our individuality or new ways of doing and seeing. Discovery and innovation come from challenging typical thoughts and actions. Creativity, imagination, and invention would be squashed if we simply acted as we were told.

Throughout every stage of my kids' childhoods, I observed some unusual, sometimes risky, and often hilariously creative behaviours. Had I not had a sense of humour and the ability to move beyond linear thinking, I could have gone bonkers with some of my children's ideas and experimentations. My attitude toward allowing, accepting, and encouraging unusual or different behaviours and thinking nurtured lateral thought in my children and saved my sanity.

In hindsight, my four children's teenage hood was mild in comparison to many others I've heard about. I find myself wondering why this is so.

There are actually many factors I consider relevant, from genetic traits to environmental influences. I will never know for sure, but I'd say one of those influencing factors was our family dynamics and the foundation I laid in their early childhood, which nurtured an attachment to me. Other factors could include living in a small town, being educated in a French immersion program with smaller class sizes, their participation in sports, school clubs, and activities, consistent extended family connections and support, persistent sibling growth challenges as well as sibling camaraderie, and two parents constantly involved in hands-on parenting that continued extensively, even when we were separated and divorced. The list goes on. And just maybe "luck" had something to do with it. Lol.

There were numerous external environmental factors that reduced the risk of delinquent behaviour as teenagers. If one or more of those influences affected each child differently and prevented them from becoming involved in crime, drugs, or other troubles, I will never know. If I had to narrow down the influences to what I believe were most important, I would say two things: they knew they were loved, and we constantly communicated about anything and everything.

I verbalized my thoughts and feelings and showed the kids through my actions that they were my most important priorities. My work, friends, studies, and other activities were important but they were a means to an end. My kids were number one! This included providing food, clothing, and shelter and supporting them emotionally, physically and psychologically. I cared for and loved them deeply and said "I love you" often. We may not have had the beautiful, modern home with every gadget you could think of, but we had a loving family and a commitment to each other.

I attended all their school science fairs, parent-teacher interviews, plays, sports events, day outings, field trips, and camping trips. I even went as a chaperone on longer trips, like when David's band travelled to play at Disneyland in California or Lisa's art class went to Vancouver to see a Leonardo da Vinci exhibit. I was interested and involved in every aspect of their lives. I believe my close connection and involvement created a security that guided them through any turbulent growth and learning experiences or experimentation that happened as teenagers.

From the very beginning of my children's school years, from kindergarten to Grade 12, I walked with them to school on the first day. When they were in the early grades, I walked them every day to and from school. When Lisa began school, I would walk her while carting the others in a stroller or with them toddling along. Walking with them to school became a habit and a tradition we enjoyed.

When they grew older and could safely do the walk without me, they walked together. In their older years, I would only walk them on the first day. When it came time for Lisa to go to high school, she was terrified! She wanted me to walk with her, but she didn't want to look like a mommy's girl or a baby or a wimp. We compromised. John, Dave, Rach, and I walked Lisa to the edge of the field that led to the high school. She gave us all hugs, we wished her luck, and she ventured into the unknown—the big, scary high school where she didn't know everyone like she had for her first nine years of schooling. As it turned out, she entered the front door of the high school, stood there for a few minutes, didn't see anyone she knew, and almost left again to return home. Then she saw a familiar face, breathed a sigh of relief, and stepped into her adolescence.

High school for Lisa was a serious time of study. She was a model student and worked hard at learning. She was passionate about freedom of speech, equality, and protecting all creatures and the environment. Lisa had several very close friends who were supportive of each other through her childhood and teenage years. Meghan, Sarena, Alexis, and Stephanie were at our home often, studying, doing projects, enjoying meals, and throwing parties. I wanted to know who my children hung out with, and I preferred them to come to my place so I could get to know their friends. If they were in my home, I knew where they were and what they were doing. I felt safer knowing what was happening in their lives.

During high school, Lisa had very little interest in boys and dating. She drank alcohol occasionally, but not in excess, and she didn't do any recreational drugs. She spent her time in academic activities, visiting friends, and working part-time. I taught her how to sew clothing and do alterations, and she worked at my shop with me. Even though she was a young teenager, she became an efficient and capable helper for me in my business. She had a lovely, helpful, and friendly personality and interacted well with customers.

It was a good arrangement. We got to spend time together, she acquired a useful life skill, and my business benefited from her hard work, skill, and dedication. It was a win-win situation.

My children's friends spent much time at our home, and some of them called me "Mama Dockman" or simply "Mama D." My place was like a second home to some of my children's friends. I enjoyed these relationships. Because of our open conversation policy, at times my kids' friends would confide in me if they were having some difficulty in life. I became a mentor, sounding board, and supporter to them.

One time when Lisa was in Grade 10 or 11, she came to me with a girl-friend's request. She knew I kept a box of condoms in my dresser drawer to promote safe sex whenever that time came for my children. Lisa said her friend was considering having sex for the first time and was afraid to speak to her mother. She was asking if she could get a condom from me. Of course I said yes and gave Lisa two condoms to give to her, one for practice on a banana and one for use if she needed it with her boyfriend. A week later, this girlfriend came to me and said thank you. She said she thought about having sex with this boy and decided against it. She also said that she had a long talk with her mother and was feeling better about her decision. She was appreciative of my support and non-judgment. Whatever choice she made, I wanted her to be safe and avoid an unwanted pregnancy at such a young age. I was happy she felt comfortable asking for help and that I was able to provide the support she needed.

Lisa had a very close friend; in fact, she was Lisa's best friend during her first few years of school, from kindergarten to about Grade 4. They spent a lot time together and had fun times. This girl changed schools, and the two of them lost touch, with only occasional contact, for about eight years. Through those years, we heard some troubling news about Lisa's old friend and her struggles with relationships and mental health problems. She saw many doctors, and they had difficulty diagnosing her. She was on different medications, and it seemed there was some hesitation in the medical system to diagnose anything specific about her mental health status. I think a diagnosis of bipolar was the final verdict, which back then was called manic/depressive disorder, which is now called bipolar.

What I remember of this friend was that she was a lovely girl, she had a sweet personality and a mischievous sense of humour, but she was also determined and stubborn. This can show itself in the ability to get things done, but the flip side is rebellion and acting out against authority. It seemed the latter became the norm for her. She got into trouble and was transferred between several schools over the years. Her mental health difficulties, I'm sure, were at the root of this instability in her life. At any rate, she struggled. In her late teens, she had a baby. The father of the child was given custody because of her inconsistent moods and behaviours. As a result of a series of events, she committed suicide.

Lisa called me extremely upset about her old friend dying, particularly because the cause was suicide. Lisa asked me to go with her to the funeral. I was saddened by the news also. Such a shame; she was such a sweet girl. We cried and told stories about memories we had of her. At the funeral mass, several speakers talked about mental illness and the tragic effects it has on the lives of many, including her. I was surprised and grateful that the family was willing to share openly some of this girl's struggle with mental illness. The fact that she was mentally ill was not swept under the carpet, as it had been in the past and still is in many families. Hiding the mental illness doesn't serve the person or their family and community. Even though her death was tragic, the fact that they openly discussed bipolar disorder became a preventative conversation for those attending.

After several discussions with Lisa and me, some of the girl's friends and family started the healing process and gave us some understanding of her life and struggles and strengths. Lisa was very upset and emotional about her friend's death—understandably, as this was the first significant person in Lisa's life who had passed away. Her death affected Lisa deeply.

Although Lisa was seriously into academics, she also had a creative side to her personality. I'm sure she got that trait from both sides of our family. My mother does lovely painting on canvas and various wood objects, as well as painting animals on rocks. My mom's work is detailed and beautiful. Mike's mother, Lisa's Nana, is also a creative and open-minded individual who encouraged my children to pursue the arts. Of course, I did artsy play with them regularly throughout their lives. In her high school years, Lisa took sculpting classes and made some lovely soapstone pieces. She also learned jewelry-making that included metalwork and welding. She learned to draw and paint well. I was impressed with her creative ability and her willingness to try alternative methods to express her creative talents.

Lisa camping and enjoying nature, and her blooming
personally through her university years

John started high school two years later. I was concerned about where
John was headed, because he was a handsome boy, and girls seemed to gather
around him and give him lots of attention. I was worried he might get caught
up in girlfriends and sexual interests and lose focus on his school and sports
activities. Many girls had been clinging to and hounding John since Grade
7. That year, a style of sweatpants by Adidas was very popular. They were
stretchy fabric with snaps going down both sides of the legs, from waist to
foot. A girl who had a crush on John in pulled at his pants, and all the snaps
came undone, leaving John standing there, mortified, in his boxer shorts.

AAAhhwwk! It was a good thing he had his boxers on. I felt that John was not emotionally ready for this barrage of female interest.

At the beginning of John's high school years, I had a sense that he was at a fork in the road in his life. He would be making decisions now that would alter his future. I know I'm putting big weight on that particular moment in John's life, but I felt his hesitation and awkwardness. His body had outgrown his mind and emotions. I could tell by his quiet, observant, and thoughtful demeanour that he was calculating his options in order to choose the next move. I watched and interjected subtly to attempt to guide him in a positive direction. I had the sense he needed to discover his path and learn from it. I was attempting to empower him.

In Grade 9, John began to have severe outbreaks of acne on his face and back. Whatever cockiness had begun as a result of his good looks was deterred by his self-consciousness about having acne. His self-confidence with girls suffered as a result. He felt that the acne marred his looks and that girls wouldn't like him. As a result, he concluded that he couldn't rely on his looks to gain the attention of girls. Therefore, he chose the path of studies and sports, and because of that decision, he avoided the path of drugs and the harmful behaviours I was worried about him getting caught up in. Four months into his Grade 9 year, I breathed a sigh of relief, because I could see that the path he had chosen was constructive, and I was grateful for whatever steered him in that direction.

John told me his perspective of this turbulent transition time in his life four years later when he was graduating from Grade 12. He said he was aware of the impending decision at the time. In hindsight, he felt he was headed in a wrong direction that could have led him into troubled behaviours and relationships. John realized years later that getting acne caused him to rethink his view of himself. He had to learn to rely on his personality and intelligence instead of just his good looks. He made a choice to become a friendly and outgoing person and develop his character along with his knowledge base. This was quite an awesome insight for any person to make at such a young age. It was a life-changing decision for John. I was also relieved because his choice brought him academic rewards and personality development that helped him avoid many of the pitfalls that tempted him and could have nega-tively impacted his life in high school.

John developed a love for computer games. It started with a GameBoy, the small, handheld version we got for him when he was about five years old. He loved Mario Brothers. We drove across Canada, from Alberta to Ontario, every summer to visit family. The drive with four young children was taxing and super challenging and John was the hyperactive child. He needed to be running and climbing and moving. Sitting in a van for twenty-four hours over three days was a ridiculous expectation for him. He was the child who said, "Are we there yet?" a hundred times each trip. Talk about driving a parent batty. I was very creative with activities in the van, but seriously, there was only so much I could do with an active child like John.

Miracle of miracles was the GameBoy! John got so absorbed with playing the games; it became hard to get him to shut it off. The electronic game was a travelling life-saver. As he grew older, John played Super Mario Bros. with this dad. Then he became interested in Star Craft, Warcraft, and World of Warcraft. We also played card games like UNO and Skip Bo, and board games like Monopoly and Risk, which sometimes were set up and played for days. Some very fierce completions happened about who was going to rule the world in Risk!

Those video games John played involved action, thinking, and strategy, and that required dexterity and skill in hand-eye coordination, skills which John practiced and developed with much expertise. John also enjoyed playing the game Magic. He collected cards that built him tactical decks with complicated strategic patterns. He played in tournaments, and his involvement became a social event as well as a challenging hobby. John enjoyed these games and spent much time playing them. He became a very good gamer.

He also continued to play hockey, and he did BMX bike racing. He loved the speed and the competitiveness of both sports. We bought John a second-hand BMX bike because of our limited funds. In the second or third season of bike racing, he had an accident while racing. I got a call at work from Mike, who was at the BMX track with John. An ambulance was on its way to get John and bring him to the hospital. A mother's worst nightmare! Don't we all worry about getting that call? Your child has been in an accident! The mind goes to a variety of horrors immediately, from visualizations of coma, paralysis, and death. Fear took over and concluded the worst in seconds, even before any words could be formulated. In my mind, I imagined the worst possible scenarios. Shock first, then disbelief. When I could finally put a few words together, I asked, "What happened? Is he okay? How serious are his injuries?" I was freaking out.

John was jumping a hill on his BMX bike; he flew in the air over the hill and fell on his bike. When he fell, he landed on one side of the handlebar, which gouged into the skin and muscle of his inside thigh. The rubber on the handlebar had been worn, so the metal was coming through. The metal tore a vee-shaped rip in his skin and leg muscle, about four inches on each side with four inches across at the top of the vee. The cut was about two inches deep. Another mom who was watching the race ran to John. She reacted quickly and pushed the skin back into place and applied pressure. She was smart and acted promptly, so no skin ended up dying while they waited for the paramedics to arrive. He was so lucky to have not hit a major artery, where he could have bleed to death. Also, the cut was inches below his groin. Had the handle been a few inches higher, he could have seriously damaged his genitals.

The phone caller reassured me that John would be fine. He was shaken up but conscious, and even though the injury was serious, it would not be debilitating. I waited and worried. Apparently John's worry was whether he'd be able to continue to play sports. He loved to run and do physical things and hoped this injury would not stop him.

John was cared for by the medics in the ambulance and taken to hospital to get stitched up. Mike drove to the hospital to meet him. Some of his muscle had to be sewn together because of the depth of the cut, and he got four internal stitches and twenty-eight external stitches. It was quite an ordeal.

The doctor said John should take it easy for two weeks and not play sports until the stitches were healed. Fortunately, John was young, healthy, and physically fit. He healed very quickly, which was a good thing, because there was no way in hell I could keep him down without tying him up, which I threatened to do, jokingly. I talked to his gym teacher about John taking it easy for a while. That was a waste of breath. John was back running and going strong physically in a few days and was playing his sports and doing gym classes. It was true his leg healed well. The injury didn't detract from his ability to use his leg at all. He has quite a scar on his leg that looks like a lobster as a reminder.

The creative spirit was alive and well in John like it was in Lisa. He enjoyed drama class in high school. John, Lisa, and David all took roles in a school musical, which had them singing and dancing to rock 'n' roll tunes. He enjoyed acting and performing, whether it was dancing, singing, or acrobatics. He didn't mind being the centre of attention. I was happy to see his creativity develop, which I felt brought balance to his personality.

John had a few close friends and several girlfriends through high school, but no serious relationships or long-lasting girlfriends. I knew him well, so I was aware of the looks he got and things he did when he was scheming a plan. One evening when he was thirteen, he asked me if he could have a sleepover at a friend's house. In my normal fashion, I asked who this friend was. He evaded my question, so I asked if it was a male or female friend. He said she was female. I said no, he could not sleep over with a female friend at thirteen years old. He asked why, and I gave him a look.

"Mom, I'm not going to do anything with her."

"Okay, so if she took her clothes off and was naked, what would you do?"

"I would do nothing."

The answer was still no! He could not go to her house.

After dinner, John went to his room a bit early, and I could see his mind working. I was suspicious. Half an hour later, I went to check on him. He was gone, as I predicted. He'd left his window wide open after he'd climbed out, my first clue. He'd used the oldest trick in the book. He had stuffed pillows and blankets under his comforter to make it look like he was asleep. I concluded that he had gone to his "friend's" home. I did the last number recall on the phone and got the girl's number. I rang it, and her father answered. He said John was not there, and his daughter was in bed. Well, I never told him that she may not be alone.

I lay on John's bed and waited for him to sneak back into his window. It didn't take long before I saw his legs coming through the window frame. He stood on the floor, saw me, and froze! He was caught in the act. I kept myself seriously stern, even though I was chuckling inside. He stammered, tried to speak, and then just stood staring at me. I said with as much stern conviction as I could muster, "John, I know what you did. I can't decide on consequences yet, so I'll sleep on it and we'll discuss your punishment tomorrow."

Fear struck and he spent the night worrying. When we had our discussion the next day, he said he'd wanted to see if he could get away with sneaking out. He asked me how I knew what he was thinking. "Mothers know," I said simply. I gave him cleaning jobs to do for going against my rule. He hated cleaning, especially the toilet. He had to clean the bathrooms. As far as I know, he never snuck out again.

John was the child who initiated the conversations about relationships and sexual behaviour. I did my best to answer the questions and be informative while welcoming an open dialogue. I had a box on condoms in my top dresser drawer that my kids knew about and that was available to them if the time came for them to have safe sex. I noticed one day that the box was almost empty. I made a few subtle queries with Lisa and David, but I was pretty sure it was John who had used them. John heard the conversation and offered that it was him who took the condoms, but not for his own use. He said he was taking a few condoms to school on Fridays and selling them for $1 each. Of course he was. What a guy! Taking the condoms I bought and making 100% profit by supplying a service to his friends. I had to suppress my laughter as I listened to his story. He was creative and ingenious.

John found that he was excellent in maths and sciences in general, but he was good at them in French. He expressed his desire to do high school in the English program, in particular language arts, where he was not as fluent as he should be and struggled. Lisa convinced John of the merits of continuing in the French immersion program through high school to get a French high school diploma. He tried, but after Grade 9 he decided to switch to the English program, and he was happier and more successful there, particularly in language arts. I supported his choice. Here he developed a love for Shakespeare, a fantastic benefit of making this decision.

Dave entered high school one year after John. The road had been paved clear for David by Lisa and John, since they all attended the same high school: Lisa in Grade 12, John in Grade 10 and David in Grade 9. David had always been a very social being. He was cute and smiley as a child and always friendly and diplomatic in his interactions with people.

Dave had developed and maintained several very close friends. He met Eddy in kindergarten and hung out and became friends with Matt, Jordan, and Blaine. The transitions to high school for David went smoothly as I recall, because of these friends who supported him. He also had Lisa and John, who showed him the ropes and eased his passage to high school and teenage hood. This transition for Dave was much less scary for him and for me because we had knowledge of how the school worked; the programs, and the teachers. Making his way in the world was simpler for David because of having two older siblings who cleared the path for him to tread upon.

David has an ear for music. As I said earlier, as a young child, he had quite an acute sense of hearing; therefore, music was one of his fascinations. He decided to play the saxophone in high school music class and join the band. His closest friends were in his music class and the band as well, so they could enjoy learning the music together and looked forward to the band trip to the Disney theme park in California.

When Dave was in Grade 11 when the 9/11 attacks took place in New York. Security for flights into the United States was heightened and related air travel was postponed. The school district decided to cancel the trip because of the risks related to the safety of the students. The following year it was deemed that safe travel to the US had resumed, and the high school band made preparations for a week-long excursion to Los Angeles, California. The trip included a day at Disneyland and one day at Universal Studios, as well as their own musical performance in a theatre in Disneyland. It was all very exciting!

I hadn't been to California or to Disney in many years, so I was thrilled to be travelling as a chaperone with David and the band on this epic journey. I was in charge of David and four of his friends, all of whom I knew well. They were all Grade 12 students, fully grown adults, and very responsible young men. The day of their performance came. They were nervous and honoured to have been chosen to play at this venue. They lulled the audience with their classical and rock tunes. It was a very special experience for these young students. Following the band's performance, they were free to explore the sights for the rest of their visit. I joined them on their excursions.

We walked to many places. Well, I should say I nearly ran to keep up to the pace of five young and fit eighteen-year-old boys/young men. We went to watch a theatre production of the movie *Aladdin* that was amazingly done. The costumes and set were spectacular. There was a full-size replica of an elephant with people inside, walking it around across the stage and through the crowd. The elephant was splendidly decorated with jewels and gold. They had Aladdin and Princess Jasmine flying through the air on a magic carpet that was suspended by wires above the audience. The production was superbly done. I brought along a huge picnic lunch with sandwiches, pickles, raw vegetables, and juice, which we ate in the theatre before the play started. The boys were ravenous, their normal state, and demolished the picnic in record time. They were teenage boys, nonstop eating machines. I spent much of my time on the trip providing breakfast food and snacks, for which they were all grateful.

We also saw a show called "It's a Bug's Life" that was entertaining and interactive. It seemed like a younger child's entertainment, but the boys weren't above letting their childlike imaginations emerge and have some fun. When the bugs in the film sprayed their enemies, we in the audience were sprayed with water also. We were startled and amused. At the end of the show, our seats moved in a rolling motion underneath us, which made it feel like there were bugs attacking us from below. It was creepy and made us all jump up in surprise. When we realized what was happening by looking at the seats with lumps moving along them, we laughed and were impressed with their ingenuity. It was a memorable trip for us all. I was happy and grateful to have had the opportunity to help and participate.

David did well in school and was particularly fond of his science classes. He also played hockey and soccer. He liked to read and figure out how things worked. He read the Lord of the Rings book series, and we went to all the movies. We attended one of the movie premiers of *Lord of the Rings* with Dave and John dressed up as Sam and Frodo. Their costumes looked authentic, and they even had the same hairstyles as their characters. They were so much fun to watch and interact with.

John and Dave dressed as Frodo and Sam for
a midnight screening of Lord of the Rings

The year Rachel went to high school, Lisa moved to Edmonton to go to the University of Alberta. John and David were attending the same high school. Rachel had a group of friends she knew and was close to from middle school, and some of them were attending the same high school. Rachel was a very smart girl, but she struggled with trying to measure up to her siblings. Even though they were older, Rachel had compared herself to them as equals. I encouraged Rachel and praised her for her unique talents and intelligence, but I'm afraid she didn't always believe me. She had such a literal way of looking at the world. What she saw was her reality, even if there were variables she didn't recognize yet. I felt she would understand in time and she would be okay. I was patient, supportive, and understanding.

Rachel and Dave deep in thought, communing with the rocks

When Rachel began high school, I had similar worries as I had with John when he started. My concern was that she was vulnerable and could easily choose friends and a path that could lead her into trouble, as far as using drugs and/or delinquent behaviour. I had faith in her as I had in all my children. I believed in her strengths and talents, and particularly the power of her conviction when she believed in something. She fought for her beliefs. When she set her mind on something, she was strong-willed and determined to make it happen.

I knew Rachel had similar intelligence as her siblings, because I watched how she approached projects with focus and ferocity, but only if she was interested in them. If she wasn't interested in the topic, really, what was the point? She still needed to understand the practicality of whatever she was learning. If she saw the value in a task, and she felt it was worth her time and effort, then she worked hard and learned. If she didn't see value or practicality, she had little interest or motivation to proceed. Because of this part of her personality, she did reasonably well in school but nowhere near her potential, the way I saw it.

Rachel tried hockey but didn't like to play the sport. We switched her to figure skating, and she shivered so badly from the cold that she just couldn't get into it. She loved to swim and became a member of the swim club. Swimming became her sport. At five years old, Rachel said she wanted to learn to swim as fast as she could back and forth through the water, which meant she was a natural for participating on the competitive swim team and racing events. The racing fit with her competitive nature, and she enjoyed the physical challenges. She was small but muscular, flexible, and athletic.

She excelled at gymnastics when she was younger and later chose to join the cheer team in high school. Cheerleading is a sport that is often shunned and looked down upon, but we learned quickly that the endurance, strength, and skill the cheer squad needed to perform their stunts was extensive. Rachel was dedicated with practices and creative with developing cheer movement sequences. Her team went to the provincial championships in Edmonton. We went to watch the teams and were impressed with the difficulty of lifts and flips done simultaneously by the different teams. Rachel's team won a first prize ribbon. It was an exciting and rewarding experience. She was thrilled.

Rachel also spent time on creative activities like jazz and tap dance classes, and she was good at both. She sculpted, drew, and painted in art classes and made some impressive pieces. One particular portrait she did with coloured pencils was of a girl with a red sari scarf and very striking green eyes. It was intricately done and was displayed at the school's public open art night. The high school had an impressive variety of creative arts that included jewelry making. Both Lisa and Rachel made some unique jewelry and learned soldering and metalwork. Making jewelry pieces set with stones was of interest to all of us. We had a fascination with rocks, semi-precious stones, and minerals. I was pleased that my kids' school curriculum included such a variety of creative arts. These unique programs developed a breadth of skills and interests in my children, as well as helped improve their self-esteem.

There were a few instances of drama and concern during Rachel's high school years. Since her personality was exploratory, she tried to push boundaries, particularly in her teenage years. There were times I could use our close connection to help her overcome some of her challenges, yet other times she chose to handle situations herself. She had a friend who said she was having challenges and conflict with her parents. Rachel explained what she knew of her friend's situation and asked if she could live with us for a few months. I wanted to support her but also made a point of talking with her parents and reassured them that she was okay. I was initially reluctant to agree, but in the end did succumb and allowed her to stay with certain rules and stipulations. After some weeks, her friend was able to talk with her parents and come to an understanding and moved back home. I felt compassion for her and for her parents. I believe I was able to help in the situation.

In Grade 9 or 10, Rachel had a falling out with her father and requested to live with me all the time. I believed her story, and she had her brother to back her up. I felt she was old enough to have her own mind, and I supported her decision. In fact, we had raised her to learn how to make choices and live with the consequences of those choices. Rachel was practicing her independence, and I wanted to empower her. When she was ready to make amends with her father, I knew she would do it. I intended to support her decision as well as her autonomy.

Rachel dated a few boys in high school, and one fairly seriously for over a year. During her early high school years, she had two cousins who had teenage pregnancies. One was female cousin was seventeen and had a beautiful baby girl. The baby's father was around for a while but had his own life problems. She raised the child herself with the help of her mother. Another of Rachel's male cousin's girlfriends got pregnant as well when they were in their mid-teens, but they did not stay together. The paternity was in question, and it seemed there was no ongoing connection between my nephew and the baby's mother. As a mother, I was worried for Rachel. I didn't want her to have an unplanned teenage pregnancy.

I made a point of having a conversation with Rachel about going to the doctor together if she wanted, or going by herself, to get a prescription for the birth control pill. I wasn't encouraging her to become sexually active. My intention was simply for her to take precautions to prevent getting pregnant before she was ready to be a mom. She resisted at first, because she said she wasn't even dating anyone at the time. I suggested it didn't matter. I thought we should take the precaution early for future prevention. She agreed and went to see a doctor and started on the birth control pill. Her having protection, on top of condoms, gave me some assurance of her protection from sexually transmitted disease and the possibility of getting pregnant. In Rachel's case, a couple of side benefits occurred from taking birth control; the acne on her face cleared up substantially, and her menstrual cycles became milder.

When Rachel went into Grade 10, Lisa was in her second year of university in Edmonton; John graduated from high school and was undecided about his career path. He decided to take some time off from school to think about what he wanted to do in life. He decided to pursue some other interests, like joining the Canadian military or becoming a firefighter. David was in Grade 12 and considering going to University of Alberta to study engineering. Lisa helped David with the applications, choosing classes, and securing a spot in the university residence.

My children were growing up all too quickly. At that time, we received some tragic news. Mary Beth was diagnosed with uterine cancer, and because of her health problems, surgery wasn't an option. She was given a drug that was supposed to get rid of the cancer in her uterus. This was a shock to me and my children. Mary Beth and I were very close friends, and she was like a second mother to my children.

The news of Aunt Beth's cancer affected all of us in different ways. John was at a place of indecision in his career path, and when he heard the news, he decided he wanted to help in a more significant way. He was nineteen years old when he decided to run across Canada to raise funds for cancer research and help find a cure. He felt this was a way he could show his love for his aunt and help others who were dealing with cancer. His goal was to raise funds but also to raise awareness about cancer in general. For all intents and purposes, John's run across Canada became his life goal, the next important phase of his life for the following fourteen months. . . certainly as important as continuing schooling, or working at a job, or any other pursuits he may have had.

Sister Love! Beth and Cathy

Incredible amounts of self-awareness and life learning came from the experience of John's Cancer Crusade run, as it was called. It was a fascinating testament to John's character, determination, compassion, and persistence, as well as the incredible generosity of Canadians across our great country. The preparations, the family and community involvement, the hardships, personal injuries, and challenges, as well as the breakthroughs, insights, and victories were all part of his incredible story.

317

John deep in thought

Back to the story of Rachel and the high school years. By the time Rachel got to Grade 12, Dave and Lisa were at university, and John was running across Canada. Rachel was a very busy girl. She was studying for her final year of high school, working part-time, and had a very busy social life. She and I rarely saw each other with me working my sewing business long hours. In essence, in three years I went from being a full-time mom to a very part-time mom. The older three had left home, and Rachel was quite independent. I thought it was great that she was taking on the responsibility for her life. She had always been ahead of her years in understanding and had the courage to try new and different things. I found myself alone much of the time at home. I didn't need to buy massive amounts of groceries. With the boys gone, I had food actually go bad and rot in my refrigerator. It was a huge adjustment for me.

Rach and I ate salads and bagels and rarely had family meals together because we were both so busy. Being alone and not having children to look after was a shock to my system at first and for a long time. I was so used to buying a full grocery cart of food every week and cooking meals for six to eight people every single day for the past twenty years. I had to change my whole outlook on my life and who I was. I went through several years of transition and turmoil as a result of empty nest and mid-life uncertainties. I wasn't even aware of the emotional and physical trauma I was experiencing and the changes that were happening in my life. Since Rachel was still living with me, I assumed I wouldn't be going through empty nest syndrome for another year at least, not to mention mid-life crisis, which I was facing but unaware of.

I used to pray to God that my children would survive to the age of twenty. I saw the dangers in life for children of all ages and felt grateful for having four, but I also knew the risks of living and leading adventurous lives. I tried to stay in the present moment as much as possible, because I believe worry is fruitless. But there were times when visions of accidents, injuries, or death entered and polluted my mind. So I thanked God, my higher power, and my guardian angels for protecting my children from harm and allowing them to continue to live and bless me with their presence in my life. As they grew, I had to adjust my prayer to "Please guide them and let them live to thirty years old." We joke about it now, but it was a serious plea for me at the time. I will by the grace of God change that prayer to forty, fifty, etc. as the years go by.

All four of my children successfully completed high school with only a few traumatic events and many minor glitches that we seemed to be able to be resolved. They had strong, bonded relationships with each other and knew the value of family. I felt I had succeeded as a mother in my efforts and goals to raise them into capable, independent, caring, and contributing members of our family and society as a whole.

How would motherhood look as they grew into adulthood? How would I spend my time? Would our relationships remain close and grow? How would I manage my emotions and mental health going through empty nest syndrome? It was an uncertain and uncomfortable time for me. I felt I had completed a huge task with no path going forward. This was the end of another phase in my life I would not recognize or be aware of until years later.

Sisters

Dave and John, Bro Twins in high school

Glamour shot with Cathy and Rachel, 2002

My teenage kids showing love to Aunt Bethy

The fantastic four in high school

# CHAPTER 24

## *University Experiences and Transition to Working Life*

Mike and I had been talking about and encouraging our children to consider continuing their education after they finished high school all of their lives. We believed that going to college and getting a trade was a good plan, and we also emphasized going to university and getting a degree and becoming a professional. It seemed the way to go at that time. Education was needed to land a good paying, secure job. This advice suited Annalisa to a "T." She embraced her education wholeheartedly. She focused on her studies in high school with the intention of achieving high grades, which she did, to prepare herself for earning scholarships and getting admission into a university of her choice. Her hard work paid off. She did extremely well academically. Lisa had the highest mark on pure math on the Grade 12 provincial exam. She also was a high achiever in all her subjects.

Lisa worked extremely hard for her marks. Working through her struggles in kindergarten to Grade 4 helped her develop excellent strategies for learning. During her Grade 12 year, Lisa did her research and applied to several universities in Canada with the intention of earning a Bachelor of Science degree. She was accepted at several schools and chose to attend the University of Alberta in Edmonton. I was happy about her decision, because she would be living away from home in a university residence, but we were only three hours away, so we could visit and keep in close contact with her for support.

Making the decision to go away to university was a huge step in Lisa's growth, maturity, and development. She was a planner and liked her life to be structured. Change for Lisa only came after much thought and preparation. Her fear of moving away from home was managed by her drive to acquire specialized education. She spent about two weeks attending goodbye parties with her friends and sorting and packing her clothes and personal items into two piles: one to take for her room in the dorm at the university, and the other to store at home.

I remember vividly that day I drove with her to move to university. It was such a major turning point in our lives and a huge change emotionally and physically. She had her car, a small white Sunbird that Grandpa had given her, and I was driving my car. Both vehicles were full to the breathing top with her most precious worldly possessions. I'm saying that literally—the trunks were jammed, and the back seat was loaded to the roof, as were the passenger seats, with plants precariously placed on top and secured by other stuff. I could barely move my gear shifter, and seeing traffic to my right or in my rear-view mirror was impossible. We managed to fit everything she chose to bring into our two cars.

We were both emotional basket cases and probably should not have been driving at that moment in that distracted, emotional frame of mind. We were on a mission and a timeline, so off we went, Lisa and I, with our memories and hopes for her better future. We had our tears of sadness and moments of excitement and pride as we left our home in Airdrie and headed to Lisa's university life experience in Edmonton. In fact, that move became significant for Lisa, the beginning of her transition from childhood to adulthood. Her move from home to university was a critically important phase of her development.

I drove my car behind Lisa in her car, on the freeway heading north to Edmonton. I hadn't realized the extent of Lisa's exhaustion until an hour after we began driving. The events of the past few weeks of preparation for the move had taken their toll on her physically and emotionally. While she was driving, I noticed erratic changes in her speed and control along the road. She would begin to slow down, and then the car would ease over onto the gravel on the right side of the road. I became very concerned, because I knew she was falling asleep at the wheel. We had no cell phones at the time to talk to each other. After some time of this, she pulled off into a restaurant parking lot about an hour outside of Edmonton. Thank God, she realized she was in no shape to be driving.

I was relieved. I was sure she would get into an accident because of her fatigue. We chose to leave her car at the restaurant parking lot, and she rode with me in my car for the rest of the drive. The problem was that my passenger seat was completely full of stuff. We had to squeeze her in amongst her stuff and pile clothes and plants on her lap. It was pretty funny; we were crammed in the car like sardines. Did she really need all this stuff? I questioned, but I knew having her things with her became a security blanket to help adjust to the changes. We did what we had to do. She couldn't drive safely any longer, and we needed to get her to Edmonton for move-in day at her residence. We decided we'd come back the next day to get her car after she'd slept. When she was rested, we could bring the other half of her belongings to her room safely and get her settled in.

We managed to find the university, the registration place, and the residence building where she was going to live—Lister Hall. It was chaos! There were masses of people and lots of activity with young eager students, stressed out parents, and cars parked everywhere, including the grassy areas around Lister. There were carts and trolleys and dollies of stuff making their way to the entrance ways of the residence buildings. Through some time and confusion, we managed to find Lisa's room and unload her things. Her room was small, about 10 feet by 10 feet in size, with cinder block walls. It was a basic boarding room.

Lisa had planned to share the room with one of her best friends from home to help ease the transition to university life. The residence had a girls' wing and a boys' wing on the each of the sixteen floors. It was a tight squeeze to get all her stuff into half of this room. She had a single bed, a student's desk, a bookshelf over the desk, and a closet. The space was minimal, simple, and barely adequate. There was a shared kitchen and a shared bathroom with showers. First time moving away from home meant freedom, independence, and excitement. Certainly the size of her room was irrelevant to Lisa. She was excited!

We had attended a parents' orientation seminar some time earlier, which was helpful, but we had much to learn. We did a grocery run to get her set up with food, toiletries, and the supplies she needed. We went to Staples to get final school supplies, and Ikea for a few shelving and organizing necessities.

Funding a university student is no small task. She had everything she needed to make her room look homey and utilize all the space. I helped her unpack food and put together shelves, put up posters, and personalize her room. She soon began to meet people on her floor. I had done everything I could to help her with her move, and it was time for me to depart. The situation brought back memories of leaving Lisa at school in kindergarten, with her crying and clinging to my leg. This time she was a young adult woman and scared to death but trying to be strong. Her motivation moved her to go for it and overcome her fear. I was so proud of her at that moment. Of course I was worried about leaving her alone in the big world, but I had done everything I could to prepare her for that moment. I had to trust her and just let go. We said a quick goodbye so we didn't break into tears again in front of her new friends, and she began her new adventure in university life and a new level of growth and independence. Her leap into adulthood.

Not long into Lisa's university experience, she changed her attitude and approach toward her education. During high school, she gave up some of her social life to focus her time on her studies. She came to a realization that she could do well in university and also enjoy an active social life. The fact that she was the top of her class in school seemed to be less relevant and less important in this university environment. Lisa's focus became more balanced. She still studied hard and achieved an excellent grade point average (GPA), but she also made many good friends and thoroughly enjoyed her university experience.

Residence life was incredibly social and full of constant activity. I'm surprised she even managed to get her studying done at all with the amount of drinking and floor parties they had. They were very creative in their party planning, with no holds barred in their pursuit of fun times. While she was learning intricate details of bird skeletons and becoming a scientist, she learned to chug beer, live on Ichiban noodles, and be active in her community building a social network of academic and personal supports. She learned much about feminism and environmental ideas and grew in confidence, solidified her ideas, and expanded her skills. Going to university for Lisa was dramatically important for her enjoyment of life, maturity, and her further development as a loving, contributing human being.

John chose to delay his further schooling and was running across Canada the year after he graduated from high school. It was August 1, 2003. Choosing to do that run across Canada was a life-changing experience for John that was full of growth and adventures. To start the run, John and David drove a thirty-year-old camper behind their dad's old van, heading east to Newfoundland.

John chose to run the same path Terry Fox ran years before. They reached the exact spot in Newfoundland that had the sign showing where Fox began his run. Dave drove the van pulling the camper each day, while John ran in front of it on the side of the road. John did two legs of running each day, at 10 to 20 kilometres per leg. Yea, that's like running a marathon a day!

Business card for John's cross-Canada run

Dave and John, at the starting point where John's running
for Cancer began in St John's, Newfoundland

Dave stayed with John to drive the van and support him for two months that summer while they got the run started. That time became another bonding experience for my two sons. Their love and respect for each other grew in depth through this experience. Living together in the small camper while travelling across Canada cemented their relationship further as young adults. Embarking on this monumental task together strengthened their brotherly connection.

Shortly after Dave had returned to Alberta, John called me one day from a dock in Halifax, full of excitement. He was standing on the shore of the Atlantic Ocean in high winds, almost being blown away, and feeling charged with the power of living. A hurricane warning was in effect. Yes, a hurricane was happening in that moment of the phone call to me, and John was thrilled to be having the experience! I was freaking out and scared for his life. He was eventually scurried away by the local police. John drove to a nearby parking lot at a mall between two large buildings and waited, anticipating the storm. There was a hurricane that devastated the area that evening. It was a horrible storm.

When John awoke the next morning, water filled the parking lot where he'd parked the camper, and the water had risen halfway up the wheel wells of the van and camper. He was surrounded by terrible flooding and wreckage. John went to the dock where he'd stood the previous day and found that it was gone, whisked away like a toothpick by the wind and water. Many buildings were destroyed and there was debris everywhere. He was lucky to have escaped the danger with no injury to himself or his vehicles. His excitement turned to horror when he saw the devastation and realized the real danger he'd been in. Living through the hurricane was one of dozens of life-changing experiences John encountered during his fourteen months of running across Canada.

There were times when John was by himself, running with no driver available to help. He would park the camper, touch a hydro pole where he finished running the previous day, and begin his day's run. He was determined not to miss one metre of Canada along his run, so he started at the exact spot he finished the previous day. When he finished for the day, he hitchhiked back to the camper and drove it to the spot he had run to in that leg. He'd find a place to park the camper nearby and then relax, eat, and sleep. Then he repeated the same thing the next day. What a challenge and a commitment! Family and friends and members of the Optimist Club volunteered to drive with John for periods of time, so we tried to have someone with him as much as possible over the fourteen months.

John running in northern Ontario

The volunteer who drove the van and camper supported John by collecting donations, buying and preparing food for their meals, and arranging for speaking engagements at local schools, hospitals, nursing homes, etc. along the route. In the larger centres, John needed police escorts to help with the traffic and safety issues. The support person called ahead to arrange for this.

Lisa had done much of the organizing with John prior to and during the run to expand awareness of it to local organizations and to set up his speaking engagements in towns and cities along the way. John met mayors, ministers, public officials, premiers like Ralph Klein, and many dignitaries throughout the country. He spoke with people at seniors' residences, schools, and service clubs. He talked about his experience to hundreds of children, youth, and cancer survivors who showed up to support him and tell their stories.

Also, John's dad helped by coordinating with the Optimist Club, of which he was a member, and got them to help sponsor John and his run. The Terry Fox Society and the Canadian Cancer Society weren't interested. I guess it was too small an endeavour to warrant their support. They said that "everyone" is running or biking across the country these days! This was unfortunate, but in the long run, it turned out to be for the best. John ran independent of those large organizations and was able to make his own choices and decisions along the way. He had a life-changing experience because of the vast amount of challenges he overcame and the victories he experienced throughout this country.

Total strangers, linked together by being fellow Canadians, connected with John and supported his cause. Many had been touched by cancer in some way and wanted to help. They gave John food, took him into their homes, fixed the van, and gave him running shoes. (He wore out eighteen pairs of running shoes during the fourteen months!) Scores of people befriended John and gave him gifts, monetary donations, and mementos from their towns or cities. Some people joined John for a time and ran beside him. The way the citizens of Canada reached out to John and supported him and his cause was mind-blowing. He was touched by people's love and compassion, by their generosity and caring. The support he was given by fellow Canadians gave him courage and faith in the human race. He was encouraged to overcome the mental, physical, and emotional challenges he faced and persist through his difficulties.

I did my part by driving the van for three weeks with John while he ran through northern Ontario. I flew to Windsor first to visit Mom, Dad, and my family. Mom and Mary Beth drove me the eight or nine hours to North Bay to intercept John. Mom and Beth visited with him, and he told us stories of his run so far. It was a great connect, since Mary Beth's cancer had been the impetus for John's run.

I began my turn the next morning driving the van and camper behind John while he ran. I recall following John on a stretch of road that was quiet and deserted. I chugged along at a couple miles an hour while John ran ahead of me. Not much different than any other day—John running 40 kilometres! Of course it was different than any other day, because this young man was striving to achieve a major feat. John was challenging his mind and his body with the goal of making a difference to the life of his aunt and others who suffered from the devastations of cancer.

One day while John was running and I was driving slowly behind him, we heard a rumbling noise and then shouting and cheering. The sound caught our attention. Soon we saw a crowd people ahead of us on the side of the road. They were holding up signs with encouraging words for John, like "Go

John Dockman!" They were congratulating him and welcoming him to their school and their town. John stopped to shake hands with the young students. It was a middle school with a hundred or so students around the ages of eight to twelve, along with their teachers, who had gathered to support John and his run. A couple of students briefly told John of their family members fighting cancer and thanked him for what he was doing to help. It was powerful. The energy, emotions, and supports were palpable.

I watched this scene unfold before my eyes. It was incredible! We hadn't even informed them of our arrival. They had simply heard that John was coming and acted. I stopped the van to observe. I couldn't see very well, because I was overcome by emotion and moved to tears by the sight before me and their unbelievable support. The moment was magical. At the end of the crowd of children stood the principal of the school, who presented John with a cheque that included donations they had collected from their community. Thinking about that scene now brings tears to my eyes all over again. Experiencing that moment with John renewed my faith in the goodness of the human race and their willingness to help. I was overwhelmed by feelings of pride and wonder, mixed with gratitude and an awe-inspiring sense of joy.

It felt like time stopped. I felt like I was watching a black and white, slow motion movie in which John was the main character. To this day I can visualize that experience and feel the joy and pride I felt for John and to be a Canadian. I had the pleasure and good fortune of being a part of that important moment and sharing it with John. Imagine the impact it had on John and his feelings of being supported. He was encouraged and inspired to persevere. He wasn't in this run alone.

In essence, I think John's resolve was reinforced with each of these community events. Experiences like this one, where the entire school came out to support him, motivated him to continue. People rallying around him and sharing their cancer stories impelled him to plug along through rain, snow, ice, and terrible weather conditions. People throughout this country met John along the way and stirred him to continue, even when he was tired or had muscle spasms or shin splints or injuries to his legs. When he saw the reactions of hundreds of people across this country, he was moved to continue and endure his hardships and revel in the joy it gave him to be helping, to be contributing in a positive way toward finding a cure for cancer. John was encouraged to endure and succeed when people showed their awareness and interest in finding a cure and supporting friends and family who suffered by supporting John and his run. There was a common link that crossed the bridges of differences and joined people's hearts to a worthy cause. Travelling with John during his run was a beautiful and fascinating experience. I was proud to be a part of that amazing journey of John's Cancer Crusade.

The story of John's run across Canada warrants a book of its own. There are literally dozens of stories that need to be told. A writer followed John's journey during those fourteen months and afterward. He interviewed John and many others and documented the Cancer Crusade Run. My hope is this writer or the Optimist Club will publish the book and include it in their ongoing fundraising efforts.

Spending the fourteen months running through urban and rural Canada gave John a new perspective of himself and our country. He spent much time alone and in deep thought and self-reflection. He had time to contemplate and evaluate himself and the meaning of his life. As I have said before, John is an old soul and somewhat of a philosopher. He doesn't spend much time on trivialities. He is keen about important matters of the heart and of life. Making the decision to dedicate fourteen months of his life to an outside cause was a demonstration of his courage and selflessness. It was an incredible undertaking for a nineteen-year-old young man, which demonstrated his empathy and compassion for others.

I mentioned John was an old soul, a mature soul. Doing the run shows how he had the capacity to feel others' pain and offer them his assistance. Before the run, when John was making his plans, he said he had started many things in his life and hadn't completed them. He made a commitment to himself that he would start and complete his run, thus he chose to create a new habit of finishing.

The young man who started his run on the east coast of Canada in St. John's, Newfoundland, was not the same young man who finished running the 9,258.3 kilometres four hundred and fifty-two days later on the west coast of Canada at Mile 0 of the Trans Canada highway, in the city of Victoria on Vancouver Island, British Columbia. He was twenty-one years old when he finished, but in reality, I believe he had matured and grown in wisdom many years beyond his physical age. There was a knowing about him, a peace and self-confidence that exuded from his being. Not only was he in optimum physical health, with his sun-browned skin, healthy glow, and incredibly muscular legs, but his inner strength and energy shone with contentment. What he had given to my sister, his aunt, and to anyone suffering from cancer was an enormous part of himself and a significant chunk of his young life. In return, he developed a satisfaction, self-assuredness, and peace of mind. He knew in his heart that he had done his very best and had succeeded. As a mother, I was very proud of him and his selfless generosity.

Determination! John running with a group of supporters

John speaking at a Cancer Crusade banquet in Airdrie, Alberta

Beth beaming with pride and gratitude with John at the banquet

Lisa who helped John organize run events, at the banquet

Dave's brilliant smile at the banquet

Mary Beth was incredibly moved by John's commitment to helping her by doing the run. She felt deeply his compassion, his love, and his support for her. She followed his run while she was taking her cancer drug treatments. Thank God these new medications worked, and by the time John finished the run, Mary Beth was cancer-free. She is alive and well. I wonder how much of her healing resulted from the support she got from her friends and family and John's run. John ran, we all helped, and Mary Beth healed. We may never know the complete effect we have on those around us. John's act of selfless love was a significant part of Mary Beth's recovery. We cannot discount love's healing power.

Cathy and gangster Beth

Lisa was attending university and John was running across Canada when David finished high school. Dave made plans to attend university to study engineering. He got accepted at University of Alberta and chose to attend on Lisa's recommendation and encouragement. It made sense to be in the same location and be able to support each other. Lisa had figured out the system of student loans, residence life, registration details, and life in general in Edmonton. Her experience was most helpful to Dave with his transition from home to university life. There I went again, making the trek up to Edmonton with a carload of possessions—Dave's this time—and helping a child move into adulthood and university life.

David told me years later that he was scared to death of moving away from home and leaving the security of his friends and family. He was much like Lisa in that way; he loved the comfort and routines of being with family and close friends. Dave enjoyed structure and predictability, so moving from home was a major step outside of his comfort zone. He clearly recalled that day at university when he decided to overcome his fears and take chances in life in order to move forward. He said he told himself to try new things; if he had the thought, he would just do it! He would overcome his fear by action. That was the attitude he had when he moved away from home into the residences at the U of A. He embraced university life and took the bull by the horns. That was a defining moment for David.

Good for David! I gave him a lot of credit for recognizing this fear and being willing to face it by taking action. That's something he can be proud of and look back on as a life-changing decision. I was so proud of him when he told me this story. It's ironic how a person can look so calm and self-assured from the outside yet have that battle of emotions raging on the inside. David possessed in him what it took to work through his fear. Possibly it was his presence of mind, or maybe his motivation to succeed and enjoy university, that allowed him to do this. His circumstances and his character and frame of mind gave him the strength he needed to take the risks and overcome those fears.

I'm sure he will recollect many experiences he enjoyed and those that challenged him, where he said to himself "I can't" or "What if I fail or look like a fool?" but made a conscious choice to try anyway. One example of Dave taking risks took place during the first week of residence life. They had many orientation events to get to know their roommates and have some fun. Dave dressed up as a woman, in a skirt, a wig with long hair, and high-heeled shoes, and traipsed around the university event. He was obviously enjoying his newfound sense of adventure.

Dale Carnegie said this well: "Inaction breeds doubt and fear. Action breeds confidence and courage. If you want to conquer fear, do not sit home and think about it. Go out and get busy." *(How to Enjoy Your Life and Your Job,* 1990).[28] David wouldn't be the scholar, the adventurer, or the world traveler he is today if he hadn't made that decision to overcome his fears and live in the moment. He also wouldn't have finished his university degree or his master's had he not taken risks by engaging in new experiences.

Following Dave's first year of university, he decided that engineering wasn't for him. Through much thought and deliberation, David decided to switch majors and continue his studies in geology. It took courage for him to follow his own path in the face of societal and family pressures. He was fortunate to have had the awareness of who he was and what his strengths and passions were, and the fortitude to change his career direction so it would match with his goals and personality. The geology program was an excellent fit for David. He especially loved the field work. He loved the outdoor adventures, hiking, climbing, and travelling to new terrains and exploring and documenting the rock and land formations.

David did some student field work in Jasper, Alberta, in British Columbia, and in the Yukon. He discovered a passion for travelling and was happy to combine work with travel. He chose to study abroad for a term with a coop-erative university in Australia. He spent a term studying at the University of Wollongong, which is along the east coast of southern Australia. He was treated superbly by the locals and made several close friends while he was in residence there. His accommodations were a few minutes away from the ocean, so he learned how to surf. He found surfing a blast. It was an amazing advantage of this experience. He and his friends had a tropical Christmas dinner that year and went surfing on Christmas afternoon. What a wonderful life experience, and quite a change from our normal cold and snowy, white Canadian Christmases.

Speaking of surfing, a new kind of surfing emerged in those years. It was called couch surfing. A person could go online and find a place to stay almost anywhere in the world and sleep on the family couch for free. It was a kind of exchange of kindness and service that wasn't directly between two people but with a pay it forward kind of attitude. By the time David finished his term at Wollongong University, he had met some friends who offered him their couch for free while he travelled and toured Australia. David offered cleaning and cooking services in return, as well as buying beer at times in exchange for their courteous accommodation.

David spent another six to seven months surfing, hiking, scuba diving, and seeing the sights of Eastern Australia. He bought an old van and used it for his travels. He visited some good friends who were native Australian whom he'd met previously in Canada in a choir he was involved with. Dave went to their family ranch in central Australia. We're talking about a large farming operation consisting of 6,000 to 7,000 acres of land. They went horseback riding and quadding over their ranch lands. They also owned a small plane to help manage the ranch. Dave was delighted to observe the ranch and livestock from above. He reveled in these activities with his friends and had a wonderful visit and enjoyable adventures. David's friend's family ranch was in the area of Australia where the wildfires were raging that year.

Warnings had come by radio and television to evacuate the area because the fire was heading in their direction. The family Dave stayed with was preparing to secure their home and outbuildings by digging trenches around them and dousing everything with water. They had a dug out where they planned to submerge themselves if and when the fire reached them. They would get into the water in the dugout up to their necks, soak a burlap bag in water, and place it over their heads to protect them from the fire. When the evacuation warning came, they told David he could evacuate to the local community centre if he wished, but the family was staying on the ranch.

David was not a local and was unfamiliar with the extent of the danger that was looming. He deduced that if his friend's family thought they would be safe, then he would trust their judgment and stay with them on the ranch and not evacuate.

Dave and his friend walked up to the top of a hill in order to get a better view of the approaching fire and judge where it was and the speed at which it was moving. While they stood there, they could see the menacing, dangerous smoke storm in the distance. They watched it speeding toward them on the horizon from a few hundred kilometres away. The wind was howling as if in warning, and the smell of smoke and devastation hung heavy in the air. They stood in fear and awe as they watched the wall of flame travel like a rushing, enormous, burning bull leaping across the hills, apparently at a speed of about 60 kilometres an hour. David's friend ran down the hill to alert his family that the fires were coming and to take shelter. David stood on that hill as the reality of the massive scale of danger smacked him hard. The thought struck him that he may not live through the day!

In those few seconds while he stood alone, terrified on that hill, awaiting destruction, abruptly all went quiet. The wind stopped. Dave said an eerie calmness settled around him. He recalled it feeling surreal, as if time paused and the world shifted. To his amazement, the wall of flame turned at a 90-degree angle and headed away from where he stood. The wind suddenly changed direction and turned the wall of flames. For whatever phenomenon occurred that forced the fire to change direction, I am truly grateful. I thank God for this miracle. Dave watched in awe as his life was given back to him. It was not his turn to leave this earth.

The horror was that when the wind turned, the direction of the fire proceeded to a nearby town, the town where Dave and this family could have been evacuated to! A very sad and frightening thought. Who would have known that decision to stay at the farm saved their lives? Many people lost their lives and their homes. David expressed his sadness and possibly guilt for having survived while so many people lost so much. They spent time helping the families who were hit hard to clean up and rebuild. It was a difficult and frightening experience for David. Who can say why these things happen? Fate? Luck? Spiritual protection? I'm not sure. I am simply grateful for whatever power kept him alive. Having been so close to death gave him a feeling of how quickly life can be gone and how precious each day was—a lesson learned for Dave about seizing the moment and enjoying today. Life is too short to have regrets, so let's live!

I had heard about the fires raging in Australia through the news. I figured Dave was on the east coast and would not be in the danger zones. I heard Dave's story after the fact, and I was obviously greatly relieved to hear he was safe and unharmed. I was grateful Dave was given more time. I was also saddened by the thought of the others who suffered.

Dave travelled more in Australia and surfed whenever he could. After a year abroad, he returned to Canada. None of our family members were aware of the day David was arriving back in Alberta. He kept his arrival a secret and individually surprised each of us by showing up at our homes and schools across central and southern Alberta. We were all most excited to see him and have him close by again. It had been the first time he'd been away from me and his siblings for that long in his life. We had all missed him tons and were thankful to have him back home safe and healthy.

Dave recalled having "after travel blues" following all the adventure and excitement of his Australia trip. He met and connected with many new friends, and overall had an excellent year travelling. When he returned to Canada, he said he kind of floated around in a sad state. The transition of adjusting to life here took some time. He finished the requirements for his geology degree and graduated with excellent grades. Many family members flew in to help celebrate his accomplishment and attend the ceremonies at the university. We had a celebratory party at the Dockman house in Edmonton, where all four of my children lived. Nana Dockman and Uncle Harry came from Brampton, Ontario, as well as Dave's aunt Christine from New Westminster, British Columbia, and Auntie Maureen from Petaluma, California. Many friends, and of course Dave's dad, his dad's partner, and step-siblings, attended and helped make preparations for meals and drinks. It was a special day of excitement, closure, and pride for all of us.

Dave had been at loose ends since his return from the Aussie trip. The evening of his graduation, a friend connected him to a person who was hiring a geologist at the Minto Mine in the Yukon. David made the contact and was hired to work in a copper and gold mine. He was thrilled to be working in his study field and to be able to travel and see more of Canada while building his work experience. He worked for this mine for two years, taking core samples and documenting them, along with other exploration and mapping tasks. It was a very big change from surfing in Australia to having an Arctic experience. Being on the Arctic Circle was a very different terrain yet no less intriguing. He accepted the challenge with the rewards of snowshoeing, polar bear and grizzly bear sightings, and learning about northern living. He accomplished his goal of getting his degree and was able to secure a job in his field of study.

Rachel graduated from high school with a load of pomp and circumstance. My last child graduating from high school was another milestone reached. Rachel and I spent much time searching for the perfect grad dress. She got hair extensions and acrylic nails. Much preparation and funds went into getting everything just right for her graduation. It was all worth it, as she was happy and looked beautiful. Her graduation day went off wonderfully well and without a hitch.

Even as a child, Rachel had logical and practical ideas about life. After high school, she had no specific ideas of what she wanted to do next. No particular passion arose from her thirteen years of schooling thus far. She had a strong personality and beliefs, yet no career path had caught her attention enough to pursue. I would say she was unique and saw the world differently than most. For example, when she was four years old, she asked for a cash register for her birthday. She clarified her request—not a play one but a real one. She wanted to set up a store. I researched and found an older second-hand cash register and gave it to her for her fourth birthday. The cash register was old-style, large, and heavy. It had special keys to perform various functions, and best of all, it had a money tray. Rachel loved it! She played store and bank manager for hours, buying and selling stuff and counting money. It turned out to be a great tool for learning about money transactions, bartering, and doing business deals.

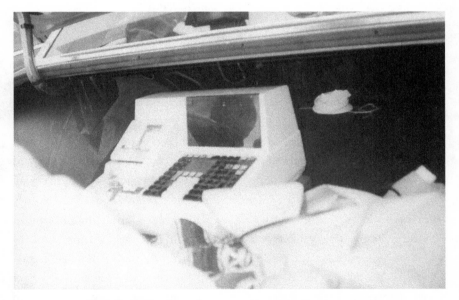

Rachel's birthday wish at four years old, a real cash register! Ta-da!

When she turned five years old, she asked for an acre of land for her birthday. Her father actually took her request seriously and looked into it, but it didn't happen. Another year when she was seven or eight years old, she asked for a typewriter as her birthday gift. You guessed it, not a toy or a play typewriter for this girl, no, but a real one. Again I figured, *Why not?* It can't hurt her to learn to type and write documents and letters. Those unusual requests gave me some insight as to how Rachel's brain worked. She identified with practical and useful things. She was a fascinating child. I don't know where she got her ideas, but she was certainly an alternative thinker.

She was very young, about six or seven years old, when she first asked me if she could get a tattoo. I said no. I was okay with funky hairstyles and different hair colours, but tattoos were too permanent. I made a rule that they could get piercings before they were eighteen, but tattoos were a hard no until they reached the age of eighteen. Rachel persisted to ask many times through the years but was respectful in listening to my rule. . . until she was almost eighteen. She was seventeen and a half years old and begged me to concede and let her get the tattoo she wanted. After all those years of her asking and listening to me, I finally weakened and allowed her to get the tattoo, especially since she was so close to eighteen.

She spent much time finding the right picture and the perfect colouring. We had a family friend who was an excellent artist, and she drew the feathery, Aboriginal style wings. Rachel got tattooed on her middle back. The wings were beautiful and tastefully done and in a spot that wasn't openly noticeable in a work environment. Rachel had me swear to keep her tattoo a secret from her father until she turned eighteen.

On the day of her graduation, Rachel wore a beautiful, burnt-orange, satin, full length dress that had criss-cross straps across her back and showed her feather wing tattoos. Her father was okay with the tattoo and didn't freak out, as she was afraid of. Her Grandpa Dockman, who was deaf and mostly blind, noticed her tattoo and hadn't seen it before. During the graduation ceremony, while the speakers were giving their talks and during a lull of silence, Grandpa asked in his loud voice, "Is that a tattoo, Rachel?" Only Grandpa! We all looked at each other with knowing looks and tried to get G-Pa to lower his voice. It was a humorous but awkward moment. All four of my children had graduated from high school, and I considered that a worthy accomplishment as a mother.

Rachel's Grade 12 graduation ceremony with her siblings

Aunt Beth and Rachel honoring her graduation

I wasn't surprised at that time when Rachel didn't pursue further education right after high school. She had some interest in math and sciences, but overall nothing really grabbed her attention. I figured it would take some time and exploration for her to find whatever it was she had a passion for, and when she did, she would go all out and achieve her aim. She worked briefly as a clerk in a liquor store, and she had the opportunity to drive a gravel loading dump truck. She was challenged and intrigued by that job. She drove the truck for that first summer and loved it. When she was learning to drive the truck, she accidentally put it into a ditch. Fortunately, her boss had a sense of humour and no harm was done. She learned and continued to enjoy and do well at the truck driving job. She made excellent money and felt great about doing what had been typically a man's occupation.

Lisa had encouraged David and John to move to Edmonton and attend the University of Alberta. Lisa also was working on Rachel to get her to go back to school and move to Edmonton with her siblings. Rachel had her friends, a boy she dated, and a social life in Airdrie. I was working out of town, and she had the run of my place most of the time. She enjoyed the freedom. I was concerned with the path she was taking and also was encouraging her to upgrade and attend school again.

About this time, Mike bought a house in Edmonton, close to the university campus. He intended that this would be a family home where all four children could live while attending college and university in Edmonton. He made them a deal. If they lived in the house for five years and paid rent each month, they would each own 10% of the home and the profits when the house sold in the future. Lisa, John, and David lived in the Dockman house, and they rented the fourth room and sometimes a fifth bedroom to friends for additional income. It was a lovely older home in a well-established area. It had hardwood floors, many upgrades, and a backyard with a garage and fire pit.

The lure of her siblings and possible return to school hadn't been enough to draw Rachel's attention to making the move to Edmonton, but the money numbers on the house caught her attention. She could end up owning 10% of the home if she lived in the Dockman house. This could be a substantial sum of money, especially if the property increased in value. She simply had to move into the house and live there for a period of time and pay reasonable rent to contribute to the mortgage payments. The financial prospects tipped the scale on her decision and she moved to Edmonton.

Rachel and Mom sharing joy and confidences

Rachel chose and pursued quite an intense and complicated path to upgrade her marks from grade 12. She enrolled in English, Math, Social and several Sciences at three separate Alberta Colleges. Her goal was to achieve the necessary course requirements and averages to attend university with the goal of becoming a geologist. After living in Edmonton about six months, Rachel reflected on her move. She recognized the partying lifestyle she'd left compared to the learning and life-advancing attitude of her environment now. Rachel was ready for specific career advancement and accepting of her siblings' support. She found her passion, which she shared with David. With her siblings' encouragement and support and her dogged determination, she overcame the obstacles and persisted in earning a Bachelor of Science, specializing in geology.

She spent her second last term of university studying abroad in Oslo, Norway at Oslo University. She had taken some time to travel with Lisa and her father in Australia when David was studying abroad and decided she wished to do the same. She spent five months studying and was able to travel to various beautiful parts of Norway during that time. She also travelled with a friend to Iceland, which she said was a geological paradise. She went to Sweden and visited the nanny we'd had in Canada when Rachel was one to two years old. Charlotte was thrilled to catch up with Rachel, whom she'd looked after for a year of their lives. Rach noted that the reunion was emotional and enjoyable for both and reunited our families, as Charlotte was now married and had three young daughters of her own. Charlotte said she learned an incredible amount from me about raising children with respect and dignity. I was very happy to hear this from her. It was a great compliment. It was wonderful to reconnect with Charlotte after so many years and still feel the connection.

Charlotte creating yummy Swedish meals for us

Charlotte joins in our Christmas celebrations

From her residence in Oslo University, Rachel was able to secure a geology job in Edmonton that started two days after she returned from Norway. How fortunate she was to be able to acquire this position online and through phone calls. She made a stop in Toronto for five days and visited her nana, who was ninety-two years old, and her special Uncle Harry. They caught up and reminisced about life and memories of years gone by. They watched videos of Rachel's childhood. One of them was the famous crinoline dancing tango, with Rachel and Lisa dancing across Nana's living room donned in layers upon layers of crinoline netting swirling crisply around. Nana had kept her round dancing costumes, and the girls loved to try them on. They alternated who was the boy and who was the girl. The girl wore multiple coloured crinolines, and the boy went shirtless. It's a super funny video to watch, definitely one that should be shown at a wedding ceremony or to grandchildren.

Rachel arrived back in Edmonton after travelling from Oslo via Toronto. We had a barbeque and welcome home celebration in David's backyard. She would resume her schooling in January to finish her degree. In the meantime, she would work as a student geologist for a local exploration company to gain experience and earn income. University is very costly in Alberta. With four children attending, I couldn't fund them financially as a single parent. I helped when I could, and so did their father, but student loans and working part-time was a necessity. Rachel had exhausted her student loan maximum and would have to work and save money for her last term of university. It's unfortunate that the province and country doesn't support further education better. Many young people finish university and begin their careers with huge student loan debt.

We justify this debt we incur for further education by saying the debt enables us to get the professional certifications to secure well-paying, meaningful work. In fact, the college and university experience provides much more. The discipline and hard work necessary to fulfill the essay and exam writing, laboratory work, and internships in the academic field are invaluable. On a social level, college and university develops maturity and growth in adult experiences. Living away from home gives them an opportunity to make decisions and gain independence. They have to take care of their finances, buy groceries, and do laundry, which many of them might not have done prior to attending school away from home. They meet new friends and develop romantic relationships. Specific knowledge is gained in their area of interest that hopefully leads to a meaningful career. Taking on debt has become a cultural norm in our country. That being said, I believe in the value of getting trained in a trade or profession. That training costs money and time and energy. Hopefully that time is spent learning useful and interesting knowledge that leads to work that adds value to ourselves and our community and gives satisfaction to those involved.

College and university became a significant part of my children's life experiences of moving from childhood to adulthood and from being dependent to independence. Lisa got two undergraduate degrees in biology, education, and French studies. She was able to secure her first job in her field right after she finished school, but she spent eight years attending university. She loved the experience and didn't want to leave it after her first degree. She had many more interests and decided to focus on education and French in her after degree. Lisa landed a job that combined education with environmental awareness for elementary school children in rural northern Alberta communities. The job was partly funded by oil and gas companies. Working for the government and for oil companies was an ethical dilemma for Lisa, since she was a strong environmentalist. The job proved to be interesting and educational. She learned much about how oil companies work and how they were trying to become greener. Lisa gained a more balanced perspective about how the world operates through that job.

After a few years travelling across northern Alberta educating Grade 5 students about our natural environment and how to preserve it, Lisa discovered a job with the University of Alberta that intrigued her. She loved the job she was doing and had a difficult decision to make. The job at the university was what she called her "dream job." She would be in a leadership position and able to develop projects to build environmental sustainability. Through much deliberation, she chose to leave her job and was hired at the University of Alberta. After some time of adjustment and creating programs, she settled into enjoying the position and its many challenges and rewards.

John elected to stop attending university after three years of studies on an education degree. He chose to switch to working in a trade. He loved taking drama courses, math, and philosophy but could not see that bringing him to a job or career he would enjoy. Teaching English or physical education had been the draw toward becoming a teacher, but the administration and organizational requirements appeared daunting to John. When he was in university, he worked framing houses for a local construction company during his summer breaks. He learned the skills of carpentry and found the physical demands energizing. Of course he would. Remember the stories of his abundant energy as a boy? Well, that energy didn't go away. It's part of his personality which is used well in the profession of building homes. After two summers of working with tools and becoming a skilled labourer, he chose to leave university and pursue a career in carpentry. He worked for a couple of years and got the hours he needed toward his apprenticeship and to acquire his carpentry ticket.

Then John chose attend college to get his carpentry training. He is in that process as I write these words. He's learning much and is enthusiastic about learning the theory behind the work he is doing. He learned how to use hand tools, about different types of wood, and how to read blueprints. In school he was required to build many projects to demonstrate his skills. He took math classes, in which he managed to get marks of over 100% on average. Definitely John has a mathematical brain, which is pretty cool. So

John works full-time for a construction company and continues to attend college two months a year in a four-year program to qualify to become a journeyman carpenter with a Red Seal certification. John was on his way. I believe he found his niche.

Dave had worked on many geological projects and had found his niche. After a couple years of travel and working intermittently, he chose to go back to school and earn his master's degree in chemical geology. He was given an excellent offer with work and scholarship funding combined to earn his master's degree. He's doing that now as I write. He has taken to operating firearms and wilderness training to prepare him for the work he will do in isolated areas of the north. You never know when you'll encounter a grizzly or a cougar while exploring and doing geological work, so safety preparation was part of the training. He headed up to Ellesmere Island in northeastern Canada for six weeks as part of his training and research. So his university education is ongoing. Dave has expressed some interest in becoming a professor and teaching geology at the university level. He may be in school for a very long time, but he's well on his way toward achieving his goals.

Rachel finished a term in Norway and has to wait until January to take the final three courses to finish her geology degree. She's working for a geological consulting company for the summer and fall in the office and in the field. She will be going to Hinton, Alberta, possibly northern Quebec, and the Crowsnest Pass in British Columbia to complete this field work. This job gives her the opportunity to gain work experience in various geological areas before she graduates next year. She is enjoying her work greatly and is pleased to be able to secure a job in her field of study.

I have concluded that for my children, their education has proven most valuable, not only in leading them to positions and work they enjoy, but for the significant value of the experience of attending university and college. I know at nineteen I thought I had the world by the horns and considered myself invincible. I learned through my twenties so much more about myself and the world. I grew into an adult gaining maturity and perspective and became more worldly wise.

The higher education for my children gave them new friends, loads of fun, wild times, and the ability to see the world through the many and varied eyes of their international friends. I am very proud to say they all attended college and university and grew and matured from the experience. So much value came from their university and college experiences, not least of which is that all four of them lived together for some of the time and ended up in the same city, where they spent much time together enjoying each other's company and supporting their siblings whenever the need arose.

For example, in the Dockman house they started a tradition of having family dinners every Sunday. They would cook together and invite friends for themed meals every week. Through this practice, they became friends as adults and began to heal and grow through some of their childhood concerns with each other. They argued and discussed and cooked and travelled and shared their lives with each other. I was grateful. It was my vision from the beginning that they develop close relationships, become good friends, and support each other throughout their lives. That was happening, and it made me smile with pleasure and hope for their connected future.

Once all four of my children complete their studies, this next phase of my mothering will be complete. Another year or so and John with be done his carpentry schooling and apprenticeship, Rachel will have completed her bachelor's degree, and Dave his master's degree. Who knows, they may attend more schooling in the future, but I feel all four of my children have an excellent base of knowledge and experience in social, academic, emotional, and spiritual growth to move them forward in life. They have meaningful relationships with each other and have been blessed with opportunities to travel the world and share many life experiences together. This completes my Bachelor's Degree in Motherhood.

# CHAPTER 25

## *The Value of Motherhood: The Life and Commitment*

I sit and contemplate time and value. I have a choice of where and with whom I will spend the time I have in my life. We all have the same twenty-four hours each day. What will we do with it? Motherhood was a choice I made that I felt to be valuable, and I committed my life to this profession. At this moment, Lisa is planning the party for her thirtieth birthday celebration. It's difficult for me to wrap my mind around the idea that it will soon be thirty years since her birth. I say this with a heart full of love that I lived these years with joy and appreciation for the time I was blessed to share with these four lovely human beings. I don't take this gift of motherhood for granted. I appreciate the fact that I have been blessed with four healthy children, and I am grateful to have ongoing relationships and open communications with them. We cherish and nurture these relationships by having regular gatherings and conversations. How sweet is that?

I could not imagine life without my four children. My heart swells with pride when I say these are my children and introduce them to someone. They make me laugh. They make me think. They help me see the world in new ways. They challenge me to move forward and not be stuck in the past. They worry me when they're off on their many adventures discovering the world, and I breathe a sigh of relief when they return home. I find joy in spending time with them, whatever the activity or inactivity. We share our feelings and ask each other's advice. Sometimes we are sounding boards for each other's frustrations. Whatever the need, there is always one of us willing and available to offer support. It's most comforting to know we have each other no matter what happens in our lives.

My journey of motherhood has been a path of many unexpected high and low experiences. Some happenings startled me; some amazed me, and some I feared. Although many of the questions I sought to answer and understand have been resolved, still a few remain unsolved. Do not fear. I have not given up my learning or queries about motherhood. I remain committed to motherhood in this next stage of being a mother to young adults. I have accepted the fact that I will not get everything answered. I will be continually seeking further understanding until my dying day. My motherhood experience will continue to grow and evolve.

New questions popped up along my journey. As it is said, we don't know what we don't know. As I became a more knowledgeable and experienced mother, my learning accumulated and went deeper, and my questions became more intricate and specific to situations. In that way, the seeds that grow into richness extend to expertise in motherhood. I hope I may grow in this wisdom with age and experience through the next stages of my motherhood.

Sometimes people have asked me, "How did you do it? How did you manage when you had all four children under five years old?" Then later, "How did you manage as a single parent of four young children and later teenagers?" How did I cope? How did I manage to survive and succeed at motherhood? Well, I think situations look worse from the outside looking in. It was my life, and I found the necessary strength deep inside to push through the challenges that presented themselves. I dealt in the moment one thing at a time, and I had lots of help from friends and family. I would say many personal characteristics came into play that helped me to cope, such as endurance, courage, compassion, my sixth sense, flexibility, curiosity, humour, commitment, patience, and a fiercely protective and all-encompassing love. I was committed to being the best mother I could be.

I stress that having a sense of humour as essential. I needed and used my humour often to enable me to enjoy my children's curious natures. Instead of becoming angry or frustrated with their constant experimentation and alternative thought processes, I went along with them and followed their lead to learn a new way of thinking. For example, John was curious about how a toilet functioned when he was about three years old. His mind wanted to know where the poop disappeared to, so he investigated. I went into the bathroom to find the back lid of the toilet water reservoir off and sitting on the counter. Interesting, I looked inside and found poop floating in the water inside the toilet reservoir behind the toilet seat. I stood back and smiled, because I could see John's mind working and him balancing above the tank, concentrating on having a bowel movement into the water to try to satisfy his inquisition. Then I visualized him proceeding to watch the tank as he flushed to see if the poop disappeared and if it went into the toilet bowl. Just where did the poop disappear to? Fascinating. Then he would get that perplexed look on his face and wonder why it didn't go into the bowl with the water. Yes, I had to clean up and disinfect, but that was little to me compared to the intrigue I felt about how a child's mind will try to understand their surroundings. And it was comical. I didn't get angry or question him or put him down for the mess he made. I felt he had a legitimate question about how this toilet worked, and he acted with the intent of relieving his curiosity. My intention was to support his inquiring mind. My sense of humour saved me more times than I can count or even recall.

I did not bring these children into this world lightly or without thought. I had an idea of the commitment I was making. At the same time, I had no idea at all, seriously clueless of the magnitude of the commitment I was making. My children were born one at a time, not all four at once. I had time to adjust to the needs and demands of each additional child as they were born. I grew into learning the skills of motherhood with time. My growth came progressively in all areas of my life—emotionally, mentally, spiritually, and physically as I adapted in my roles of motherhood.

If I had known all the work it would take to become a successful mother, I still would not have reconsidered or changed my mind, because with the hardships came my growth, and with the growth came awareness, joy, and fulfillment. Also, I would not have known the extent of the rewards I would receive through motherhood. That's how life works. We learn by doing. The experience changes us, and we become better for rising to the challenge, or maybe bitter if not. I became in tune with my children. I grew connected to them physically, emotionally, and in spirit. The feelings I have for them are inexpressible. People talk of love. Sure, I love them very much, but the word love lacks the immense emotion I feel for my children. Love is part of how I feel for them, but I also feel a multitude of other emotions. They are separate yet a part of me. I feel pride, joy, connection, curiosity, understanding, and hope. The feeling is all-encompassing and consumes me through each cell of my being. My children are so much a part of who I am. I couldn't imagine my life without any of them and all of them.

The team

My undergraduate degree at the University of Motherhood is complete. I have graduated. How can I tell? I get no marks. There are no bars to measure my success or failure. There are no time limits or deadlines, no standard rules or policies I had to obey. How do I know I succeeded? The result of who these children will be takes time. There is no immediate gratification except the small steps along the way. I implore you to please enjoy the journey. Enjoy each day when your child smiles and gurgles at you, when they begin to walk and talk, enjoy each phase of life as you live it, and really enjoy every single moment you share with your children. Time goes by quickly, and here I am with a thirty-year-old daughter. I remember and cherish all those times I spent with them as they grew. The motherhood part of me is happy with who I am and who my children became.

You may be wondering how I can say that I have graduated in motherhood when my role is not over, not completed. Be settled, I am aware. There is more. I am considering the Undergraduate degree of Motherhood as my children's youth and school years. I intend to continue the story with a book I will call *The University of Motherhood: Master's Degree*, which will include my experiences of motherhood through the years of my children's young adulthood, our growth and challenges during the years of partnering, possible childbearing, career, and social experiences. I again will reflect on how my changing role as a mother will best guide them through these life experiences. I can only imagine the joy and learning of becoming a grandmother and mother-in-law. Sharing life with them will continue to be life changing.

I envision my continuum through to graduate school with a third book *The University of Motherhood, PhD*, sharing my learning as I age, and my experiences of motherhood as my children grow into middle age. I will further document, write, and reflect on how my views and methods have affected their lives. So much more of my journey through motherhood will come with time. I anticipate this passage with excitement. I hope to continue with an open mind and heart. Until then, enjoy the moment, and happy mothering!

# ENDNOTES

1   *The Secret Life of the Unborn Child*, Dr. T. Verny, 1981. Simon & Schuster, New York, NY.

2   *Dare to Discipline,* Dr. J. Dobson 1970, Tyndale House Publishers, Inc. Wheaton, Illinois

3   *Children: the Challenge,* R. Dreikurs 1990, Penguin Books, Toronto, Ontario.

4   *Parents* magazine, monthly, 1983, Meredith Corporation, New York, N.Y.

5   *Mr. Mom*, 20th Century Fox, 1983

6   *The Birth Order Book, Why You Are the Way You Are*, Dr. Kevin Leman, 1985. Fleming H. Revell, a division of Baker Publishing Group, Grand Rapids, Michigan

7   *Jonathon Livingston Seagull,* Richard Bach, 1970. Macmillan Publishers Inc. New York, N.Y.

8   *Rollerball*, Norman Jewison, United Artist, 1975

9   *The Nutcracker*, Alberta Ballet Company, Southern Alberta Jubilee Auditorium, 1990

10  *The Bible*, KJV, The New Testament, Matthew 25:31–46

11  *Quest Study Bible*, Matthew 25:31–46, New International Version, Zondervan, Grand Rapids Michigan, 2003

12  *Dare to Discipline,* Dr. J. Dobson, 1970, Tyndale House Publishers, Inc. Wheaton, Illinois

13  *The Discovery of the Child*, Maria Montessori, 1973, Ballantine Books Inc. New York, N.Y.

14  *Think and Grow Rich,* Napoleon Hill, Global Grey, 2018, pp.72.

15  *Final Harvest, Emily Dickinson Poems*, Emily Dickinson, 1961. Little, Brown & Company Inc. Toronto, Ontario

16  *Siblings Without Rivalry*, Adele Faber & Elaine Mazlish. 1987, W.W. Norton & Company, Inc. New York, N.Y.

17  *Chatelaine's Adventures in Cooking, 1969, Maclean-Hunter, Ltd. Toronto, Ontario*

18  *More-with-Less Cookbook,* Mennonite Central Committee, 1982, Herald Press, Waterloo, Ontario

19  *Traditional Ukrainian Cookery,* Savella Stechishin, 1979, Trident Press Ltd. Winnipeg, Manitoba

20  *The Joy of Cooking*, Irma S. Rombauer, 1964 paperback edition, Bobbs-Merrill Company, New York, N.Y.

21  *Adult Children of Alcoholics,* Janet Woititz, 1983, Simon & Schuster, New York, NY

22  Maya Angelou, BrainyMedia Inc, 7 August 2020. https://www.brainyquote.com/quotes/maya_angelou_392897

23  Dr. Angelou, May 2013 issue of *O, The Oprah Winfrey magazine*

24  *Think and Grow Rich,* Napoleon Hill, 1960, Fawcett Books, New York, NY

25  *The Discovery of the Child*, Maria Montessori, 1973, Ballantine Books Inc. New York, N.Y.

26  Albert Einstein, *What Life Means to Einstein,* George Sylvester Viereck, Saturday Evening Post, 1929

27  *Adult Children of Alcoholics,* Janet Woititz, 1983, Simon & Schuster, New York, N.Y.

28  *How to Enjoy Your Life and Your Job,* Dale Carnegie, 1990